"Rally, Once Again!"

Selected Civil War Writings of

"Rally,

Alan T. Nolan

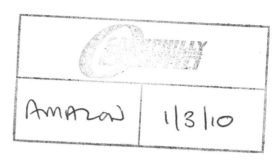

Once Again!"

 Madison House Publishers
Madison, Wisconsin

DEDICATION

In memory of my father Val
and my mother Jeannette
*   and*
to my brother Val, Jr.
and sister Kathleen
God, I've been lucky!

—ALAN T. NOLAN

Nolan, Alan T.
"Rally, Once Again!": Selected Civil War Writings of Alan T. Nolan

For acknowledgment of permission to reprint individual articles and for full
citation of where articles appeared originally, see page 295.

LIBRARY OF CONGRESS CATALOGING-IN-PUBLICATION DATA

Nolan, Alan T.
    "Rally, once again!": selected Civil War writings of Alan T. Nolan.—1st ed.
      p. cm.
    Includes bibliographical references and index.
    ISBN 0-945612-71-0 (hardcover: alk. paper)
    1. United States—History—Civil War, 1861–1865.   2. Generals—United
States—Biography.   3. Generals—Confederate States of America—Biography.
4. Gettysburg (Pa.), Battle of, 1863.   5. United States. Army. Iron Brigade
(1861–1865)   6. United States—History—Civil War, 1861–1865—Book
reviews.   I. Title.

E464.N65 2000
973.7—dc21   99-089974

ISBN 0-945612-71-0 (cloth: alk. paper) ISBN 978-0-945612-71-1

Designed by William Kasdorf

Printed in the United States of America on acid-free paper

Published by
Madison House Publishers, Inc.
P.O. Box 3100, Madison, Wisconsin 53704
www.madisonhousebooks.com

FIRST EDITION

Contents

I. Leaders

II. Gettysburg

III. The Iron Brigade

IV. Selected Reviews

Illustrations

Cover: Alonzo Chappel's 1865 *Battle of the Wilderness Attack at Spottsyl-vania Court House.* Courtesy of Chicago Historical Society.

Title Page: Company C of the Second Wisconsin Volunteers. Raised in Grant County, Wisconsin, the company is pictured at an unidentified date, wearing the distinctive uniform ordered by General John Gibbon for the Iron Brigade. Photo courtesy of State Historical Society of Wisconsin.

Page xii: Robert E. Lee, posing for a famous photo portrait by Mathew Brady. Photo courtesy of Library of Congress.

Page 130: Abraham Lincoln. Photo courtesy of Alan T. Nolan.

Page 174: Charles A. Keeler of St. Joseph, Michigan, of Company B of the Sixth Wisconsin. He wears the uniform prescribed by General Gibbon, May 7, 1862. Photo courtesy of Alan T. Nolan.

Page 242: William Garl Brown's 1869 *General Thomas J. "Stonewall" Jackson.* Courtesy of Stonewall Jackson Foundation, Lexington, Virginia.

Preface

We are told on all sides of the significance of the American Civil War, that it was the defining experience of our country, the Second American Revolution, etc. I believe these things are true. Further, by a happy coincidence I was introduced to the war as a child on a trip to Gettysburg and Antietam with my history-loving father. I also learned from him about my own Irish Civil War grandfather. A famine refugee, he arrived in the United States in about 1850 and settled in Indiana. When the war came, he volunteered in 1862 for Company I of the Sixty-sixth Indiana Volunteers. He was wounded and captured at the Battle of Richmond, Kentucky, in August 1862. Paroled, he was later exchanged and returned to the field. He was then stricken with dysentery, and hospitalized in a Federal hospital in Corinth, Mississippi. He died there on November 1, 1863, and is buried in the National Cemetery there. The cemetery record book accurately identifies him as interred there, but his grave is unidentified. He is one of several hundred soldiers buried there with a stone that simply says "a Union soldier." The practice at the time of his death was to install a wooden headboard painted with the soldier's name, unit, and date of death. These boards weathered and ultimately disappeared. I have a letter from Mrs. E. E. George of Fort Wayne, Indiana, an Indiana Sanitary Commission nurse, who was with him when he died. She wrote to the oldest of his seven children telling of the father's last wishes:

> He wished your mother to keep the children together and teach them to love their God and the Country their father had given his life to save. He repeated the words *to save*, for Madam, It will be saved.

My maternal great-grandfather Jacob Covert had a somewhat checkered career as a lieutenant in the Twenty-fourth Indiana Volunteers, a regiment that was at Shiloh.

Sensitive to my family's stake in the Civil War, I have been studying, writing, talking, and thinking about the war for sixty years. I am hopeful that others may be interested in my thoughts, represented here by previously published essays, book reviews, and articles.

Years of Civil War study have resulted in conclusions of my own about the subject. In the first place, contrary to the Hollywood and Margaret Mitchell image, I do not see the war as at all romantic or glorious. It was in fact a grim and inhumane experience for the Americans involved, although its decisive results—emancipation and the maintenance of the Union—were surely positives. Other, indeed all, of the contentions of the Southern myth of the Lost Cause are also offensive to me and unhistoric.

Northern racism has caused Northern people generally to accept the trivializing of slavery as the cause of the war. In fact, slavery *was* the source of the sectional conflict. The South seceded to protect the institution from a disapproving national majority. Thus, the romantic cliché that "both sides were right" is absurd. The Lost Cause tradition has also ignored the fact that African-Americans participated vigorously in their own emancipation; indeed 180,000 of them joined the Federal armies. On examination, General Lee is not the paragon of the Civil War myth. He was a staunch believer in slavery and personally enmeshed in the institution, owning and trafficking in slaves, and seeing to the capture of fugitive slaves. His frequently remarkable military feats were unusually costly in terms of his army's irreplaceable and disproportionate losses. He was not respectful of the North's wartime effort; instead, he hated the North and its people. Nor was he a postwar conciliator as is customarily claimed.

Postwar reconstruction is another victim of the Civil War mythology. It was not a Southern crown of thorns but an effort that was flawed and failed in large part because of Southern and Northern racial bigotry and Southern intransigence. In short, except for the valor of Confederate common soldiers, I find almost nothing in the Confederate culture or tradition to admire or celebrate.

EDITOR'S NOTE ON THE TEXT: All annotation has been left as in the original text, and all original illustrative material has been deleted.

"Rally, Once Again!"

I

Leaders

Lawyer Lincoln— Myth and Fact

The lives of famous political men are invariably surrounded by a mythology. The ordinary man in whom no one is interested at least has the benefit of an unargumentative reputation. But in the case of the extraordinary man, especially the extraordinary public man, this is not the case. During his life, the more articulate citizens are related to him as advocates. At best they display his strengths and obscure his weaknesses, or vice versa, and at worst they make up facts about him as they go along. Even after the great man is dead, his enemies and friends busy themselves in making history fit the myths.

This phenomenon creates a contradiction for the historian. On the one hand, the historian is told that he cannot write sound history until much time has passed and a perspective developed about the subject. But because of the mythmaking process, the later historian is compelled to dig through the myths in an attempt to find the facts from primary materials. When the subject of the historian's inquiry is a man of controversy, the conflicting character of the secondary materials—the pros and cons—may be helpful. They provide a test from which a sense of judgment or an insight into truth may develop. The historian's most difficult assignment is presented when the subject has become a genuine folk hero. There are a few of these, and Abraham Lincoln is surely the primary one to modern Americans.

Perhaps the most prevalent Lincoln romance concerns his career as a lawyer. A study of Lincoln the lawyer should be of interest to lawyers—simply because we share his professional experience. And Lincoln the lawyer is also worth considering for a larger reason. In his recent exceptional study, *Lincoln As A Lawyer*, John P. Frank notes that

Lincoln actively practiced law for twenty-five of the thirty-five years of his adult life. As Frank says it, practicing law "in terms of time and energy and preoccupation . . . was in bulk the largest single factor of his life . . ." Accordingly, an understanding of Lincoln as a lawyer is a means of learning more about him as a human being. Considering Lincoln as a member of our profession affords new insights into the character and personality of the man.

The mythology about Lincoln the lawyer has several noteworthy attributes. Among these is the fact that it has not developed because of any neglect of this aspect of his life. In the vast body of Lincoln literature, Abraham Lincoln the lawyer has been a frequent subject. In addition to a number of reminiscences, articles and pamphlets, four major works have been concerned with his professional career. In 1906, Frederick Trevor Hill published *Lincoln The Lawyer,* a study of Lincoln's period at the bar and the legal aspects of his later career. In 1936, on the eve of the centennial of Lincoln's admission to the bar, Albert A. Woldman published a second full-scale analysis. In 1960, John J. Duff, a New York practicing lawyer, issued a new book, and the book by John P. Frank was released in the following year. Lawyer Lincoln has also been described in the major biographies by Beveridge, Sandburg, Thomas and others.

With the exception of the Duff book and that of John P. Frank, most of the writing about lawyer Lincoln has been of limited worth. It has been marked by a number of unhistoric characteristics, including implicit apologies for the fact that he was a lawyer at all. Popular mythology would clearly have preferred that he had been a soldier, an Indian scout or, God forbid, a physician. Authors Duff and Frank are free of these limitations, but the myths are deeply rooted and even sophisticated men—even sophisticated Harvard lawyers—have presumably been influenced by them.

A nother interesting characteristic of what Duff calls the "stained glass" approach to Lincoln as a lawyer is that it has surely been unconscious on the part of some of the previous writers. It was not unconscious on the part of Sandburg who follows the venerable and even biblical tradition of dishonoring lawyers as a class. Anyone who has read Sandburg's poem, about the snickering of the horse pulling the hearse as he hauls a lawyer away, would expect Sandburg to have difficulty when confronting his hero as a lawyer. But other writers without Sand-

burg's problems have also assisted in the mythmaking. Albert A. Woldman, for example, began his work with the express intention of avoiding
the halos and what he called the "silly twaddle" which pictured Lincoln
"as a Don Quixote of the judicial circuit . . . an oafish country lawyer . . .
naïve almost to the point of simplicity . . ." But Woldman, like the others
who preceded Duff and Frank, became enraptured as he went along.
The story—the true story—of the journey of this unpromising backwoodsman, from Kentucky to Ford's Theatre, was too much for Woldman, as it has been for so many conscientious writers. Ultimately, like
them, he rationalized those events which did not fit the myth of Lincoln,
the folk hero.

What are some of the more significant myths? Perhaps the basic one,
in Frederick Trevor Hill's words, is that Lincoln would not accept professional employment unless he "really believed in the justice of his
cause." Granting that the word "justice" is an argumentative one, lawyers
at least should be pleased to learn that Lincoln accepted employment in
a number of cases in which the law and the facts were stacked against
him. Also satisfying is the knowledge that he was never reluctant to resort to highly legalistic and technical arguments when these seemed to
be the likely course.

Another popular picture of Lincoln is that of the poignantly sympathetic man—the man without aggressive instincts. Having studied all of
the materials, including the primary ones, John P. Frank finds that Lincoln the lawyer had ". . . unbridled enthusiasm for combat." Among
other evidence of this fact are amusing handwritten notes outlining Lincoln's argument to the jury in a case in which he represented a plaintiff
in a suit for money. Lincoln's client was the widow of a Revolutionary
War veteran, and Lincoln's outline shows that he opened his argument
with a discussion of this fact, surely irrelevant to the issues in the case.
And the last point on his outline was short and sweet—"skin defendant,"
he told himself, an argument which was surely not that of the sweet and
soft man that many of us picture.

L incoln is also universally pictured as a joke-telling, folksy man, and
the implication is that he was nothing more. He was unquestionably a funny man, and he unquestionably was folksy. But his mind was
orderly, and it was also sensitive, both to the technicalities and to the equities of the legal conflicts to which it was applied. Of greater contrast to
the storytelling, hayseed image is his attribute of diligence. The records

show that Lincoln was an extremely hard-working practicing lawyer, and when the occasion presented itself he was capable of careful and thoughtful workmanship over a sustained period of time.

The myths even extend to the character of Lincoln's practice. Thus, numerous biographers have repeated Hill's assertion that Lincoln had little relationship with criminal matters and that, in Hill's words, he was "not well qualified for work of this character and . . . avoided the practice of criminal law as far as possible." The fact is that Lincoln was frequently employed in the criminal practice and he unhesitatingly represented the defense in homicide matters.

A consideration of the so-called *Matson Slave Case* provides the sharpest contrast between the myth and the fact of Lincoln's legal career. The treatment of the case by various writers also admirably illustrates the method in which the myths are made and carried on. The record shows that one Robert Matson of Kentucky was the owner of a farm in Coles County, Illinois. Matson farmed the land with slaves which he brought from Kentucky each spring and returned to Kentucky after the harvest. This technique prevented the Negroes from acquiring a situs in Illinois, which would have jeopardized their status as chattels. There was one exception in Matson's arrangement. This was Anthony Bryant, a former slave who remained continuously in Coles County, acting as an overseer for Matson and thus becoming a freeman. In 1847, Matson brought his slaves from Kentucky to Coles County. Among them were Anthony Bryant's wife and their four children. During the course of the sojourn, Matson's white housekeeper became annoyed with Mrs. Bryant and threatened to have her and the children sent to Kentucky and sold to a plantation in the deep South. When Bryant learned of this, he contacted local Abolitionists and with his family went into hiding under their protection in Illinois. Matson invoked the law, employing Usher F. Linder, a skillful lawyer and a contemporary of Lincoln's, and eventually Lincoln himself became associated with Linder in behalf of Matson. Opposing them were other well-known lawyers of the area, Orlando B. Ficklin and Charles H. Constable. Ultimately, the issue was presented in a *habeas corpus* proceeding, on petition filed on behalf of the Negroes, who by this time were in jail in response to the slave owner's writ for possession.

On the merits, Matson's case depended on whether the Negroes had acquired a situs in Illinois or were simply seasonal workers, chattels carried into the state and intended to be returned to Kentucky in accordance with their owner's practice. Lincoln and his co-counsel divided their presentation into two parts. Lincoln argued that the slaves were in fact *in transitu* and thus that Matson's ownership was entitled to protection. He also challenged the form of the petition on technical grounds, contending that in any event the action was defective. At length the court decided against Matson and the slaves were freed.

Before Duff's book, many of the writers simply overlooked the Matson case, although its existence was surely known to them. Those who concerned themselves with it uniformly resorted to elaborate apologies in an effort to exorcise an episode which collided so sharply with the Lincoln image. The apologies took two principal forms. Some, like Woldman, found the Matson case evidence of Lincoln's paramount devotion to due process and his ability to overcome his antislavery principles because of a deeper and more significant commitment to a system of law. Others, including Beveridge and Benjamin P. Thomas, rationalized on the ground that Lincoln was ineffective in his presentation, hinting at least that Lincoln intentionally "threw" the case. Those writers who have taken this view have said that Lincoln's devotion to freedom either overpowered his professional commitment to Matson and his oath as a lawyer or deprived him of his skill as an advocate.

But on honest examination, one is convinced that Lincoln presented the Matson case with both vigor and skill. The theory that he either compromised his client or was paralyzed in his efforts does not stand up. The other apology—that Lincoln accepted the employment because of some overriding commitment to the legal system—implies the real question. Having in mind Lincoln's lifelong and consistent antislavery views, why did he accept the employment in behalf of the slave owner? Although it is a nice thing to want to believe, there is not the slightest *evidence* that he was asserting some absolute moral in taking the case. Why did he take it? John J. Duff's book concerns itself at length with this question and his ideas are meaningful. He grants that Lincoln may have had misgivings about the position of his client (and what lawyer has not?), and he concludes that Lincoln accepted Matson's case simply *because he was a lawyer*. As Duff states it, Lincoln was, after all, a member of that "cruel calling" which requires its members "to repress their own sometimes deep-seated convictions and become, at times, articulate advocates of ideas and clients abhorrent to their own inner feelings." Thus, the uncomplicated answer to the question of why Lincoln represented Matson is based on the elemental proposition that the lawyer's essential role in our legal system assumes that he will accept employment in an honest cause, regardless of what Duff calls "an inherent or emotional bias which predisposes (him) . . . in favor of one side or the other." In considering Lincoln as a lawyer it may be parenthetically noted that the economic self-interest of the lawyer may be consistent with this role. But surely it is understood that a system of laws requires this status for lawyers. It is apparent that laymen, even sophisticated ones, do not understand this, and it becomes increasingly apparent that many lawyers themselves either do not understand it or cannot take the consequences. This has led to an always increasing tendency of the citizen to merge the identities of lawyers and their clients and an always diminishing number of lawyers willing to maintain an independence from the views and interests of their clients. A system of due process assumes the availability of the technicians who know how to operate it. But the growth of the dependent bar tends to wither due process, and the unpopular cause or unpopular client, including those of an unorthodox political flavor, have more and more difficulty in invoking the system of law. Insofar as Lincoln was concerned, it should be understood that Abolitionism was by no means a majority point of view in the place of his practice in the 1840's. On the other hand, slave-catching was even more unpopular than Abolitionism. Thus, Lincoln in the Matson case was acting in the essential and traditional lawyer's role in spite of the unpopularity of working for the slave-catcher.

So much for the myths and the facts and what they tell us about lawyer Lincoln. He may not have been a "great" lawyer, whatever that means, but he was surely a competent one, and during his career he progressed from the small and unremunerative cases to a number of substantial matters, including the then landmark utility and water rights cases which demonstrated his professional growth. It is surely unhistorical for the legal profession to claim that it created Lincoln. Although the lawyer's life at the time and in the place did afford a training ground for those attributes which were to mark Lincoln as a great political President. In John P. Frank's words the profession did "more to polish than to create his native skills." But it did polish the native skills and made them into lawyer's skills, and surely it was fortunate that Lincoln was a lawyer and that he was a good one. His administration was unusually beset with desperate and fundamental issues which were essentially legal issues: the nature of the Union, Emancipation, the power of the Executive, and the status of civil liberties in the midst of massive rebellion. Lincoln approached these and all of the problems of his administration in terms of legal concepts and in the way that a lawyer works. John P. Frank is right when he states that from the practice of law, Lincoln carried with him to the Presidency his incredible industriousness; an ability to absorb, retain, organize, and use facts; a capacity for effective expression, and an aptitude for making correct decisions on the basis of the facts, instead of hopes and appearances.

As a lawyer and a President, Lincoln also suggests an interesting contradiction. As is well known, he was an intensely complicated man personally. But his acts as a lawyer and as a lawyer who was President were direct and uncomplicated. As President, this meant that he was able to find his own common denominator to the enormously complex situation which surrounded him. This common denominator was the defeat of the Rebellion. Having found that single goal, he pursued it indefatigably, throwing off the distractions which would have pulled him from it. From the beginning, and in spite of the most extreme pressures from without and what surely must have been strong emotional pressures from within himself, all issues and all men were measured by Lincoln by the single standard: would they help or hurt in the defeat of the Rebellion? This was the cornerstone of Lincoln's conduct of his office, and he clung to it as surely no one else could have. This was Lincoln's ultimate gift, and it is worth noting that it is a lawyer's gift: he could find the heart of the issues and could pursue the heart of the issues relentlessly and single-mindedly.

General Lee—
A Different View

I believe that Lee's generalship hurt the Confederates' chances for victory. I do not fault his tactics or operational strategy. I do fault his sense of the South's *grand strategy*. Tactics, of course, refers to *how* a battle is fought. Operational strategy concerns the plan of a campaign or battle. *Grand strategy* pertains to the use of military forces in order to win the war.

I concede that Lee was an effective and sometimes brilliant field commander, but his towering reputation results from viewing his leadership a campaign or a battle at a time and disregarding considerations of grand strategy. I argue that in grand strategic terms Lee did not understand the war, an ultimate failure that his sometimes brilliant operational strategy and tactics simply do not overcome.

In order to evaluate my thesis, one has to identify his or her own opinion as to how the South could have won: with an offensive grand strategy that risked the depletion of its inferior numbers in an effort to defeat the North militarily, or the defensive, that is, fighting the war so as to prolong it and punish the North so that it would have decided that coercion was impossible or not worth the cost. Because of its relatively limited manpower and manufacturing base, the Confederacy was never in a position to defeat the North militarily. Its only chance was to make the war so costly to the North that the North would give it up. To do this, it was essential for Lee to observe a conserving, defensive grand strategy, the counterpart of Washington's grand strategy in the Revolution. The Americans could not and did not militarily defeat the British regulars, but within a grand defensive context they kept armies in the field and harassed the enemy until it gave up the contest.

In arguing for the defensive grand strategy, I am not advocating a perimeter war, a war of position or the exclusively defensive operational strategy and tactics of General Joseph E. Johnston in the Atlanta campaign. Nor do I believe that Lee could simply have remained idle. Within a defensive context he could have maneuvered and raided, as did Washington, and still avoided the expensive battles that his offensives induced. Occasional reasoned operationally strategic offensives and tactics could have been undertaken within the framework of the grand strategic defensive. Washington's leadership is again the model.

Lee's grand strategic view was set forth in a letter of July 6, 1864, to President Davis:

> If we can defeat or drive the armies of the enemy from the field, we shall have peace. All of our efforts and energies should be devoted to that object.

This is a statement of offensive grand strategy. Lee believed that to win the war the South had to overpower the North militarily, to decimate and disperse its armies. A reference to 1862–63 is appropriate. Having taken command of the Army of Northern Virginia on June 1, 1862, for two years Lee vigorously pursued the strategic offensive in an effort to defeat the North militarily: the Peninsula, the Second Bull Run Campaign, the Maryland Campaign, Chancellorsville, and the Pennsylvania Campaign. He either attacked or, in the case of Second Bull Run and the Maryland Campaign, maneuvered offensively so as to precipitate large and costly battles. He did this although he had predicted that a siege in the Richmond defenses would be fatal to his army. In order to avoid being fixed, to avoid a siege, an army must be mobile. And mobility, the capacity to maneuver, requires numbers in some reasonable relationship to the enemy's numbers. In the course of his offensives, Lee took disproportionate, irreplaceable and unaffordable losses that undermined the viability of his army, deprived it of mobility, and ultimately committed it to a siege. A comparison of Lee's and the Federals' losses is instructive:

	Federals	*Confederates*
The Seven Days	9,796	19,739
	10.7%	20.7%
Second Bull Run	10,096	9,108
	13.3%	18.8%
Antietam	11,657	11,724
	15.5%	22.6%
Chancellorsville	11,116	10,746
	11.4%	18.7%
Gettysburg	17,684	22,638
	21.2%	30.2%

Fredericksburg, Lee's only 1862–3 genuinely defensive battle, provides a significant contrast: Burnside lost almost 11,000 killed and wounded (10.9%) as compared to Lee's 4,656 (6.4%).

Classic examples of Lee's mistaken offensive grand strategy are provided by his decisions that led to the battles at Antietam and Gettysburg. Having been victorious at Second Bull Run, Lee was in an ideal position in September 1862 to desist from a prompt offensive move. In spite of statements by some writers that he had no alternative to moving into Maryland, even Freeman concedes that after Second Bull Run he could have moved a "slight distance southward" from Manassas, "to Warrenton, for instance. . . . That would put the Army of Northern Virginia on the flank of any force advancing to Richmond, and would give it the advantage of direct rail communications with the capital." In spite of this alternative, Lee moved into Maryland, which forseeably drew the Federal army after him and resulted in the costly battle at Antietam. Lee knew that substantial casualties were inevitable in that battle whether he won or lost. The situation immediately after Chancellorsville is also illuminating. In that battle, Lee had demonstrated his offensive tactical brilliance—and he had taken heavy losses in the process. According to his aide, Col. Charles Marshall, and Lee's own comments, Lee then had three options: to attack Hooker across the Rappahannock, to position himself to defend against another Federal effort to attack him across the Rappahannock, and to raid into Maryland and Pennsylvania. Having wisely rejected attempting to attack Hooker across the river, Lee chose the Northern raid option. This choice ended at Gettysburg where, to quote Freeman, Lee's army was "wrecked." Surely Gettysburg, requiring a crossing and recrossing of the Potomac and with extended lines of communication, was the most risky of the options. As in the case of the 1862 move into Maryland, win, lose or draw, the Maryland-Pennsylvania move of 1863 was bound to result in substantial casualties.

Lee's offensive view of the war also appears in his dispatches after Gettysburg. On August 31, 1863, in a letter to Longstreet he said that "I can see nothing better to be done than to endeavor to bring General Meade out and use our efforts to crush his army." On October 11, 1863, he wrote the Secretary of War from near Madison Courthouse that, "Yesterday I moved the army to this position with the hope of getting an opportunity to strike a blow at the enemy." Less than a week later he informed President Davis from Bristoe Station as follows: "I have the honor to inform you that with the view of bringing on an engagement with the army of Gen. Meade . . . this army . . . arrived near Culpeper on the 11th." Later in 1863, he spoke of "preparations made to attack (Meade)," which were frustrated by Meade's retreat. In February of 1864, he wrote Davis of his desire to "drive him (the enemy) to the Potomac." Even after the Wilderness and Spotsylvania, Lee wrote Davis that "it seems to me our best policy to unite upon it (Grant's army) and endeavor to crush it." Also in 1864 he told General Jubal A. Early that "we must destroy this army of Grant's before he gets to the James River." Already reduced by his 1862–63 offensives, it was simply not possible for Lee to "crush" or "destroy" Grant's overwhelming force. He could injure or slow it down, but not destroy it. The point is that, as had been true from the beginning of his army command, even at this late date Lee thought strategically in Armageddon terms. Early's Shenandoah Valley campaign in 1864 is significant in another respect. Early was sent to the valley to draw Federal forces away from Petersburg and Richmond. To draw Federals into the valley and *keep them there*, Early's force had only to be present in the valley. But Lee's offensive spirit caused him to tell Early to attack the Federals' valley forces. Early pursued the offensive. His outnumbered army took heavy losses and was ultimately decimated and resoundingly defeated. This permitted the Federals to be returned to Grant before Richmond. The offensive urged by Lee countered Lee's purpose in sending Early to the valley.

Lee's 1862-63 costly offensive warfare defied his own concern about relative manpower. His correspondence with Davis and the Secretary of War is replete with statements of that concern. During the 1862-63 period, he wrote regularly of the "superior numbers of the enemy," the necessity to "husband our strength," "the falling off in (his army's) aggregate shows that its ranks are growing weaker and that its losses are not supplied by recruits," and that the enemy "can be easily reinforced, while no addition can be made to our numbers." Some may contend that Lee's grand strategy was defensive, an offensive defensive. To make this claim, they must somehow exorcise Lee's own words, his consistent advocacy of the attack, and the way he used his army for two years, until its losses deprived him of mobility and the offensive option.

Forced to the strategic defensive by 1864, Lee demonstrated the value of that posture, exacting such a price from the North that it came close to abandoning the war. I contend that had he carried out his leadership in this way during the two costly offensive years, as he did only at Fredericksburg, he would have slowed the enemy's increase in numerical superiority to the extent that it arose from Lee's heavy, disproportionate, and irreplaceable losses. He would have saved a substantial portion of the approximately 100,000 soldiers that he lost on the offensive. With these additional numbers, he could have maintained mobility and avoided a siege. Maneuvers like Early's 1864 movement in the valley could have been undertaken with sufficient numbers to be effective. The Federals, on the offensive, could have suffered for an earlier or longer period the ceaseless Federal losses that began in May of 1864. The Northern people could have politically abandoned their support of the war.

Some who disagree with me argue that the defensive would not have punished the North more than the 1862-3 offensives did. That may be so, but, as indicated by Fredericksburg, the defensive would not have wasted Lee's own force, which was the principal defect with his offensives. My detractors further contend that traditional military doctrine advocates the offensive because it permits selection of the time and place of the battle. But the endemically outnumbered Lee was not in a traditional situation that afforded him a chance of winning the war militarily. It is also said that the Southern people would not have accepted the defensive. There is no evidence that Lee or the Confederate Administration relied on this factor in pursuing the 1862-3 offensives. Further, if Lee had believed that the offensive was destructive to his chances, his obligation, and that of the Administration, was to bring the public along with them. Time, the duration of the war, was a problem for both sides, the South because of its relatively limited supply base and the North because of the risk that the public would abandon the contest as hopeless.

In short, I believe that Lee's offensive grand strategy was destructive to the South's chances. Lee's task was not to win great battles, to be spectacular, but to win the war. The military historian Lt. Col. George A. Bruce states that "the art of war consists in using the forces of a nation to secure the end for which it is waged, and not in a succession of great battles that tend to defeat it." In 1862–63 Lee sought out the great battles. He went on the defensive in 1864 against his own strategic sense, only because his prior losses forced this posture. Maj. Gen. J. F. C. Fuller, the English military historian, seems to me to have fairly characterized Lee's leadership during the first two years of his command: Lee "rushed forth to find a battlefield, to challenge a contest between himself and the North." In this process, he unilaterally accomplished the attrition of his army that led to its being besieged and ultimately surrendered. His losses ultimately prevented his sustaining his army and punishing the North sufficiently to induce it to abandon the war—the only chance the South had to win.

The Price of Honor: R. E. Lee and the Question of Confederate Surrender

I

The meaning and significance of the doggedness with which Robert E. Lee pursued the Southern cause all the way to Appomattox have never been seriously analyzed by historians, who seem to assume that his persistence was wholly admirable. The general's place in history has been established without questions about the consequences of his persistence and without inquiry into his motives. Such an inquiry is, however, appropriate. Whether the South could have won the war and, if so, why it lost, are not at issue in the inquiry; rather, the relevant questions concern what Lee himself believed at various times about the risk of losing the war, how he carried out his leadership in view of what he believed, his motivation, and the consequences of his acts.

Lee's biographers have candidly reported Lee's view of the Confederacy's chances of winning the war. They have credited two 1865 statements attributed to Lee concerning his beliefs at the outset of the contest. The first of these was reported by John S. Wise, son of a former Virginia governor. According to Wise, Lee spoke to him in April 1865, near Farmville, as the Army of Northern Virginia moved toward Appomattox. Referring to the Confederate disaster at Saylers Creek, Lee said, "A few more Sailors' Creeks and it will all be over—ended—just [as] I have expected it would end from the first." The second statement was reported by General William N. Pendleton, at one time chief of artillery of the Army of Northern Virginia and a confidant of Lee's. According to Pendleton, immediately prior to the surrender Lee said to him: "I have never believed we could, against the gigantic combination for our subjugation, make good in the long run our independence unless foreign powers should, directly or indirectly, assist us."

Because the Pendleton report contained the proviso regarding foreign assistance, it is necessary to inquire of Lee's expectations in this respect. Douglas Southall Freeman stated that Lee did not believe that foreign assistance would be forthcoming, but there is more direct evidence. Lee wrote to his wife on 25 December 1861, at the time when the *Trent* affair threatened war with England; rejecting her suggestion of the possibility of British intervention in the war, he asserted: "We must make up our minds to fight our battles and win our independence alone. No one will help us." And in November 1865 he told the Englishman Herbert C. Saunders that "taking . . . the well-known antipathy of the mass of the English to the institution [of slavery] into consideration, . . . he had never expected help from England."

Taken at face value, these statements indicate that Lee believed from the beginning that war was in vain. But the statements were made after the reality of defeat. Perhaps Lee did not feel as hopeless in April 1861 as he did in April 1865. Setting these reports of his 1861 feelings aside, it is instructive to trace his beliefs about the South's chances of winning as the war progressed—and for the purposes of analysis, it is useful to examine those beliefs at three particular periods of time: in 1863, after the defeats at Gettysburg and Vicksburg; in 1864, as of the early weeks of the siege of Petersburg; and during the period following Abraham Lincoln's reelection in November 1864.

On 10 June 1863, prior to Gettysburg, in a letter to Confederate president Jefferson Davis, Lee commented on the mounting odds against a Southern victory. In portions of the letter Lee entrusted the South's cause to Heaven and to prayer; additionally, he wrote:

> Conceding to our enemies the superiority claimed by them in numbers, resources, and all the means and appliances for carrying on the war, we have no right to look for exemptions from the military consequences of a vigorous use of these advantages. . . . We should not, therefore, conceal from ourselves that our resources in men are constantly diminishing, and the disproportion in this respect between us and our enemies, if they continue united in their efforts to subjugate us, is steadily augmenting.

Lee went on to discuss the importance of encouraging the Northern peace movement. According to Freeman's interpretation, the letter reveals that "twenty-two months before Appomattox" Lee "could see no other outcome of the struggle than the ultimate defeat of the Confederacy by the more powerful Union," unless the Northern people became so discouraged that the North would no longer support the war.

Although Lee's letter does not constitute a statement of hopelessness, it is at least a statement of grave doubt. Significantly, the statement was made after the victory at Chancellorsville but before the Gettysburg and Vicksburg defeats. The reality of Lee's pessimism at that time has been described by Edwin B. Coddington. Referring to Chancellorsville, he said, "Although the Northern army had suffered heavy losses, it still was intact and could renew the offensive if given a breathing spell. . . . Even as they celebrated the glorious triumph at Chancellorsville they saw ominous developments unfolding in the Mississippi Valley. General U. S. Grant had . . . gotten his army on the same side of the river as the defenders of Vicksburg." These facts were among several that, however imperfectly, led to the Pennsylvania campaign, on which the Army of Northern Virginia embarked on 3 June 1863.

Whether or not Gettysburg and the chronologically coincidental surrender of Vicksburg were the decisive events of the war, they were of great significance in the final analysis. The loss of John C. Pemberton's army of 29,491 men and the similar casualties suffered by Lee at Gettysburg were plainly heavy blows, and they were recognized as such by thoughtful Confederate leaders. Thus, on 28 July 1863, General Josiah Gorgas, chief of ordnance, wrote in his diary: "One brief month ago we were apparently at the point of success. Lee was in Pennsylvania threatening Harrisburgh, and even Philadelphia. Vicksburgh seemed to laugh all Grant's efforts to scorn. . . . Now the picture is just as sombre as it was bright then. . . . Yesterday we rode on the pinnacle of success—today absolute ruin seems to be our portion. The Confederacy totters to its destruction."

The Confederate military disasters of July 1863 were followed by other disasters. British domestic politics, bungled diplomacy between the British and French governments, and the setbacks at Gettysburg and Vicksburg put to rest any serious possibility of European recognition of the Confederacy. On 23 July 1863, Henry Adams reported from London "that all idea of intervention is at an end." The British, responding to American pressure and their perception of the South's waning hopes, in

September 1863 detained the Laird shipyard's rams, then being built in England for the Confederacy. At home, Braxton Bragg's Army of Tennessee, after a September victory at Chickamauga, was routed at Chattanooga and Missionary Ridge in November. And on 4 December 1863 the Confederates abandoned their costly effort to seize Knoxville.

Lee did not at the time record his views of the impact of these events on the war's outlook; but given that he had in June adverted to the fact that "our resources in men are constantly diminishing, and the disproportion . . . between us and our enemies . . . is steadily augmenting," Lee's sense of defeat must have been intensified by this series of misfortunes. It is reasonable to conclude that at some point between mid-July and mid-December 1863, from twenty-one to sixteen months before Appomattox, Lee was aware that the cause was lost.

The whirlwind of 1863 raged into 1864. William T. Sherman struck for Atlanta in May, and in the same month the Army of the Potomac crossed the Rapidan to enter the Wilderness in Virginia. After grievous losses on both sides, in mid-June the Federals invested the Richmond defenses at Petersburg. The siege of Petersburg began.

Lee believed that being besieged in the Richmond defenses signaled the surrender of his army. Former Confederate artillery officer Edward Porter Alexander was in his memoirs quite specific about the meaning of what transpired. Referring to Grant's eluding Lee and to his successful move from Cold Harbor to the James River and Petersburg in mid-June 1864, Alexander commented that Grant "gained a strategic position of such controlling value that the fall of Richmond, and with it of the Confederacy, was, after that, only a question of a few moves more or less." With this event, according to Alexander, "the last hope of the Confederacy died down & flickered out." Amplifying his conclusion, Alexander stated, "The position which [Grant] had now secured, & the character of the military operations he now contemplated, removed all risk of any serious future catastrophe, however bold we might be, or however desperately we might fight. We were sure to be soon worn out." Insight into Lee's personal sense of ultimate defeat during the Petersburg siege can be gained from his correspondence. According to Freeman, Lee's letters from Petersburg "give more than a hint that he believed the Southern cause was becoming hopeless." On 23 August 1864 he told the secretary of war, "Without some increase of strength, I cannot see how we are to escape the natural military consequences of the enemy's numerical superiority." On 2 September 1864, Lee warned President Davis,

"As matters now stand we have no troops disposable to meet movements of the enemy or strike when opportunity presents, without taking them from the trenches and exposing some important point."

A note of desperation also marked Lee's communications as the siege progressed. On 26 September 1864, in a letter to Braxton Bragg about his failure to receive enough men to replenish his immediate losses, he wrote, "If things thus continue the most serious consequences must result." Pleading to Bragg for slaves to replace army teamsters, cooks, and hospital attendants, he said that if the slaves did not arrive promptly, "it may be too late." And on 10 October 1864 he told Adjutant and Inspector General Samuel Cooper that, "I fear it will be impossible to keep [Grant] out of Richmond."

In his foreword to *R. E. Lee,* Freeman discussed the summer of 1864 and Lee's sense of the risk of defeat at that time. He wrote: "Looking backwards, it is obvious, of course, that the reduction of the food supply, the death of Jackson, the defeat at Gettysburg, the virtual starvation of the horses in the winter of 1863–64, the inability of Lee to force Grant back across the Rappahannock after the battle of the Wilderness, and the failure of conscription in the summer of 1864 marked definite states in the approach of defeat. . . . *Lee saw clearly and without illusion*" (emphasis added).

It appears, therefore, that, leaving aside his conclusions in 1863 about the likelihood of defeat, by the time of the siege of Petersburg in June 1864, ten months before Appomattox. Lee believed that his surrender was inevitable. It was simply a question of when he would surrender. Alexander's analysis of the situation in June 1864 is informative:

> Of this period the future historian will doubtless write that by all the rules of war & of statecraft the time had now fully arrived for President Davis to open negotiations for peace. Now was the time to save his people the most of blood, of treasure, & of political rights. The last chance of winning independence, if it ever existed, had now expired, & all rules must condemn the hopeless shedding of blood.
>
> . . . And, perhaps, by a peace he might have saved the South five hundred, or even a thousand million dollars, & doubtless also some thousands of lives.

It is fair to suggest, however, that there may have been an unstated proviso to Lee's belief that the war was lost. This proviso concerned

Northern war-weariness, a factor to which Lee was sensitive. His letter of 10 June 1863 to President Davis, after describing the growing manpower disadvantage of the South, addressed the issue of the North's will. He wrote that "under these circumstances, we should neglect no honorable means of dividing and weakening our enemies, that they may feel some of the difficulties experienced by ourselves. It seems to me that the most effectual mode of accomplishing this object, now within our reach, is to give all the encouragement we can, consistently with truth, to the rising peace party of the North."

In practical terms, Northern war-weariness was to be at issue in the presidential election in November 1864. If Lincoln and the Republicans and Union Democrats were defeated, it was at least possible that there would be some sort of effort to end the war on terms acceptable to the Confederacy. This proviso was eliminated when Atlanta fell and Lincoln and his party were overwhelmingly reelected. It was plain then that a military decision was to be made, not a political one, and that the North would carry on the war to victory. Historian Clifford Dowdey remarked that "with the passing of the possibility of a political change bringing peace, no rational hope remained for the Confederacy to gain its independence." As characterized by Alexander, "The re-election of Mr. Lincoln . . . might well have been generally recognized as the very funeral of our last chances." Surely by November 1864, with this election result, Lee knew unconditionally that the war had been lost. Appomattox was five months away.

The question at hand is, when did Lee come to believe that defeat was inevitable? At the very latest, it must, of course, have been when he in fact decided to surrender his army in April 1865. But was there an earlier time—between April 1861 and April 1865—when this was his conviction? In view of his own statements, it is plain that Lee was at no time optimistic of a Southern victory. Indeed, he at all times seemed to feel that defeat was likely. If he is to be judged on his 1865 statements to Wise and Pendleton, it appears that he believed from the beginning, as he left the United States Army and traveled to Richmond, that the war was bound to be lost. But disregarding these expressions after the fact, the evidence composed of his own wartime statements points to at least three periods of time when he seems to have believed, perhaps with varying degrees of certainty, in the inevitability of the loss of the war. The first of these, presumably when his conviction of defeat was most tentative, was in 1863 following Gettysburg and Vicksburg. The second was in June 1864 at the outset of the Petersburg siege, approximately ten months prior to Appomattox. At that time he characterized his conviction as categorical and unqualified, but in fact he may have harbored some hope that the South would be aided by the results of the November election in the North. The third was in November 1864, five months from the end, when Lincoln was reelected.

At each of these times, Lee persisted in the fight despite what he believed about ultimate defeat. The implications of his persistence went far beyond the Army of Northern Virginia; they affected the continuation of the war as a whole. Freeman accurately portrayed the effect of Lee's resolve in fighting on:

> The final major reason for Lee's successes ... was his ability to maintain the hope and fighting spirit of the South.... As months passed with no hopeful news from France or from England, while the Union forces tightened their noose on the Confederacy, the Southern people looked to their own armies, and to them alone, to win independence. Vicksburg fell; the Confederacy was cut in twain. The expectations raised by the victory at Chickamauga were not realized. The Army of Tennessee failed to halt the slow partition of the seceded states. Gradually the South came to fix its faith on the Army of Northern Virginia and its commander.... On the Rapidan and the Rappahannock there was still defiance in the flapping of each battle flag. The Southern people remembered that Washington had lost New York and New England, Georgia and South Carolina, and still had triumphed. Lee, they believed, would do no less than the great American he most resembled. As long as he could keep the field, the South could keep its heart.... Morale behind the line, not less than on the front of action, was sustained by Lee.

Dowdey echoed Freeman's conclusion. Referring to the autumn of 1864 and the relatively high morale in Petersburg, he wrote: "It was not that the spirit in Petersburg promoted any illusions in Lee. The issue remained for him 'a question of time.'... He, a solitary mortal ..., had become the primary factor in prolonging a war with the United States." Historian Frank Vandiver has commented on another aspect of this phenomenon, Lee's awareness that the Southern people pinned their hopes on him and the Army of Northern Virginia. Lee, he wrote, "understood the special position that his army came to have in relation to Congress and to the Confederate people. . . . He knew he and his men embodied Southern hopes in the public mind. He, and by extension his army, were more symbols than realities."

The consequences of Lee's persistence are plain. They included civilian hardship, North and South; heavy casualties in the several armies of the Confederacy and Federal casualties, East and West; and severe economic losses. Given the vantage point from which Lee himself viewed the situation, it is unnecessary to quantify all of these factors; it is enough to measure the price of persistence simply in terms of casualties in the Army of Northern Virginia.

As is well known, Lee's casualties frequently were not officially reported. Without attempting to rationalize the always-conflicting data about casualties, we can let former Federal colonel Thomas L. Livermore's estimates of Confederate losses in several of the battles after Lee came to sense defeat serve to make the point:

Wilderness (5–7 May 1864)	7,750
Spotsylvania (12 May 1864)	9,000–10,000
Petersburg (15–18 June 1864)	2,970
Weldon Railroad (18–21 August 1864)	1,619
Winchester (19 September 1864)	3,921
Cedar Creek (19 October 1864)	2,910

This list omits other 1864 engagements such as Cold Harbor, the Petersburg Mine, Deep Bottom, and Boydton Plank Road. It also excludes casualties suffered after Lincoln's reelection. In addition to the casualties resulting from the almost-constant deadly sniping in the Petersburg-Richmond siege lines, the Army of Northern Virginia suffered unascertainable but severe losses at Hatcher's Run in February 1865. Lieutenant Colonel Walter H. Taylor, adjutant general of the army, reported that during the last thirty days of the siege of Petersburg "the loss to the army by desertion . . . was . . . an average of one hundred per day"; nevertheless, on 25 March 1865 Lee ordered the unsuccessful attack on Fort Stedman. Freeman conceded that Federal estimates of 4,800 to 5,000 casualties incurred by the Confederates at Fort Stedman are not "greatly exaggerated."

And finally, Lee moved west with Richmond burning behind him as a result of Confederate efforts to prevent Federal use of its manufacturing and stores. On 20 April 1865 Lee himself characterized the state of his army before Richmond. To Davis he reported

> The operations which occurred while the troops were in the entrenchments in front of Richmond and Petersburg were not marked by the boldness and decision which formerly characterized them. Except in particular instances, they were feeble; and a want of confidence seemed to possess officers and men. . . . On the morning of the 2d April, when our lines between the Appomattox and Hatcher's Run were assaulted, the resistance was not effectual: several points were penetrated and large captures made. At the commencement of the withdrawal of the army from the lines on the night of the 2d, it began to disintegrate, and straggling from the ranks increased up to the surrender on the 9th.

But Lee led this army on to Appomattox, fighting all along the way. The "still defiant Lee," according to biographer Marshall W. Fishwick, "still . . . held out," as his army "lurched westward" and "staggered toward Appomattox." In the process of this hopeless effort, from 29 March to 9 April, the Confederates, according to Livermore, needlessly lost another 6,266 men.

How many men the Confederacy lost remains unclear. One thing is certain: casualties were horrendous. R. E. Lee's Army of Northern Virginia, for example, although it consistently inflicted far more casualties than it sustained, nevertheless in twelve major battles between 1862 and 1865 lost proportionately many more killed and wounded—one of every five men engaged. Former Union colonel Thomas L. Livermore analyzed census returns, official army records, earlier studies of casualties, state muster rolls, pension records, and veterans' postwar estimates to compile *Numbers and Losses in the Civil War in America 1861–65*, first published in 1900. Livermore estimated that perhaps as many as 1,082,119 men served multiyear enlistments in the various Southern armies. Of those, approximately 329,000—or nearly one of every three—fell killed or wounded. Many thousands more died of disease. By the spring of 1865, casualties, disease, desertions, expired enlistment terms, and other losses had left the Confederate armies with only 174,223 men present at the surrenders that occurred during the last days of war. Lee, for instance, commanded only 30,000 men on his army's final march.

II

Robert E. Lee's belief in the inevitability of his final defeat, and the contrast between that belief and his combative persistence, together raise the question of his motivation. There are several worthwhile lines of inquiry regarding his motives, but before examining them it is necessary to consider briefly the question of his authority to surrender: did he have the authority to surrender his army and, if so, what circumstances permitted him to exercise that authority?

It is plain that Lee did have the right to surrender and was aware that he did. Between 7 April and 9 April 1865, as his correspondence with U.S. Grant proceeded, Lee consulted certain trusted aides and debated with himself the issue of surrender. But he insisted that, "if it is right, then *I* will take *all* the responsibility." On 9 April, the deed was done at Appomattox. On 12 April, Lee reported the surrender to Jefferson Davis, explaining that maintaining the battle "one day longer . . . would have been at a great sacrifice of life, and at its end I did not see how a surrender could have been avoided." In short, on 9 April 1865, believing that ultimate surrender was inevitable, he could not justify the sacrifice of life that further prolonging the combat would entail.

The situation at Appomattox was surely grim, but as has been noted, Lee had viewed the South's situation in the same grim terms for anywhere from twenty to five months prior to 9 April 1865. He had the same authority then to surrender as he had on 9 April. As the casualties and other losses—physical, financial, and emotional—mounted, what interest did Lee believe he was serving in continuing the hopeless struggle? His own statements suggest four possible answers to this question: he believed that the North was such a monstrous tyrant that defeat and death were the only moral responses; God willed his continuing to fight in spite of the inevitability of defeat; he was bound to persist because he was subject to Confederate civilian control, which did not want him to surrender; or his personal sense of duty demanded it.

The first answer suggests the philosophical proposition that there are worse fates than defeat and death. Americans in Lee's day, as well as today, were the heirs of a liberty-or-death tradition. Lee identified with this tradition. Despite his personal opposition to secession, he is quoted as having said, "We had, I was satisfied, sacred principles to maintain and rights to defend, for which we were in duty bound to do our best, even if we perished in the endeavor." On 7 April or 8 April, sometime within two days of the surrender, General William N. Pendleton, representing a group of officers, suggested surrender to Lee. Lee rejected the idea, stating that rather than surrender "we must all determine to die at our posts." But the liberty-or-death motive does not adequately explain Lee's prolonging the war after he adopted a belief in its futility, bearing in mind that he did in fact surrender, despite his prior rhetorical flourishes. Furthermore, he flatly rejected General Edward Porter Alexander's suggestion of guerrilla warfare as an alternative means of continuing the war because of its deleterious effect on the country as a whole. His 20 April 1865 letter to President Davis also discouraged Alexander's guerrilla warfare suggestion and urged Davis to seek a general peace. And on 13 June 1865, Lee applied for amnesty and the "benefits and full restoration of all rights and privileges" as a citizen of the United States. Each of these facts contradicts the notion that Lee was motivated by the belief that ultimate resistance to the Federals was the appropriate moral position.

Untroubled by any questions concerning the correctness of Lee's conduct, his biographer Douglas Southall Freeman comes close to suggesting that Lee persisted in the war because he believed that, regardless of the odds and the inevitability of defeat, God wanted him to keep fighting. Thus, Freeman stated that "nothing of his serenity during the war or of his silent labor in defeat can be understood unless one realizes that he submitted himself in all things faithfully to the will of a Divinity which, in his simple faith, was directing wisely the fate of nations and the daily life of His children." It is certainly true that Lee had a strong personal sense of the presence of God and God's responsibility for human events. But given the general's Herculean efforts, and his reliance on God to give him victories, it seems unreasonable to suggest that he persisted in futile combat because of some sense that God intended him to do so. Had this been his conviction, he presumably would not have surrendered on 9 April 1865.

Freeman was at pains to point out that Lee accepted wholeheartedly the American constitutional premise of military subordination to the civil government: "Lee ... applied literally and loyally his conviction that the President was the commander-in-chief." This constitutional principle was consistent with one of the general's life principles, described by Freeman as "respect for constituted authority" and "his creed of obedience to constituted authority." Biographer Clifford Dowdey's description of certain events in February and March 1865 provides an interesting insight into the question of Lee's deference to authority. Referring to the period following the Hampton Roads meeting of 3 February 1865, between Confederate representatives and Abraham Lincoln and his aides, Dowdey wrote:

> Lee had held a private conversation with Virginia's Senator R. M. T. Hunter. . . . Lee urged him to offer a resolution in the Senate that would obtain better terms than, as Hunter reported Lee as saying, "were likely to be given after a surrender." Hunter claimed that Davis had already impugned his motives for seeking peace terms, and told Lee, "if he thought the chances of success desperate, I thought he ought to say so to the President." Though Lee held frequent conversations with Davis during February, it is unlikely that he ever brought himself to introduce a subject which would be so distasteful to the President.

Dowdey then recounted the views of Secretary of War James A. Seddon, his successor in that office, John C. Breckenridge, and James Longstreet, all of whom shared Lee's recognition of the fact the war was lost and peace was needed. Dowdey concluded by observing, "The crux of the matter was that men in a position to know recognized that the South was defeated, *but no one was willing to assume the responsibility of trying to convince Davis of this*"! (emphasis added). Lee had by this time become general-in-chief of the Confederate armies. Considering Dowdey's unflinching admiration for Lee, his attributing Lee's position and that of the others mentioned to an unwillingness to take responsibility is surely an unintended indictment. In any event, although it is evident that Lee accepted subordination to civilian authority, he ultimately took responsibility for the surrender and simply announced it to Davis. It cannot, therefore, be said that civilian control was the reason for Lee's persistence.

Finally, can Lee's resolve to fight on in the face of certain defeat be explained by his sense of duty and honor? Historian Gaines M. Foster has described the South as "a culture based on honor," and Bertram Wyatt-Brown has detailed the entire complex white culture of the South in terms of a code called "Honor." The authors of *Why the South Lost the Civil War* have attempted to give a short definition of the concept:

"When Confederates talked of honor they did not mean pride so much as moral integrity, personal bravery, Christian graciousness, deference to and respect for others, and self-worth, recognized by their peers."

In Lee, honor and its companion, duty, were, to be sure, highly and self-consciously developed; so too was their consequence, the self-regard that Wyatt-Brown describes. All biographies of Lee quote at length his many aphorisms about these values. He said, for example, that the Confederates were "duty bound to do our best, even if we perished." On 22 February 1865, in a letter to his wife, he stated, "I shall . . . endeavour to do my duty & fight to the last." In a March 1865 interview with General John B. Gordon, he spoke of "what duty to the army and our people required of us." Preparing to evacuate the Petersburg-Richmond line and move west toward Appomattox, "he acted," Lieutenant Colonel Walter H. Taylor noted, "as one who was conscious of having accomplished all that was possible in the line of duty, and who was undisturbed by the adverse conditions in which he found himself."

In regard to the effort to escape the pursuing Federals between Richmond and Appomattox, Freeman observed: "So long as this chance was open to him, his sense of duty did not permit him to consider any alternative" and "as long as there was a prospect of escape Lee felt it was his duty to fight on. He would not yield one hour before he must." Freeman also noted approvingly Lee's memorandum to himself: "There is a true glory and a true honor: the glory of duty done—the honor of the integrity of principle." Commenting on "the dominance of a sense of duty in [Lee's] actions," Dowdey stated that "this is not so much a sense of duty in the abstract as a duty to do the best he could. The point can clearly be seen when duty, *as a sense of the pride of a professional in his craft,* caused him to practice meticulously the techniques of command *long after any military purpose could be achieved"* (emphasis added).

Such a narrow definition of Lee's sense of honor and duty seems to be another unintended indictment by Dowdey. However defined, this sense of honor appears, after all, to have been an essentially personal emotional commitment that compelled Lee to fight on, regardless of the cost and long after he believed that it was futile to continue the contest. Referring to the Confederacy's hopeless situation during the winter of 1864–1865 and sympathetic to his personal commitment, Dowdey recognized "the moral obligation that required [Lee] to act as though defeat could be held off."

In a chapter entitled "The Sword of Robert E. Lee," Freeman set forth "an accounting of his service to the state." Having noted Lee's mobilization of Virginia, the Seven Days, the repulse of Federal offensives against Richmond, and his victories in six of ten major battles from Gaines's Mill through Spotsylvania, Freeman proceeded,

> During the twenty-four months when he had been free to employ open manoeuvre, a period that had ended with Cold Harbor, he had sustained approximately 103,000 casualties and had inflicted 145,000. Holding, as he usually had, to the offensive, his combat losses had been greater in proportion to his numbers than those of the Federals, but he had demonstrated how strategy may increase an opponent's casualties, for his losses included only 16,000 prisoners, whereas he had taken 38,000. Chained at length to the Richmond defenses, he had saved the capital from capture for ten months. All this he had done in the face of repeated defeats for the Southern troops in nearly every other part of the Confederacy. . . . These difficulties of the South would have been even worse had not the Army of Northern Virginia occupied so much of the thought and armed strength of the North. Lee is to be judged, in fact, not merely by what he accomplished with his own troops but by what he prevented the hosts of the Union from doing sooner elsewhere.

In reciting what Lee had accomplished, Freeman did not allude to the fact that for perhaps the last twenty months of these efforts, and surely for a substantial lesser period, Lee was proceeding in a cause that he personally believed was lost.

James M. McPherson has summarized the ultimate consequences of the prolonging of the war, to which Lee's accomplishments made a significant contribution:

> the South was not only invaded and conquered, it was utterly destroyed. By 1865 the Union forces had . . . destroyed two-thirds of the assessed value of Southern wealth, two-fifths of the South's livestock, and one-quarter of her white men between the ages of twenty and forty. More than half the farm machinery was ruined, and the damage to railroads and industries was incalculable. . . . Southern wealth decreased by 60 percent (or 30

percent if the slaves are not counted as wealth). These figures provide eloquent testimony to the tragic irony of the South's counterrevolution of 1861 to preserve its way of life.

In conjunction, the statements of Freeman and McPherson raise reasonable questions regarding Lee and history and Lee's role as an American idol. On the one hand, the Lee tradition projects a tragic hero, a man who courageously pursued a cause that he believed to be doomed. On the other hand, this heroic tradition must be balanced against the consequences of Lee's heroism. There is, of course, a nobility and poignancy, a romance, in the tragic and relentless pursuit of a hopeless cause. But in practical terms such pursuit is subject to a very different interpretation.

In reality, military leadership is not just a private or personal activity. Nor is a military leader's sense of honor and duty simply a private and personal impulse. Military leadership and the leader's sense of duty are of concern not only to the leader, but also to the followers and to the enemy, ordinary people, many of whom die, are maimed, or otherwise suffer. In short, military leadership involves responsibility for what happens to other persons. There is, therefore, no matter how sincerely a leader may believe in the justice of a cause, a difference between undertaking or continuing military leadership in a cause that the leader feels can succeed and undertaking or continuing such leadership in a cause that the leader feels is hopeless. In the latter circumstance, the leader knows that his order "once more into the breach" will kill or injure many of his soldiers as well as the enemy's and also realizes that his order and these deaths and injuries are without, in Dowdey's phrase, "any military purpose." Lacking a military purpose, they also have no political purpose. Thus they are without any rational purpose.

The absence of any rational purpose behind Lee's persistence is suggested by his sense of the meaning of the deaths of his men as revealed by his early advocate, the Reverend J. William Jones. Among the general's wartime papers that Jones found after his death were "maxims, proverbs, quotations from the Psalms, selections from standard authors, and reflections of his own." One of these, in Lee's own hand, read, "The warmest instincts of every man's soul declare the glory of the soldier's death. It is more appropriate to the Christian than to the Greek to sing: 'Glorious his fate, and envied is his lot, Who for his country fights and for it dies.' "

As suggested earlier by McPherson's description of the war's impact on the South, the conflict involved catastrophic consequences for the people of the United States, both North and South. During the war as a whole more than half a million soldiers died. Untold thousands were maimed. The families of all of these men also suffered grievously. Whatever portion of the catastrophe occurred after the time when Lee had become convinced that the war was lost—whether Lee came to believe this twenty, fifteen, ten, or only five months before the end—significant harm took place, in the West as well as the East, before Lee finally called a halt to the fighting. For the plain people who suffered, Lincoln's "him who shall have borne the battle, and . . . his widow, and his orphan," the consequences of the war were dire in the extreme.

Freeman wrote bitterly about Southerners who were fearful or doubtful or who wished for peace, comparing them unfavorably to the dauntless Lee and to President Davis. But the authors of *Why the South Lost the Civil War* made a different observation: "By late 1864, very likely earlier, those Confederates who argued for an end of war, even if that meant returning to the Union, did not include only the war-weary defeatists. Many among those who took that statesman-like position may have lost their will, but they weigh more on the scales of humanity than those who would have fought to the last man."

The Lee orthodoxy insists that the Confederate officers and soldiers at Appomattox were tearful and heartbroken at their surrender—they wanted to keep fighting. But even purveyors of the orthodoxy occasionally, perhaps unwittingly, contradict the tradition. Thus, quoting Lieutenant Colonel Charles Venable, Dowdey wrote that soldiers who learned of Lee's intent to surrender were "convulsed with passionate grief." But Dowdey also reported that "Lee was aware that many of his soldiers, officers and men, were ready to end 'the long agony.' . . . He could sense the attitude." He also described enlisted men who, en route to Appomattox, "overcome by exhaustion . . . were lying stretched out flat or sitting with their heads on their knees, waiting to be gathered up by the enemy." A suggestive Federal account by an eyewitness agreed with Dowdey's report. "Billy," an enlisted man in the 1st Michigan Volunteers, wrote to his family from Appomattox on the day of the surrender. He described the pursuit to Appomattox and then added, "The best of it is the Rebs are as pleased over the surrender as we are, and when the surrender was made known to them cheer after cheer went up along their whole line."

If one steps back from the romantic tradition, the intensity of Lee's resolve seems startling. By the early weeks of 1865, the Confederacy was an empty shell. Its ports and, except for Richmond, its major cities were in Federal hands. Its western army had been effectively dispersed in the December battle at Nashville. Having marched across Georgia at will, William T. Sherman was poised to start from Savannah into the Carolinas, and no significant force was prepared to oppose him. Lee was trapped in the Richmond defenses. Much of the civilian population was suffering serious hardship and civil order was at the breaking point. In these circumstances, Lee on 11 January 1865 sent to Senator Hunter a letter regarding the enlisting of slaves as soldiers. He wrote of "our duty to provide for continued war and not for a battle or a campaign." He sounded the same note in discussing the same issue in his letter of 18 February 1865 to Congressman Ethelbert Barksdale: "I believe that we should provide for a protracted struggle, not merely for a battle or a campaign." On 19 February 1865 he advised the secretary of war, "I fear it may be necessary to abandon all our cities, & preparation should be made for this contingency." On 14 March 1865, with Appomattox less than a month away, he wrote to Davis concerning the necessity to avoid the "destruction of our armies. If they can be maintained, we may recover from our reverses." Ten days later, he requested from Virginia all "negroes, slave and free, between the ages of eighteen and forty-five, for services as soldiers ... to enable us to oppose the enemy." Lee's army was shrinking daily as a result of desertion. His letter to Davis of 20 April 1865 acknowledged that his army had been demoralized "in the entrenchments in front of Richmond and Petersburg." After Saylers Creek on 6 April 1865, where approximately eight thousand of the harried Confederates fleeing westward from Petersburg were overpowered and surrendered, Lee spoke to General William Mahone of his remaining soldiers as "true men." In Lee's mind the captured men were by implication untrue; a "true man" was one who could somehow stay in the fight as long as Lee's personal sense of honor demanded it. So Lee fought on regardless of the consequences to the Southern people and in spite of the absence of any rational purpose.

There is every reason to question the aspect of the Lee tradition that has glorified and does not reconsider his pursuit of the war even after he believed it was lost. What has not been addressed here, however, is the implicit question of whether, prior to Appomattox, Lee had an alternative to continuing the fight as of the time he knew that such continuation had no rational purpose. In terms of military law and custom he had the technical authority to surrender his army when he believed its situation was hopeless. General Order No. 9 and the 12 April letter to President Davis were drafted on the premise of this authority: defeat was inevitable and postponing surrender would uselessly bring additional deaths to the soldiers for whom he was responsible. But in practical terms, although the same premise had existed for some months, the exercise of that authority prior to Appomattox would doubtless have presented serious problems because of the views of President Davis and at least some of the Confederate political leadership and the opinions and expectations of the army and the Southern people. Granting that Lee had to take these factors into account, what were his practical alternatives to carrying on the war until Appomattox? This question is essentially philosophical. Perceiving that useless death and destruction are the consequences of an army commander's continuing to fight, but that his government or the army or people expect him to continue, the issue concerns the commander's personal responsibility.

In stating that the war was effectively lost in June 1864 at Petersburg and that President Davis should have sought peace at that time, Confederate officer Edward Porter Alexander said that "both the army and the people at that time would have been loth to recognize that the cause was hopeless. In the army, I am sure, such an idea was undreamed of." But he then wrote, "Gen. Lee's influence could doubtless have secured acquiescence in it, for his influence had no bounds; but nothing short of that would." This, then, is the first answer to the question of Lee's practical alternatives to continuing the fight. He could have surrendered and persuaded the government and the people to accept the fact of the loss of the war. But assuming that his sense of personal responsibility did not extend to this exercise of his technical authority, and prior to Appomattox it obviously did not, he could have confronted the civilian authorities with his views of the hopelessness and tragic consequences of fighting on and recommended that the fighting cease. Lee did not do this. Indeed, as late as the winter of 1864–1865, as noted by Dowdey, he would not take that responsibility. Had Lee done this, and had the civilian authorities ordered him to fight on, two choices would have then been available to him. He could have fought on and borne history's judgment for having done so, with credit for his effort to avoid the continuation. Or he could have resigned and escaped that judgment.

Readers may form their own opinion as to the time—twenty, fifteen, ten, or five months before the end—when Lee's personal responsibility became an imperative. That responsibility was not in fact assumed by Lee until 9 April 1865. The issue of Lee's personal responsibility cannot be escaped by romanticizing his continuation of the war. As a responsible actor in the events of the war, Lee must be fully subject to history's gaze and must be accountable for his acts.

An apologist for Lee may point out that all wars have gone on too long, that all wars have invariably been lost long before the losing side has surrendered or abandoned the war. This is true, but, as regards the matter considered here, it is beside the point. The point is this: the Lee literature uniformly expresses admiration for the general's having carried on the war, despite its devastations, long after the Confederate cause was hopeless and long after Lee himself knew that it was hopeless. That this was heroic on his part, that it is part of his glory, is Lee dogma. This dogma is dubious, however, within the context of the American Civil War, in view of the common nationality and culture of the North and South, the political circumstances of the sections, Lee's prewar disapproval of secession, and his prompt postwar application for amnesty. Taking these factors into account, the harm to Americans, North and South, should surely be considered in reference to Lee's status in American history, as should questions concerning the personal character of his motives for continuing the contest.

It may be easier to grasp the irony and cost of Lee's persistence if one moves from gross statistics to what happened in microcosm to Southern soldiers. On 25 March 1865, Lee ordered the Confederate attack on Fort Stedman, a Federal stronghold in the Petersburg line. After initial success, the assault was beaten back. Federal reports estimated Confederate casualties to have been between forty-eight hundred and five thousand men, and General George G. Meade reported to General U. S. Grant that "permission was granted the enemy . . . to remove their dead and wounded, under flag of truce." On 2 April 1865, as the Confederate Petersburg line was at last pierced, some four hundred to six hundred men from Cadmus M. Wilcox's division and Nathaniel H. Harris's brigade were put into Fort Gregg and told to hold it to the last extremity. They were assaulted by a full division of Federals and ultimately defended themselves with bayonets in hand-to-hand fighting. Finally surrounded, the survivors capitulated, but the Federals also found fifty-five dead in the fort. In a report reminiscent of Lee's "glory of the soldier's death" document, Freeman cited a source stating that during the Fort Gregg struggle Lee called his staff around him and asked them to witness "a most gallant defense."

Two weeks after Fort Stedman and a week after Fort Gregg, Lee surrendered. On the following day he issued General Order No. 9, revered in history, the farewell to his army that included these words: "Feeling that valor and devotion could accomplish nothing that could compensate for the loss that may have attended the continuance of the contest, I determined to avoid the *useless sacrifice* of those whose past services have endeared them to their countrymen" (emphasis added). And as has been previously stated, he then reported to President Davis that he had surrendered because to maintain the battle "one day longer . . . would have been at a great sacrifice of life, and at its end I did not see how a surrender could have been avoided."

The dead and wounded Confederates at Fort Stedman and Fort Gregg, and the Federals killed and wounded there, are symbolic of the problem of the prolongation of the war and General Lee's military accomplishments. As of 9 April 1865, Lee himself believed that further casualties would be a "useless sacrifice," but it was too late for the several thousand who had gone down since he had concluded that the war was futile. Among these, of course, were the 6,266 of his soldiers killed and wounded in the Appomattox campaign itself.

On 9 April 1865, Lee apparently felt that he had fully and finally served his personal sense of duty. He had fulfilled, at last, what Dowdey described as his personal sense of "duty to do the best he could, . . . a sense of the pride of a professional in his craft." He was prepared, at last, again quoting Dowdey, "to assume the responsibility" for introducing a subject "distasteful" to Jefferson Davis. The awful human cost of his persistence had, of course, been paid by countless other people, including his own soldiers.

Giving Lee full credit for good faith and high personal character, the historian must nonetheless—as a practitioner of a discipline regarded as one of the humanities—take into account the human and social consequences of his continuing to lead others in a war that he believed was lost. It is fair to observe that Virginia, reputedly the focus of Lee's primary interest, suffered especially devastating losses of life and property because it was the scene of almost constant warfare. The facts cast serious doubt on the traditional assumption that Lee's persistence was wholly admirable.

Confederate Leadership
at Fredericksburg

In terms of Confederate leadership, Fredericksburg may be summed up by the old saying, "shooting fish in a barrel." That is what happened at Fredericksburg. Two official communications in the *Official Records* provide an excellent summary of the battle. On November 14, 1862, General in Chief Henry W. Halleck notified Ambrose E. Burnside as follows regarding Burnside's proposed Fredericksburg movement: "The President has just assented to your plan. He thinks it will succeed if you move rapidly; otherwise not." Lee's report of Fredericksburg, dated April 10, 1863, says this about Burnside's assault on December 13, 1862: "The attack on the 13th had been so easily repulsed, and by so small a part of our army, that it was not supposed the enemy would limit his efforts to an attempt, which, in view of the magnitude of his preparations and the extent of his force, seemed comparatively insignificant."[1]

In the late fall of 1862, on the eve of Fredericksburg, the fortunes of the war had tilted dramatically against the Confederacy, even in the Virginia theater. The Confederate movements into Maryland and Kentucky had been frustrated at Antietam and Perryville, and Lee and Bragg, respectively, had retreated. Perhaps even more significantly, the raids into Maryland and Kentucky had dispelled the Southern notion that these border states were anxious to join the Confederacy or contribute heavily to its support. In the West, the North continued to penetrate along the Mississippi River and therefore to threaten Vicksburg. The issuance of

[1]U.S. War Department, *The War of the Rebellion: A Compilation of the Official Records of the Union and Confederate Armies,* 127 vols., index, and atlas (Washington, D.C.: GPO, 1880–1901), 19(2):579, 21:555 (hereafter cited as *OR;* all references are to series 1).

Lincoln's preliminary proclamation of emancipation had radically changed the dynamics of the war and at least suggested that the Confederacy was to be perceived less favorably in Europe.

It is plain that, as specifically related to the Army of Northern Virginia, Lee's Maryland venture had significantly damaged that army in casualties and morale. Lee had lost approximately 13,000 men (including missing), more than 26 percent of his force, at Antietam, on the heels of the loss of approximately 9,000 (19 percent) at Second Bull Run and significant losses at South Mountain.[2]

Lee candidly reported the symptoms of morale deterioration. On September 21 he addressed President Jefferson Davis about the state of the army: "Its present efficiency is greatly paralyzed by the loss to its ranks of the numerous stragglers. I have taken every means in my power from the beginning to correct this evil, which has increased instead of diminished." On September 22 Lee again wrote to Davis about this subject. "In connection with . . . straggling . . . the destruction of private property by the army has occupied much of my attention," he stated. "A great deal of damage to citizens is done by stragglers, who consume all they can get from the charitable and all they can take from the defenseless, in many cases wantonly destroying stock and other property." Three days later Lee told the president that after withdrawing from Maryland on September 18 he had intended to cross the Potomac again, "to advance upon Hagerstown and endeavor to defeat the enemy at that point," but had changed his mind, he said, because the army did not "exhibit its former temper and condition."[3]

Casualties, including those in the officer corps, required a reorganization of the Army of Northern Virginia. Douglas Southall Freeman titles a chapter in *Lee's Lieutenants* "A Crisis in Reorganization." Referring to the army's general officers of lower rank, Freeman observes that "that organization now had to be rebuilt."[4] To this process General Lee's attention was committed over a period of weeks in the late fall. The first and easiest step was the appointment of James Longstreet and

[2]Thomas L. Livermore, *Numbers and Losses in the Civil War in America, 1861–1865* (1901; reprint, Dayton, Ohio: Morningside, 1986), 92–93, 88–89.
[3]*OR* 19(1):143, (2):627.
[4]Douglas Southall Freeman, *Lee's Lieutenants: A Study in Command,* 3 vols. (New York: Charles Scribner's Sons, 1942–44), 2:250.

Stonewall Jackson to head the now officially authorized corps commands.[5] This was followed by the formal structuring of the corps and promotions to the ranks of major general and brigadier. When the process was completed, the army included Maj. Gen. J. E. B. Stuart's cavalry division, comprising four brigades and Maj. John Pelham's horse artillery, and Brig. Gen. William Nelson Pendleton's reserve artillery, together with the artillery in the two corps. Longstreet had the First Corps, composed, in addition to corps artillery, of five divisions: Maj. Gen. Lafayette McLaws's, Maj. Gen. Richard H. Anderson's, Maj. Gen. George E. Pickett's, Maj. Gen. John Bell Hood's, and Brig. Gen. Robert Ransom, Jr.'s. Jackson's Second Corps had four divisions, commanded, respectively, by Major Generals D. H. Hill, A. P. Hill, and Jubal A. Early (commanding Ewell's division) and Brig. Gen. William B. Taliaferro (commanding Jackson's division).[6]

The period after Antietam also saw changes in the Army of the Potomac, the most profound involving George B. McClellan's removal and replacement. But that army had also been refitted and substantially reinforced during McClellan's long delay in Maryland, from September 17 to October 30. On the latter date the Army of the Potomac finally moved south into Virginia. Ambrose E. Burnside's appointment to replace McClellan on November 7, as well as communications between Washington and the army, made it plain that the administration expected Federal action.[7] Reacting to the administration, Burnside promptly prepared a plan of campaign.[8]

In the late fall of 1862 Lee was not in a position to mount a strategically offensive move. Confederate leadership, for the time being, was to be reactive to Federal aggressiveness. These were the circumstances that led to the battle of Fredericksburg.

As of Burnside's appointment to replace McClellan, the Army of the Potomac was encamped near Warrenton, Virginia. The Army of Northern Virginia was divided. Jackson's corps was in the Winchester area in the Valley; Longstreet was near Culpeper Court House, between the Rapidan and the Rappahannock.[9]

[5] *OR* 19(2):643.
[6] *OR* 21:538–45, 19(2):683.
[7] *OR* 21:82–83.
[8] *OR* 19(2):552.
[9] *OR* 21:83, 550–51.

The interesting thing about the battle of Fredericksburg, and about Confederate leadership at the battle, involves what happened between Burnside's communication of his plan on November 9 and his launching attacks at Fredericksburg on December 13, 1862. We speak from time to time about accidental battles. In June and July of 1863 the armies were on a collision course in Pennsylvania, but Gettysburg was the place of collision by chance and circumstances. Fredericksburg surely ranks as another prominent accidental battle of the war. Neither army intended to fight there. This becomes obvious if one consults the communications of the leadership prior to the battle, during the period between November 9 and December 13.

McClellan had exhausted the Lincoln administration's patience with his inaction by November 5, the day on which the Federal change-of-command order was issued and Halleck dispatched a highly pregnant letter to Burnside: "General: Immediately on assuming command . . . you will report the position of your troops and what you purpose [*sic*] doing with them."[10] On November 7 (but not sent until November 9 through Chief of Staff Gen. G. W. Cullum) Burnside advised Halleck of his plan to concentrate his army near Warrenton, "impress upon the enemy a belief that we are to attack at Culpeper or Gordonsville, and . . . then to make a rapid move of the whole force to Fredericksburg, *with a view to a movement upon Richmond at that point*" (emphasis added).[11]

This statement makes it plain that Fredericksburg was to be the base for a Federal move on Richmond rather than the point of attack. Burnside's November 9 communication also referred to "moving by way of Fredericksburg," stated that Fredericksburg lay "on the shortest route to Richmond," and projected "a rapid movement . . . direct upon Richmond." In short, Burnside's plan was premised on his ability to cross the river at Fredericksburg promptly and with little or no opposition, and then to move toward Richmond.

Because of his plan to cross the Rappahannock, Burnside requested that pontoon trains be sent to Fredericksburg. On November 12 Halleck ordered Brig. Gen. Daniel P. Woodbury of the engineer brigade in Washington to instruct the chief quartermaster to transport "all" pontoons and bridging materials to Aquia.[12] On November 14 Burnside's chief

[10] *OR* 21:83.
[11] *OR* 19(2):552.
[12] *OR* 19(2):553, 572.

engineer twice telegraphed General Woodbury to inquire about the progress of the pontoons. Woodbury's response acknowledged delay but also described a plentiful supply of pontoons and stated that the first train would start for Falmouth on the sixteenth or seventeenth.[13] Burnside was reassured.

Lee intended at all times to confront any Federal move south. Initially uncertain regarding Burnside's intent, he was ultimately persuaded that Fredericksburg was to be Burnside's route. Even then Lee did not plan to fight at Fredericksburg. Instead, he contemplated meeting the Federal army at the North Anna. At Culpeper on November 19 Lee wrote to Jackson at Winchester. He was not decided on Burnside's route but possessed enough evidence to start Longstreet's corps to Fredericksburg. In spite of this he announced that "I do not now anticipate making a determined stand north of the North Anna."[14]

After the battle, in a December 16 letter to the secretary of war, Lee reiterated that fighting at the North Anna had been his intent. He was then anticipating another crossing of the Rappahannock by the defeated Burnside, perhaps at Port Royal. In announcing his own intent Lee said, "I think it more advantageous to retire to the Annas and give battle than on the banks of the Rappahannock." He then stated that that had been his intent initially, when Burnside first arrived at Fredericksburg. Lee also noted that the narrowness and winding character of the Rappahannock made it unlikely that he could prevent a Federal crossing in the vicinity of Fredericksburg. He had fought at Fredericksburg, he wrote, not because of any military advantage to that site but because he did not like to open the area south of Fredericksburg to Federal "depredation" and because he wanted to collect forage and provisions in the Rappahannock Valley.[15]

The North Anna idea had persisted. General Longstreet's article in *Battles and Leaders* says that after Jackson's arrival at Fredericksburg the commander of the Second Corps stated a preference for fighting at the North Anna because he believed that a victory there, unlike a victory at Fredericksburg, would permit pursuit of the enemy.[16]

[13] *OR* 21:84–85.

[14] *OR* 21:1021.

[15] *OR* 21:549.

[16] James Longstreet, "The Battle of Fredericksburg," in *Battles and Leaders of the Civil War*, ed. Robert Underwood Johnson and Clarence Clough Buel, 4 vols. (New York: Century, 1887–88), 3:71–72 (hereafter cited as *B&L*).

With the Confederate army widely divided, and in pursuance of his plan of crossing at Fredericksburg and then moving south toward Richmond, Burnside started his army toward Fredericksburg. The march went well, and the Federals promptly arrived on the northern side of the river: Edwin V. Sumner's two corps were at Falmouth on November 17, and William B. Franklin's on the eighteenth. Joseph Hooker's corps reached Stafford Court House, six miles from Falmouth, on November 19, the day Burnside himself arrived. Pontoons were not there, and the river was not believed to be fordable.[17]

Lee's move to Fredericksburg was much less direct. His planning must be described because it is very much a part of his leadership. His communications especially demonstrate two aspects of that leadership: first, his carefulness as a defensive planner, and second, his high level of responsibility for the Virginia theater of the war.

Although a field army commander, Lee had broad responsibility for overall Confederate strategy and troop movement in the Virginia theater. In a letter of November 14 to Secretary of War George Wythe Randolph, after reciting a Federal movement out of the upper part of Fauquier County to the north of Manassas and Warrenton, the Confederate commander wrote that he "thought it probable that he [the enemy] would change his line of approach to Richmond and make a sudden descent upon Fredericksburg, from which point his line of communication with Washington would be comparatively safe." Lee also told Randolph of his consideration of ways of frustrating Burnside's use of Fredericksburg as a point of concentration, noting that he had ordered the destruction of the railroad from Fredericksburg to Aquia Creek. Providing evidence that, like Burnside, he saw the Federal move to Fredericksburg as simply the base for a move to Richmond, Lee discussed ordering the destruction of the railroad from Fredericksburg to Hanover Junction. But he was uncertain regarding Burnside's intent: "Were I certain of the route he will pursue, I should commence immediately to make it as difficult as possible."[18]

On the following day, November 15, Lee directed Brig. Gen. W. H. F. Lee to send a mixed reconnaissance force to Fredericksburg. If they found it occupied, they were to proceed south to the railroad crossing of the North Anna. Also on the fifteenth he advised Col. W. B. Ball, commanding

[17] *OR* 21:101 – 2.
[18] *OR* 19(2):717.

at Fredericksburg, of the ordered reconnaissance and said that "it is probable that he [the enemy] is marching upon Fredericksburg."[19]

Lee changed his mind two days later regarding Burnside's intent. To President Davis he stated that he had apprehended a Federal shift to Fredericksburg to use it as a base, but there was no evidence of such a move. "I have heard of no preparation to build the wharves at Aquia Creek," he wrote, and there were no apparent provisions for subsisting a large army. This provoked new speculation. On the same day as his November 17 letter to President Davis, Lee wrote to the secretary of war: "I think it, therefore, probable that the movement in execution is with a view of transferring the army south of the James River, and the appointment of General Burnside to command favors this supposition." Late on the seventeenth he advised Secretary Randolph that his scouts reported three Federal brigades advancing on Fredericksburg, but he speculated that this might be a feint.[20]

On the following day, November 18, Lee reported to Adjutant and Inspector Gen. Samuel Cooper that his scouts reported Sumner's corps moving toward Fredericksburg. Two divisions of Longstreet's corps and W. H. F. Lee's cavalry brigade had been started for Fredericksburg, according to Lee. Also on November 18, from near Culpeper Court House, Lee wrote to Jackson, who was still near Winchester in the Valley. Lee told his subordinate that the cavalry reported Federals moving in force to Fredericksburg, but the Confederate plan, he said, "awaits confirmation of intelligence." Lee further stated that there was no observable preparation for a transfer to south of the James River. Finally, he told Jackson that it was advisable to put some of his divisions in motion across the mountains and "advance them at least as far as Sperryville or Madison Court-House."[21]

On the nineteenth Lee told President Davis that two divisions of Longstreet's corps had moved to Fredericksburg on the eighteenth and two more were to follow that day. Still apparently uncertain regarding Burnside's Fredericksburg destination, Lee said, "I shall wait to hear again from Stuart, and then proceed as circumstances dictate." Also on the nineteenth, writing to Jackson at Winchester, Lee noted that

[19] *OR* 21:1013–14.
[20] *OR* 21:1014–16.
[21] *OR* 21:1017, 1019.

"Longstreet's corps is moving to Fredericksburg, opposite to which place Sumner's corps has arrived." He then expressed his preference for a North Anna battle site, as previously noted. Lee also told Jackson on the nineteenth of a November 18 message from Stuart that the entire Federal army had marched to Fredericksburg and advised Jackson that Stuart "considers the information he received as conclusive" on the issue. Lee said further that he was waiting for a report from Stuart on November 19. He would "then start for Fredericksburg, if circumstances warrant." Jackson was not told to move from Winchester.[22]

Finally, on November 22, Lee could report from Fredericksburg to General Cooper that the entire Federal army was before him on the other side of the river. On the following day he told Jackson this and asked him to move east of the Blue Ridge "and take such a position as you may find best." Jackson also learned that Lee remained uncertain of enemy plans and expressed the fear that Federals would be transferred from Fredericksburg to some other location.[23]

Lee's anxiety about Federal intent was briefly piqued on the twenty-second. Reporting to Davis on the twenty-fifth he told of Federals moving to their rear on November 22, virtually disappearing from the heights opposite Lee. It had not been a transfer of operations, Lee wrote, but for the purpose of avoiding Confederate artillery fire and for subsistence convenience. Lee stated that he now believed the Federals did propose to go south by way of Fredericksburg. He did not know where the crossing would occur but believed that Hanover Junction was an object of the movement. He intended to break up the railroad south of Fredericksburg but was reluctant to do so because of the effects of the damage on civilian morale. He tendered to Davis the issue of concentrating closer to Richmond and explained that he had waited to order Jackson to Fredericksburg because Jackson's presence on Burnside's flank was tactically valuable.[24]

Lee also wrote twice to Jackson on the twenty-fifth. His first dispatch reiterated his view that a move by Jackson to Culpeper would be advantageous and stated that Burnside apparently intended to advance on Richmond from a Fredericksburg base. He stated further that although Jackson's corps "may, therefore, be needed" in Fredericksburg, he need

[22] *OR* 21:1021–22.
[23] *OR* 21:1026–28.
[24] *OR* 21:1029.

not hasten his march. The second dispatch of the twenty-fifth carried a 7:00 P.M. time. It recapitulated the earlier dispatch and recommended the Culpeper destination for Jackson, but suggested that Jackson's advance troops march as far as Rappahannock Station and that his cavalry cross the river. These moves, Lee said, would deter an advance by Burnside.[25]

On November 26, in another letter to Jackson, Lee adverted for the first time to the possibility that Burnside might attempt to cross the river in front of Fredericksburg. He also said that "some other point on the river" might be the place of crossing. He requested that Jackson advance "by easy marches" to Fredericksburg. In view of the possibility of Burnside's crossing, Lee believed "that the whole army should be united." On the following day, having forwarded a status report to President Davis, including word of the arrival on the Stafford Road of a Federal pontoon train, Lee wrote again to Jackson designating the area of Massaponax Creek as Jackson's appropriate destination. On the twenty-eighth Lee reiterated to Jackson the Massaponax Creek destination and added that he was busy in a personal reconnaissance of the river. He did *not* expect Burnside to cross in front of Fredericksburg and speculated that the Port Royal area might be the planned site because of the possibility of support from gunboats and ready access for the Federals to the Old Richmond Road for a movement south.[26]

As a part of his reconnaissance, under date of December 2, 1862, Lee received a very interesting report from a captain of engineers. Lee, of course, had requested the report, which reflected "an examination of the Rappahannock River with reference to positions suitable for forcing a passage from the north side." Incorporating references to "Coast Survey Charts" and detailed observation, it seems a sophisticated document.[27]

On December 6 Lee again reported to the president. He cited Burnside's inaction and set forth a comprehensive statement of Federal troops elsewhere in the theater. The communication indicates that Burnside's inaction played on Lee's fear of Federal operations elsewhere, including south of the James River.[28]

---

[25] *OR* 21:1031–32.

[26] *OR* 21:1033–35, 1037. This road had three names at the time: the Old Richmond Road, the Bowling Green Road, and the Port Royal Road. In this essay, it is called the Old Richmond Road.

[27] *OR* 21:1042–43.

[28] *OR* 21:1049–50.

Lee did not know that there was an objective reason for Burnside's inaction. It was the Federal judgment on or about November 17–19 that the river was not fordable[29] *and* Federal command failure to deliver the pontoons on which Burnside's plan relied. On November 22 a Burnside dispatch unwittingly acknowledged that the premise of the Federal plan had already been compromised, and predicted what was to occur on December 13. Referring to his pontoon requisition in the initial statement of his plan on November 9, Burnside said:

> It is very clear that my object was to make the move to Fredericksburg very rapidly, and to throw a heavy force across the river before the enemy could concentrate a force to oppose the crossing, and supposed the pontoon train would arrive at this place nearly simultaneously with the head of the column. Had that been the case, the whole of General Sumner's column—33,000 strong—would have crossed into Fredericksburg at once over a pontoon bridge, in front of a city . . . garrisoned by a small squadron of cavalry and a battery of artillery which General Sumner silenced within a hour after his arrival.
>
> Had the pontoon bridge arrived even on the 19th or 20th, the army could have crossed with trifling opposition. But now the opposite side of the river is occupied by a large rebel force under General Longstreet, with batteries ready to be placed in position to operate against the working parties building the bridge and the troops in crossing.
>
> The pontoon train has not yet arrived, and the river is too high for the troops to cross at any of the fords.[30]

Thus, Burnside's plan, and opportunity, to cross on November 18, with the pike to Richmond open and Hanover Junction vulnerable, was gone. The pontoons story goes on and on. They began to arrive on November 25, but there was still inadequate bridging material.[31] On November 26 Burnside met Lincoln and Secretary of War Edwin M. Stanton at Aquia Creek. On November 28, in Washington, Burnside again

[29] *OR* 21:85.
[30] *OR* 21:103.
[31] *OR* 21:85, 798.

discussed the situation with the administration.[32] Despite the evaporation of the whole strategic idea, a crossing in the face of the Army of Northern Virginia was to occur.

Although neither commander was yet aware of it, they were now committed to the accidental battle at Fredericksburg. There was, however, one more decision that sealed this eventuality. The Federals had made preparations to cross at Skinker's Neck, fourteen miles below Fredericksburg, but Confederate demonstrations there changed Burnside's mind. In addition, Burnside came to the belief that the enemy would be most surprised by his crossing at Fredericksburg.[33]

On December 11, the day the Federal bridges were finally laid, Burnside issued orders to the Federal grand division commanders. These orders have an eerie quality because they do not advert to the radical change in circumstances between Burnside's initial planning for his campaign and December 11, that is, the arrival of the Army of Northern Virginia across the river. Sumner was told to cross at the upper bridge and to take "the heights that command the Plank road and the Telegraph road." His "first corps" was to move directly to the front, supporting it by "your other corps." Franklin was to cross, move immediately to the front, and take "the heights which command the Plank and Telegraph roads." He was to "move down the old Richmond road, in the direction of the railroad." Hooker was to cross and hold himself in readiness to support either Sumner or Franklin.[34] What had been intended as a change of the Federal base *to* Fredericksburg for an advance on Richmond had become the battle *of* Fredericksburg.

Burnside's forces crossed on December 11 and 12.[35] Two of Jackson's divisions were still moving up, and the other two, Early's and D. H. Hill's, were quite remote. The latter two were not ordered up until late afternoon on December 12, and both divisions had to make night marches to join Lee's defensive line. But Burnside did not attack on the twelfth.[36]

The logistics of the armies were dictated by the terrain. As Lee stated in his report, "The plain on which Fredericksburg stands is so

[32]Kenneth P. Williams, *Lincoln Finds a General: A Military Study of the Civil War,* 5 vols. (New York: Macmillan, 1949–59), 2:508.

[33]*OR* 21:87.

[34]*OR* 21:106–7.

[35]*OR* 21:88–89.

[36]*OR* 21:622, 630, 663, 643, 1057.

completely commanded by the hills of Stafford (in possession of the enemy) that no effectual opposition could be offered to the construction of the bridges or the passage of the river without exposing our troops to the destructive fire of his numerous batteries. Positions were, therefore, selected to oppose his advance after crossing."[37] The heights on the Federal side of the river dictated Lee's initial defensive tactics.

General Longstreet has left us a specific impression of Lee's position:

> The hills occupied by the Confederate forces, although over-crowned by the heights of Stafford, were so distant as to be outside the range of effective fire by the Federal guns and, with the lower receding grounds between them, formed a defensive series that may be likened to natural bastions. Taylor's Hill, on our left, was unassailable; Marye's Hill was more advanced toward the town, was of a gradual ascent and of less height than the others, and we considered it the point most assailable, and guarded it accordingly. The events that followed proved the correctness of our opinion on that point. Lee's Hill, near our center, with its rugged sides retired from Marye's and rising higher than its companions, was comparatively safe.[38]

On the Confederate right a plain extended about a mile from the heights held by Jackson's soldiers to the riverbank, on which the Federals south and east of the town were to be exposed. Timber covered the ground toward the Massaponax. On the Confederate left Marye's Heights rose immediately behind the town. The Confederates had cut a military road along the crest of the high ground to facilitate communication and movement from one part of the line to another. A convenient bend in the Rappahannock three miles above Fredericksburg allowed Lee's left to rest at the river. His right touched the Massaponax where it flowed into the Rappahannock, approximately three miles below the lower Federal pontoon bridges. There existed a nine-mile theoretical front for Lee to defend, but only approximately six or seven of these miles could be readily attacked. Kenneth P. Williams, believing that Lee had approximately 60,000 infantry available, estimates that the

[37] *OR* 21:546.
[38] Longstreet, "Battle of Fredericksburg," 73.

Confederates therefore had roughly six men per yard to defend the vulnerable part of their front. In *Lee's Lieutenants* Freeman computes on the basis of 68,000 Confederates but reaches the same figure of six men per yard.[39] Stuart's cavalry and horse artillery, with infantry support, anchored Lee's right in the valley of the Massaponax, occupying ground on both sides of that stream.[40]

Although Lee had no expectation of preventing the Federal crossing, he did intend to make it costly. From McLaws's division of Longstreet's corps, William Barksdale's brigade on the eleventh took position in the town and skillfully fired on the Federal bridge builders. The Federal response included bombarding Fredericksburg in an unsuccessful effort to drive off Barksdale's Mississippians. Barksdale's activities, concluded in the late afternoon, set Burnside's timetable back the better part of a day. Ultimately the bridges were completed, but the Federals mustered on the western bank of the river only after most of Lee's troops were in position. Had Sumner's troops crossed unopposed on schedule, Franklin's force could have been across at the lower site by midday and would have faced only two of Jackson's divisions.[41]

The fighting at Fredericksburg began on the Confederate right, in the sector defended by Jackson's corps. Jackson had approximately 35,000 infantry and 50 guns, including Stuart's on his right, to defend a front of about two miles.[42] His men occupied a wooded ridge that was inland from the Richmond, Fredericksburg & Potomac Railroad. The ridge was dominated by Prospect Hill. Jackson's first line of troops were those of A. P. Hill's Light Division. The divisions of Early and Taliaferro formed a second line. D. H. Hill's division, identified as the reserve, was still farther back. Jackson's formidable line was approximately one mile deep.[43] In front of Jackson was the railroad, then the Old Richmond Road, a half-mile farther east. Another 800 yards in front of A. P. Hill's men was the Rappahannock. The ground from the railroad to the river was level and open with one significant exception. Approximately 1,300

---

[39] Williams, *Lincoln Finds a General*, 2:527; Freeman, *Lee's Lieutenants*, 2:341 n. 17.

[40] *OR* 21:547.

[41] Freeman, *Lee's Lieutenants*, 2:336–38; *OR* 21:546, 552.

[42] *OR* 21:1057, 636.

[43] *OR* 21:630–31, 643.

yards to the left front of Hamilton's Crossing was a wooded ravine. The base of the woods, approximately 200 yards wide, abutted the Confederate side of the railroad tracks, and the woods then extended inland.[44] The placement of A. P. Hill's line in reference to this woods represents the only significant Confederate leadership error of the day. Instead of occupying the woods at the ravine, James H. Lane's brigade of A. P. Hill's division was placed approximately 250 yards to the left of the woods, and James J. Archer's brigade was placed at the woods' right corner, leaving approximately 500 yards of unoccupied front between Lane's right and Archer's left. Maxcy Gregg's brigade of A. P. Hill's division was placed behind the woods, that is, on the Confederate side, in A. P. Hill's line.[45]

In discussing Confederate leadership, some comment is appropriate concerning who was at fault for this gap. A. P. Hill was the immediate commander. Jackson and Lee performed a reconnaissance of the Confederate line on December 12. According to Robert L. Dabney of Jackson's staff, his commander became aware of the gap on the morning of the thirteenth and predicted that the Federals would attack at that point.[46] Dabney and the other early church fathers of the Confederacy are not very reliable witnesses. Dabney's story is intended to show us that Jackson was prescient. If the story was true, I am convinced that Jackson would have promptly plugged the gap. I am therefore skeptical of Jackson's awareness of the gap. Its existence would seem to be A. P. Hill's problem. Jackson and Hill were in the midst of one of their embarrassing conflicts, and Jackson's report is plain as to the blame for the costly struggle at the gap. He refers to "the interval which he [Hill] had left between Archer and Lane." In any event the Federal divisions of Meade and Gibbon assaulted the gap, penetrated the line, and presented a significant threat to Hill's position.[47] Jubal A. Early's division, supported on his left by General Taliaferro's brigades, drove the Federals back and pursued them to the plain, until checked by Federal artillery. The crisis passed perhaps by 2:30 or 3:00 P.M. Conspicuous in

[44]The distances are from Freeman, *Lee's Lieutenants,* 2:341–42.

[45]Ibid., 2:342–43; *OR* 21:631–32.

[46]Freeman, *Lee's Lieutenants,* 2:343, 347; Douglas Southall Freeman, *R. E. Lee: A Biography,* 4 vols. (New York: Charles Scribner's Sons, 1934–35), 2:450–51.

[47]*OR* 21:632, 511, 480.

Early's action were the brigades of A. R. Lawton (Col. Edmund Atkinson), Early (Col. James A. Walker), and Isaac R. Trimble (Col. Robert F. Hoke).[48]

Both James I. Robertson, Jr., and A. Wilson Greene assert that A. P. Hill had "disappeared" all afternoon on December 13. But Hill's report, dated January 1, 1863, speaks in the first person as if he was an observer. It further refers to an "interval" in his line between Archer and Lane.[49]

That this fighting on Jackson's front was significant is indicated by casualty data. Meade lost 1,800 of his 4,500 men. For the day, Jackson's corps lost approximately 3,400 men, two-thirds of them from A. P. Hill's division.[50]

On the Confederate left, Longstreet's front, Lafayette McLaws's division of the First Corps was posted on Marye's Heights with Richard H. Anderson's division on its left. The divisions of George E. Pickett and John Bell Hood were on McLaws's right. Robert Ransom's division, initially designated the reserve of the First Corps, was then assigned to support McLaws's left in the defense of Marye's Heights. Under Longstreet's direction, the corps batteries were placed in pits. Firing trenches and abatis were added. The famous sunken road at the foot of the heights lay behind the equally famous stone wall.[51] As is well known, the Federal bloodletting on the Confederate left was severe.

In terms of leadership, even Freeman says that Longstreet "observed everything, kept his eye on everything." Several of the general's actions suggest that that was the case. Prior to the Federal assault, Longstreet noted that Cadmus M. Wilcox's brigade, on the left of Anderson's division, seemed exposed. He communicated this to Anderson but also realized that T. R. R. Cobb's brigade of McLaws's division needed to be aware of Wilcox's situation so as not to be exposed if Wilcox moved.[52] Responding to Longstreet, Joseph B. Kershaw dramatically led two of his regiments to Cobb's line as Cobb was dying and his soldiers seemed to falter. In mid-afternoon, under Longstreet's direction, E. Porter Alexander's artillery battalion and additional guns from

[48] *OR* 21:547, 554, 664.

[49] *OR* 21:645–48.

[50] *OR* 21:140, 635.

[51] *OR* 21:568–70; Freeman, *Lee's Lieutenants*, 2:359–65.

[52] Freeman, *Lee's Lieutenants*, 2:364; *OR* 21:611–13; William Miller Owen, "A Hot Day on Marye's Heights," in *B&L*, 3:97–98.

Virginia and Louisiana batteries replaced the Washington Artillery because the latter guns were out of ammunition.[53] In short, there was no Confederate crisis on the left.

December 13 closed on a scene of utter defeat for the Federals. Federal losses were more than 12,500 men, in excess of 11 percent of Burnside's force.[54] As I have said, it was an accidental battle, brought on in the final analysis by Burnside's insistence on crossing the river and attacking in the face of the Confederate army, which was almost ideally positioned to defend. The Federals did not resume their attacks. They recrossed the river on the night of the fifteenth, and the Confederates did not pursue.[55]

There was some criticism in the Southern press about the absence of a counterattack or pursuit by the Confederates. Jackson reported that on the thirteenth he had prepared to counterattack from the Confederate right with infantry following artillery. He waited until late in the evening so that if the move were unsuccessful, his retreat would be "under the cover of night." He reported further that "the first gun had hardly moved forward from the wood 100 yards when the enemy's artillery responded, and so completely swept our front as to satisfy me that the proposed movement should be abandoned."[56] I see no reason to doubt Jackson's judgment.

In his article in *Battles and Leaders* Longstreet addressed the issue of pursuit:

> It has been asked why we did not follow up the victory. The answer is plain. It goes without saying that the battle of the First Corps, concluded after nightfall, could not have been changed into offensive operations. Our line was about three miles long, extending through woodland over hill and dale. An attempt at concentration to throw the troops against the walls of the city at that hour of the night would have been little better than madness. The Confederate field was arranged for defensive battle. Its abrupt termination could not have been anticipated, nor

[53]*OR* 21:570, 588–89, 571.
[54]Livermore, *Numbers and Losses,* 96.
[55]*OR* 21:95.
[56]*OR* 21:634.

could any skill have marshaled our troops for offensive operations in time to meet the emergency. My line was long and over
broken country,—so much so that the troops could not be
promptly handled in offensive operations.

Lee also responded persuasively to the point in his report, part of
which has been set forth at the beginning of this paper. He wrote:

> The attack on the 13th had been so easily repulsed, and by so
> small a part of our army, that it was not supposed the enemy
> would limit his efforts to an attempt, which, in view of the mag-
> nitude of his preparations and the extent of his force, seemed to
> be comparatively insignificant. Believing, therefore, that he
> would attack us, it was not deemed expedient to lose the ad-
> vantages of our position and expose the troops to the fire of his
> inaccessible batteries beyond the river, by advancing against
> him; but we were necessarily ignorant of the extent to which he
> had suffered, and only became aware of it when, on the morn-
> ing of the 16th, it was discovered that he had availed himself of
> the darkness of night, and the prevalence of a violent storm of
> wind and rain, to recross the river.[57]

I have been critical of Lee's generalship because of his offensive
grand strategic sense of the war, his aggressiveness.[58] He believed that
the Confederacy could win the war by defeating the Federal armies, by
militarily overpowering the North. This is what he said he believed; this
was the thrust of the way he directed his army. In my view, Lee was
wrong. The South simply did not have the strength to win the war militarily. Its only chance to win was to prolong the war and make it so
costly to the North that the Northern people would give it up. The analogy, of course, is Washington's strategy during the Revolution. It is the
strategy of wearing the other side out, of winning by not losing. It would
have required Lee to embrace a strategically defensive strategy, undertaking only occasional promising offensive moves, and thereby conserving his outnumbered and limited manpower. Instead of this grand strategy, Lee was typically on the strategic offensive in 1862 and 1863. He

---

[57]Longstreet, "Battle of Fredericksburg," 82–83; *OR* 21:555.
[58]Alan T. Nolan, *Lee Considered: General Robert E. Lee and Civil War History*
(Chapel Hill: University of North Carolina Press, 1991), 59–106.

also directed Jubal Early to fight offensively in the Valley in 1864. Lee's actions, no matter how brilliantly conducted and whether his battles were won or lost, led to his heavy, disproportionate, and irreplaceable casualties that ultimately resulted in his being besieged. They destroyed the viability of his army. His leadership was therefore destructive to the Confederacy.

Having in mind the foregoing, my opinion is that Fredericksburg was Lee's most intelligent and well-fought battle during 1862 and 1863. In the first place, unlike Second Manassas and Antietam and Gettysburg, for example, it was not borrowed trouble, an inevitably costly offensive campaign. Burnside's plan posed a genuine immediate threat to Richmond and to Lee's army. Strategically, it was necessary for Lee to frustrate that plan.

Second, Lee suppressed his risky and Napoleonic bent, his costly aggressiveness. He accepted the strategic and tactical defensive and was not only highly successful but also did not suffer the massive and disproportionate casualties that frequently marked his battles. His casualties were 4,600 men, 6.4 percent of his force, as opposed to Burnside's 12,500, 11.8 percent of his force. General Pendleton commented in his report that the "loss of valuable life [was] so much less than usual."[59]

Lee also planned carefully, taking excellent advantage of the bastions that Burnside's actions had provided him. He seems to have taken personal charge of the wise placement of his army. To me, it was Lee at his best.

Ironically, the Confederate victory at Fredericksburg had very different meanings for Lee and Longstreet. Longstreet deemed the battle a success, and it was a factor in persuading Longstreet of the wisdom of the tactical defensive. Freeman identifies Longstreet as "an unqualified advocate of a tactical defensive by the Army of Northern Virginia." Lee, on the other hand, was disappointed with Fredericksburg. To his wife he wrote on December 16 that the Federals "suffered heavily as far as the battle went, but it did not go far enough to satisfy me. Our loss was comparatively slight. . . . The contest will have now to be renewed." Freeman writes at some length of Lee's and Jackson's chagrin that there had not been more to Fredericksburg, quoting Lee as having later written, "We had really accomplished nothing; we had not gained a foot of

[59]Livermore, *Numbers and Losses,* 96; *OR* 21:567.

ground, and I knew the enemy could easily replace the men he had lost."[60] Fredericksburg, in short, did not mute Lee's commitment to the Armageddon theory of battle and the offensive, strategically and tactically.

The differences between Lee and Longstreet surfaced in Pennsylvania in 1863, with Longstreet referring expressly to Fredericksburg to support his objection to Lee's offensive tactics at Gettysburg. After the war, Longstreet commented that in discussing tactical options in Pennsylvania he called Lee's "attention to the Battle of Fredericksburg as an instance of defensive warfare, where we had thrown not more than five thousand troops into the fight and had beaten off two-thirds of the Federal army with great loss to them and slight loss to my own troops."[61]

Descartes wrote that "a thousand questions do not make a doubt." Longstreet learned that one question, or maybe two or three, would bar him from the pantheon of the cult of the Lost Cause.

[60]Freeman, *Lee's Lieutenants,* 3:45–46; Robert E. Lee, *The Wartime Papers of R. E. Lee,* ed. Clifford Dowdey and Louis H. Manarin (Boston: Little, Brown, 1961), 365; Freeman, *R. E. Lee,* 2:472–73.

[61]Freeman, *Lee's Lieutenants,* 3:46–47; James Longstreet, "Lee's Invasion of Pennsylvania," in *B&L,* 3:247.

Iron Brigade General: John Gibbon

At last we have a biography of General John Gibbon, and it is a fine one, filling a significant void in the literature of the Civil War. And, because of Gibbon's large involvement, the book also adds to our knowledge of the sad story of the Indian fighting after the war.

Gibbon initially attracts our attention as a North Carolina resident, a regular from West Point, who stayed with "the old Flag" while his three brothers enlisted with the Confederacy. He was a lifelong Democrat, a McClellan loyalist, and from a slaveholding family. It is always difficult to determine with certainty what caused such men to stand by the Union; perhaps they did not themselves know precisely why. In Gibbon's case, it seems ultimately that his oath of allegiance as a soldier tipped the balance in behalf of the North.

A brief reference to Gibbon's military career provides more substantial reasons for his entitlement to our interest. An excellent artillerist, he started the war as Captain of historic Battery B of the 4th United States Artillery. As an infantry officer, he proceeded during the war from a brigadier generalship of volunteers to a major generalship. He commanded the Iron Brigade, a division of the Army of the Potomac's First Corps, a division in that army's Second Corps, and temporarily commanded the Second Corps. Transferred then to the Army of the James, he temporarily commanded the XVIII Corps and finished the war as commander of the XXIV Corps in that army. Along the way he was wounded twice and participated in the battles at Brawner Farm, Second Bull Run, South Mountain, Antietam, Fredericksburg, Chancellorsville, and Gettysburg. He was then significantly involved in Grant's 1864–65 Overland Campaign. On hand at Appomattox, he was one of three Federal Commissioners appointed by Grant to carry out the terms of the surrender document. Inevitably, his personal experiences involve the story of the war in the Virginia theater. His story after the war is that of the Indian Wars. His command buried Custer's dead at the Little Big Horn and fought Chief Joseph and the Nez Perce at Big Hole in 1877. He finished his career directing the army in essentially police activities, protecting the Chinese in the northwest at the time of riots against those immigrants.

What kind of a man was Gibbon? The authors are not writing a *Life of the Saints* biography and they present Gibbon, warts and all. The individual reader can make his own decision. To this reader, he appears as a family man of high personal character and habits, a brilliant combat leader, an effective commander, and an honest and courageous person. He was direct, "no nonsense," and followed the book in his leadership. As the authors note, he was not a "twentieth-century man in his attitudes" and this meant that he had a Victorian's touchiness about his "honor"—he was outspoken and contentious and participated actively in the well-established game of army politics. These characteristics led him into celebrated, unseemly, and virtually endless controversies with Generals Hancock, McDowell, and Pope, several of which were to his personal disadvantage. On the other hand, he presented an admirable modern side; he had keen psychological insights in pre-Freudian times and was humane, departures from the traditions and practices of the army of the time. Most noteworthy in this regard are his attitudes toward the Indians he was fighting after the war. The authors authenticate their statement that Gibbon was "a sensitive human being" when they set forth his statements about the war against the native American, "a people forced into war by the very agents of the government which makes war upon them." In addition he wrote:

> The Indian, although a savage, is still a man with . . . quite as much instinctive sense of right and wrong as a white man. . . . He argues this way: the white man has come into my country and taken away everything which formerly belonged to me. He even drives off . . . and destroys the game which the Great Spirit gave me to subsist on. He owes me something for this, but refuses to pay.

If more white Americans had shared these perceptions, the Indian story might not haunt American history.

Biography is a useful form because it permits the telling of "the times" of its subject. The authors have done a fine job of informing the reader from the context of Gibbon's life: the impact of the Sumter news on officers from the North and South stationed at an isolated United States military base; the emotionally charged relationships between soldiers and their commanders at brigade level; the nature of Civil War tactics; Federal morale problems incident to the incessant combat and casualties of Grant's Virginia Campaign; how a family divided by conflicting loyalties carried on; and details of the Appomattox surrender.

Of particular interest to this reader is the book's description of the relationship between Gibbon and the Iron Brigade, the relationship that dictated the title of the book. Promoted from a captaincy in the artillery to Brigadier General of Volunteers on 2 May 1862, Gibbon took command of a brigade of Indiana and Wisconsin volunteers, the only all-Western brigade in the Eastern armies of the Union. As a result of Gibbon's training and under his leadership—he led the brigade at Brawner Farm, Second Bull Run, South Mountain, and Antietam—these soldiers earned the sobriquet "Iron Brigade." Fighting typically with Gibbon's old battery, B of the 4th U.S., the brigade was reinforced after Antietam by the 24th Michigan Volunteers, thus retaining its distinctive regional identity. The brigade carried forward its storied career after Gibbon's promotion to division command. The eminent T. Harry Williams has called these Western soldiers "probably the best fighting brigade in the army." Gibbon retained his relationship with the Iron Brigade all of his life. The veterans selected him as the permanent President of the Iron Brigade Association.

Following his final service in the Northwest, Gibbon retired in 1891 and settled in Baltimore. Dying there in 1896, he was buried in Arlington Cemetery, his monument marked by the Iron Brigade Association's badge and paid for by veterans of the brigade.

This book is marked by outstanding research. Official government records, obscure primary documents, family papers and correspondence, and appropriate secondary reports give the book authority. Having mined these sources, Messrs. Jordan and Lavery have given us a rich, detailed, and excellent account of the life and times of a significant and neglected soldier of the Union.

Joshua Lawrence Chamberlain

This is a superb book. It is, on the one hand, a biography. But because the writer has firmly placed her protagonist in the social, political, and military history of his times, it is also an exceptional narrative history. Three essential elements seem to me to account for the excellence of the book: the historical milieu of the life of Joshua L. Chamberlain, the facts of his remarkable life, and the author's skill in research and in the telling of Chamberlain's life.

Robert Penn Warren has written: "The Civil War is, for the American imagination, the great single event of our history. Without too much wrenching, it may, in fact, be said to *be* American history." At first blush, Warren's statement may strike one as an exaggeration, but the fact is that it is difficult to overstate the significance of the Civil War in our history. Translated into an equal proportion of today's population, Civil War fatalities from combat and disease would account for five million American deaths. It is estimated that three soldiers were wounded for each soldier killed in combat, another staggering loss. In spite of our efforts to rationalize, even to romanticize it, the Civil War is the American holocaust, standing like a giant and grotesque statue in the midst of our generally optimistic national experience. The consequences of the war were surely profound. The American nation was saved and redefined. Slavery was abolished. In the latter regard, let us once and for all acknowledge that the South seceded to protect slavery and that, however flawed and inept the trial, freedom was at stake.

The presence of the issue of freedom sets up the startling contradiction of the war: it was at the same time tragic and redemptive. Denis W. Brogan has captured this contradiction. The war, he writes, "put the American people, decisively, once and for all, among the peoples who have lived in interesting times and who have paid an extravagantly high price for this experience." Brogan says further, "I do not for a moment suggest that the American Civil War was a good thing—merely that it was and is felt by the unregenerate (a majority of the Western races now and for as long as we can inspect the past) to be the most moving, interesting, dignified thing that has ever occurred in America." The war and the period of the war are the milieu of this book. That is the first element of its excellence.

By any standard, Joshua Chamberlain is a fascinating human being, an ordinary man of his times who, in the context of the war and its aftermath, was somehow *extraordinary*. An academic at Bowdoin College, a seminarian with no significant military background or education, he had a natural gift for soldiering and for military leadership. Essential to this gift in the kind of personal war in which he became involved, Chamberlain had exceptional physical courage and the capacity, whatever it is called, to withstand the searing pain of wounds and the primitive discomforts of Civil War soldiering.

Chamberlain started his Civil War career as the lieutenant colonel of the Twentieth Maine Volunteers. He progressed to the rank of brigadier general, not by brevet but by commission. He commanded a regiment, a brigade, and a division. Along the way he was wounded six times, grievously at Petersburg. Perhaps his best-known wartime exploit occurred at Gettysburg. Great events like Gettysburg are made up of a number of "little events," particular incidents that were unusually dramatic. A few of these particular, dramatic little events were also decisive in terms of the outcome of the battle. In the case of Gettysburg, the defense by the Twentieth Maine of the Federal left at Little Round Top on the second day of the battle was clearly decisive. Chamberlain commanded the Twentieth in this fight.

Although Chamberlain returned to academia after the war, his distinction during the war inevitably drew him into politics, in which his career was also remarkable. He was four times elected governor of Maine before becoming the president of Bowdoin College. His fascination with the war caused him to be one of the most studious and prolific postwar writers and lecturers about his own experiences and the larger aspects of the war. This is the citizen-soldier about whom Alice Rains Trulock writes. His significance, his many-faceted character, and his rich experiences are the second element in the strength of this book.

To the promising milieu and fascinating protagonist, Ms. Trulock brings exceptional skills. First there is her research. She has found a wide range of hitherto unknown primary sources, including Chamberlain's personal and family papers and other manuscript materials in obscure repositories and in private hands. She has studied the substantial body of Chamberlain's own writings, published and in manuscript. She has mastered the *Official Records* and the vast secondary literature of the war.

Research alone, however well done, does not make a book. Ms. Trulock also writes exceptionally well, but she does more. Biography can be, but sometimes is not, an excellent vehicle for describing "the times" of its subject. Ms. Trulock tells us of the context of Chamberlain's life without losing the focus on the man. In addition, without compromising the historian's detachment, she *understands* Chamberlain. I particularly admire her technique of letting him speak for himself about the great events of his life. Ms. Trulock's skills in research and in the telling of Joshua Chamberlain's tale and his times is the third element that distinguishes this book.

This, then, is the life of Joshua L. Chamberlain and his times, what is customarily called the definitive biography. It is an important book.

Considering *Lee Considered:*
Robert E. Lee and the Lost Cause

The nationally distributed *Civil War News* of October 1992 printed a reader's letter that said, in part, "I call upon every true student of the Civil War, every son and daughter of the veterans of that war, North and South, and every organization formed to study, research, reenact, preserve and remember our Civil War heritage not to purchase Nolan's book. . . . If you have already, burn it. . . . Moreover, it is noted that Nolan's name has appeared on the agenda as a presenter at certain Civil War symposiums. . . . I recommend that you not attend and write to the sponsor stating why."[1] The letter was signed by a retired general of the U.S. Army who also sent copies to a broad segment of Civil War media and organizations. The book in question was my 1991 work, *Lee Considered: General Robert E. Lee and Civil War History.*

I was intimidated to find myself included in the group of distinguished professional historians who spoke at this conference. I cite the letter as a credential, because I doubt if any of the other participants has caused such a letter to be written.

As further background, I confess that I am interested in myths and legends, especially ones that defy facts or, even more curious, coexist with facts while contradicting them. The Irish writer Sean O'Faolain tells of a woman of his acquaintance in West Cork. As is well known, the Irish have a large and colorful mythology that includes a number of mythical creatures—fairies, elves, leprechauns, and other "Wee Folk." O'Faolain asked his friend if she really believed in the Wee Folk. She responded, "Of course not, but they are there!" It is my opinion that what is deemed to be the history of the Civil War is heavily marked by this phenomenon.

[1] *Civil War News,* October 1992.

I believe that in the popular mind the Civil War exists as an American counterpart of an Icelandic saga. According to the dictionary, a *saga* is a "story of heroic deeds." Perhaps *legend* would be a more descriptive term, defined as "any story coming down from the past, especially one popularly taken as historical though not verifiable; also such stories and traditions collectively, especially of a particular people." That legends commonly persist is a fact to which I may be more sensitive than my colleagues because round tables and Civil War seminars are more my milieu than is a gathering of professional historians. I insist that the legend exists and that it is more popularly entrenched than the history of the period. Indeed, it serves as the history of the period.

Gaines M. Foster wrote of the way in which the war generation of Southerners and succeeding generations "accepted defeat and interpreted the war in the years from 1865 to 1913. . . . Their interpretation emerged in what has come to be called the Lost Cause, the postwar writings and activities that perpetuated the memory of the Confederacy." Having identified the Southern memorial organizations, Foster contends that "more Southerners formed an understanding of their past through the ceremonial activities or rituals conducted by these groups than through anything else."[2] The Lost Cause, as I will call it today, is the legend of the Civil War.

The legend, as distinguished from the history of the war, has certain characteristics. Thus, the conflict is presented as essentially romantic, a contest of honor and martial glory in which brave and valorous men and women contended over the issue of Southern independence. The romantic image of the war contrasts sharply with reality. The war was in fact harsh and cruel, producing not only astonishing fatalities—in excess of 600,000 men—but also thousands of disabled soldiers, widows, and orphans. These casualties and guerrilla warfare, border-state struggles, prison camps, and widespread destruction of Southern cities justify Robert Penn Warren's characterization of the war:

> The word *tragedy* is often used loosely. Here we use it at its deepest significance: the image in action of the deepest questions of man's fate and man's attitude toward his fate. For the

[2]Gaines M. Foster, *Ghosts of the Confederacy* (New York: Oxford University Press, 1987), 4.

Civil War is, massively, that. It is the story of a crime of monstrous inhumanity, into which almost innocently men stumbled; of consequences which could not be trammeled up, and of men who tangled themselves more and more vindictively and desperately until the powers of reason were twisted and their virtues perverted.[3]

The legend is also marked by defensive Confederate advocacy. As pointed out by Michael C. C. Adams in *Our Masters the Rebels,* long before the secession crisis, Southerners "came to see themselves as representing a minority group within the nation," in part because of "the need to justify the existence of slavery. . . . Even before the abolitionist attacks from the North, Southerners began the defense of slavery as a social system that provided unique benefits, both for the slave whom it placed under the fatherly care of a superior race and for the master who was given the freedom from toil necessary to the creation of a superior culture."[4] In short, the Southerners were placed in a defensive posture before the war, and this status has never changed. This defensive apologetic stance has been carried over into what is deemed the history of the war, what I am calling the Lost Cause legend.

Elements of the Lost Cause Legend

Slavery and the War

It has always seemed clear to me that the slavery issue was the common denominator of the national political discord in the generation before the war. And surely it is not a coincidence that the compromise efforts between the time of South Carolina's secession and the firing on Fort Sumter were concerned with the status of slavery. Despite these facts, some historians argued until recently that slavery was not the central issue between the sections; it was trivialized as the cause of the war in favor of such things as tariff disputes, control of investment banking,

[3]Robert Penn Warren, *The Legacy of the Civil War* (New York: Random House, 1961), 102.
[4]Michael C. C. Adams, *Our Masters the Rebels* (Cambridge: Harvard University Press, 1978), 3–4.

cultural differences, and conflict between industrial and agricultural societies. Today's historians seem to concede that the South seceded to protect slavery and that the North went to war to defeat secession. Slavery therefore caused the war. I believe, however, that in the popular mind slavery remains discounted as the cause of the war. We know, for example, that there was an outcry about Ken Burns's PBS Civil War series because it so categorically identified slavery as the cause of the war.

The Abolitionists

The status of the abolitionists in the legend is a corollary to the principle that slavery was not the cause of the war. The abolitionists' image is negative. They were troublemakers, provocateurs, virtually manufacturing a disagreement that was of little or no substance. Reformers are always painful people, simply because they will not cooperate, and they demand the reluctant attention of those who will. Reformers frequently provoke unpleasant feelings of guilt in others. But the abolitionists were right one hundred years ago. It is now late in the twentieth century. There is no excuse for their negative image in a historical sense, but the image persists in the legend.

The South Would Have Given It Up

A third principle of the Lost Cause teaches that slavery would have been abandoned by the South on its own. It was simply a question of time. If the war *was* about slavery, fighting was unnecessary for the elimination of the institution. This contention conveniently overlooks the agitation over the acquisition of Cuba and the filibustering about Mexican and South American territory. I believe that Allan Nevins was correct when he said, "The South, as a whole, in 1846–61, was not moving toward emancipation, but away from it. It was not relaxing the laws which guarded the system, but reinforcing them. It was not ameliorating slavery, but making it harsher and more implacable. The South was further from a just solution of the slavery problem in 1830 than it had been in 1789. It was further from a tenable solution in 1860 than it had been in 1830."[5]

[5]Allan Nevins, *The Emergence of Lincoln*, 2 vols. (New York: Charles Scribner's Sons, 1950), 2:468.

The Slaves

Related to the principles that I have mentioned are the "faithful slave" myth and what William Garrett Piston calls the "happy darky stereotype."[6] Fiction writers from Joel Chandler Harris to Margaret Mitchell and their counterparts in an earlier Hollywood are largely responsible for these historical problems. Recall Shirley Temple playing the part of a Southern plantation daughter, tap dancing in the big house with Bill "Bojangles" Robinson, who was a happy slave. *The Little Colonel* (1935) was a typical Hollywood view of slavery. Presumably, there were slaves who were fond of and sympathetic toward their owners, fitting the unknowing and uncaring "happy darky" mold. But this image was for so long the predominant portrayal that it became endemic to the popular legend. Only recently laypeople learned of the significant Federal logistical problems caused by the slaves' fleeing to the Federal lines and of the slaves' assisting Federal soldiers in the field. Despite the work of James McPherson and Dudley Cornish, the facts concerning black soldiers in the Federal army are new information to many Americans. It seems especially unfortunate to me that African Americans have not known of this heritage. When I saw the movie *Glory*, a number of blacks were in the audience. I overheard them expressing surprise that "we were in the Civil War." The actor Denzel Washington had a strong role in the film. A sophisticated and well-educated black man, he has reported his own amazement when the script was initially sent to him because he was unaware that black soldiers had served in the Union army.

The Nationalistic/Cultural Difference

Having eliminated slavery as the source of sectional contention, the South created a nationalistic/cultural basis for the disagreement. This theory was instituted on the eve of the war and became a staple of the Lost Cause theory after the war. An extensive statement of the argument appeared in June 1860 in the *Southern Literary Messenger*. The Northerners were said to be descended from the Anglo-Saxon tribes that had been conquered by the Norman cavaliers. The Norman cavaliers were, of

[6]William Garrett Piston, *Lee's Tarnished Lieutenant: James Longstreet and His Place in Southern History* (Athens: University of Georgia Press, 1987), 157–58.

course, the ancestors of the Southerners, according to this theory. It was written that the cavaliers were "descended from the Norman Barons of William the Conqueror, a race distinguished in its earliest history for its warlike and fearless character, a race in all times since renowned for its gallantry, chivalry, honor, gentleness, and intellect."[7] As described in *Why the South Lost the Civil War,* the South "simply appropriated as their own the history they shared with the Union and recreated it. . . . Without its own distinctive past upon which to base its nationality, the Confederacy appropriated history and created a mythic past of exiled cavaliers and chivalrous knights that owed more to Sir Walter Scott than to the flesh and blood migrants from the Old World."[8] Kenneth Stampp has commented on this fiction, "Fundamentally [the Confederacy] was not the product of genuine Southern nationalism; indeed, except for the institution of slavery, the South had little to give it a clear national identity . . . and the notion of a distinct Southern culture was largely a figment of the romantic imaginations of a handful of intellectuals and pro-slavery propagandists"[9] Grady McWhiney, David M. Potter, and other current historians share Stampp's opinion.

Military Analysis

The legend has also rationalized the Confederate loss in the war's military aspects. It was asserted, in effect, that the South could not have won the war because of its manpower and material disadvantages.[10] On the other hand—never mind the contradiction—it was stated that if the Confederacy had won at Gettysburg, it would have won the war. The Gettysburg loss was attributed to General James Longstreet. By extension, Longstreet was responsible for the loss of the war. Foster calls this the "Longstreet lost it at Gettysburg" theory. It became part of the legend.[11]

[7] *Southern Literary Messenger* 30 (June 1860): 401–9.

[8] Richard E. Beringer, Herman Hattaway, Archer Jones, and William N. Still, Jr., *Why the South Lost the Civil War* (Athens: University of Georgia Press, 1986), 76.

[9] Kenneth M. Stampp, *The Imperiled Union* (New York: Oxford University Press, 1980), 255–56.

[10] Foster, *Ghosts,* 57.

[11] Ibid., 58.

Understanding the Reason for the Legend

Warren wrote that "the Civil Was is our only 'felt' history—history lived in the national imagination."[12] I believe that imagination is the stuff of legend. Bruce Catton has expressed the same idea in a different way: "For above and beyond everything else, the Civil War was a matter of emotions. It came about because men's emotions ran away with them; it was borne, North and South, for four mortal years because these emotions remained strong; and its first significance, nowadays, is often more a matter for the heart than for the head."[13] These insights set up a psychological source for the legend. The imaginative and predominantly emotional sense of the Civil War arose because it was marked by such intense contradictions and traumas.

The primary contradiction was that between the Declaration of Independence and the existence and flourishing of slavery. It is important to acknowledge that both sections were mired in this conflict. Although a majority of the Northern people believed by 1860 that slavery should not be extended, the same majority accepted slavery where it existed and would not and did not go to war to extinguish slavery. Secession to protect slavery precipitated the war, and slavery became a victim of the war for a combination of military and political reasons.

With further regard to contradictions, predominant Northern attitudes about race were not, of themselves, significantly different from those in the South. The free black population was severely discriminated against in civil and social rights. In several states, notably those of the Midwest, state constitutions prohibited the immigration of free blacks. Abraham Lincoln said in 1858 that he opposed "the social and political equality"[14] of the races, surely the predominant attitude of the Northern people. Thus, the antislavery movement in the North struggled with an interior conflict—a conviction that slavery was wrong side by side with a crude and virulent racism.

---

[12]Warren, *Legacy,* 4.

[13]Bruce Catton, *Prefaces to History* (New York: Doubleday, 1970), 96.

[14]Roy P. Basler, Marion Dolores Pratt, and Lloyd A. Dunlap, eds., *Collected Works of Abraham Lincoln,* 9 vols. (New Brunswick, N.J.: Rutgers University Press, 1953–55), 3:145.

Southern supporters of slavery also had contradictory feelings. On the one hand, Southern leaders and theologians proclaimed that slavery was a positive good for master and slave alike. On the other hand, the Southern leadership class was religiously orthodox. The Southerners sensed a discrepancy between their historic faith and the new faith in slavery. In addition, lascivious connections between masters and female slaves lingered in the system. In a society that boasted of chivalry, morality, and racial purity, the sexual side of slavery was a disturbing, dirty, and open secret. Further, the whole Western world was arrayed against the Southern view, as many of the Founding Fathers had been, and they were much respected and imitated by the planter aristocracy. The mixture of religious tradition, the standards of Western culture, and the theories of the supporters of the institution created what Bell I. Wiley identifies as a widespread "sense of guilt" in the Southern leadership.[15] Calling this "crypto-emancipationism," Warren describes it as "a deep moral, logical, and economic unease" about slavery.[16] That this ambiguity existed in the South is suggested by the Confederate constitution. While expressly protecting the ownership of slaves, it forbade the slave trade, an implicit acknowledgment that something was wrong about slavery.

But there is more to the story of contradictions. The South had an ancient loyalty to the United States and culture that it shared with the North, at least in broad terms. Again to quote Warren, "the nation share[d] deep and significant convictions and [was] not a mere hand basket of factions huddled arbitrarily together by historical happenso."[17] The sections shared the same revolutionary experience, heroes, and Founding Fathers. The South departed from the Bill of Rights in its efforts to protect slavery but at bottom shared a sense of political values with the North. It is worthwhile again to refer to Stampp:

> Fundamentally [the Confederacy] was not the product of genuine Southern nationalism; indeed, except for the institution of slavery, the South had little to give it a clear national identity. It had no natural frontiers; its white population came from the

[15]Bell Irwin Wiley, *The Road to Appomattox* (Memphis, Tenn.: Memphis State College Press, 1956), 102.
[16]Warren, *Legacy,* 8.
[17]Ibid., 83.

same stocks as the Northern population; its political tradition and religious beliefs were not significantly different from those of the North; it had no history of its own; and the notion of a distinct Southern culture was largely a figment of the romantic imaginations of a handful of intellectuals and pro-slavery propagandists.

Even after a generation of intense sectional conflict over slavery, the South was still bound to the Union by heritage of national ideals and traditions.[18]

This Southern inability to separate itself emotionally from the common ground it shared with the North had a predictable result. As the authors of *Why the South Lost the Civil War* point out, "A truly nationalistic movement will not be confused about where its loyalties lie. Yet this was a great source of Confederate confusion.... Southerners did indeed suffer a confusion of loyalties."[19] This confusion provided another significant contradiction to add to the list.

Common nationalism and culture drew the participants into another contradiction. Although fighting with incredible ferocity, enlisted men and officers tended to trust one another and had difficulty identifying each other as genuine enemies. The books are full of stories of meetings and friendly personal contacts between picket lines. Many general officers had been at West Point together or had been stationed together at isolated prewar military posts and regarded themselves as friends. Grant's *Memoirs* and Porter Alexander's *Fighting for the Confederacy* describe the immediate postsurrender fraternization of officers and men of both armies at Appomattox.

Finally, regarding trauma as a source of the legend was the awfulness of the event. I have already quoted Warren about the scope and depth of the tragedy, "a crime of monstrous inhumanity." The recent and relatively sophisticated advances in ordnance and the contrasting primitiveness of the sciences of medicine, nutrition, and sanitation combined to create unusual deprivation and suffering. In short, the Civil War as a human event was so rife with contradictions and traumas, and so confused and painful in its images, that the participants were moved to manufacture a history of the event. They were psychologically impelled to

[18] Stampp, *Imperiled Union,* 255–56.
[19]Beringer et al., *Why the South Lost the Civil War,* 76.

obscure the truth with tales and traditions that were essentially romantic and more palatable than the facts. This phenomenon constitutes one
of the sources of the legend.

Another source of the legend lay in the participants' need to rationalize the war in social terms. Somehow they had to account for themselves.
While proclaiming the righteousness of the cause, the South had to accept
a bitter and destructive defeat. James M. McPherson has accurately
summed up the war's consequences for the South: "The South was not
only invaded and conquered, it was utterly destroyed. By 1865 the Union
forces had ... destroyed two-thirds of the assessed value of southern
wealth, two-fifths of the South's livestock, and one-quarter of her white
men between the ages of twenty and forty. More than half of the farm
machinery was ruined, and the damage to railroads and industry was in-
calculable.[20] The South needed to justify itself.

The North had more complicated rationalizing to do. On the one
hand, it needed to establish that it had been right, that the war had been
worth the cost. But insisting that the two sections comprised one nation,
the North needed to reclaim the allegiance of the South, creating an implicit Northern disposition to protect the dignity of the South to bind it
again to the Union. The North surely perceived that this apology would
be difficult because of the Southern wounds.

There was, to be sure, an initial period of bitterness and a protracted
period of maneuvering as the national political parties sought to establish their Southern constituencies. In the North, "bloody shirt" politics
was practiced in the interest of Republican political control. Prior to the
Hayes-Tilden compromise of 1877, there were Federal efforts to guarantee and protect the rights of the freedmen. But in the longer run, the
South's need to dignify its defeat and losses and the Northern need to
credit the Southern cause in the interest of political union prevailed.
Just as the psychological motive produced a romantic mask for the war's
inhumanity, the participants' need to justify themselves dictated the al-
teration of critical facts concerning the war.

Because the long-standing disagreement, and the war itself, had
been about slavery and the status of the black race, it is not surprising
that the social rationalizations about the war started with these matters.
Two significant themes were developed in the South. The first con-

---

[20]James M. McPherson, *Ordeal by Fire* (New York: Knopf, 1982), 476.

cerned the role of slavery. The second involved changing the sense of the slave and the freedman.

Stampp commented that Southerners "denied that slavery had anything to do with the Confederate cause, thus decontaminating it and turning it into something they could cherish. After Appomattox, Jefferson Davis claimed that slavery 'was in no wise the cause of the conflict,' and Alexander H. Stephens argued that the war 'was not a contest between the advocates or opponents of that peculiar institution.' "[21] According to Robert F. Durden, this denial became "a cardinal element of the Southern apologia."[22] Indeed, James L. Roark found that Southerners had "a nearly universal desire to escape the ignominy attached to slavery."[23]

The new picture of the Southern black also required a stark reversal. In place of the slaves and freedmen that existed in fact, there emerged, as previously noted, the "happy darky stereotype." This person—unaware, unknowing, and uncaring—became universally known, North as well as South.

By eliminating slavery as the issue that had divided the North and South and led them into the war, and by changing the image of the real black person to that of the happy darky, the Southern leadership facilitated Northern acceptance of the honor of the South. It is, of course, not surprising that the South discarded the protection of slavery as the reason for its conduct. States' rights, liberty, and the Constitution were surely more likely rationales for secession. It also is not surprising that the South was anxious to create the happy darky, who replaced a much more complex and threatening person, the real slave and freedman.

The revisionism in regard to slavery as a cause of the war and the nature of the slaves could have remained a Southern theme. It could not have become part of the national legend without Northern complicity, and the North, including its historians, did accept the South's rewriting of the record. It let the South substitute a war for liberty for the war for slavery, and the North ceased to think of the slaves and freedmen as serious persons. This Northern contribution to the legend resulted in part from its implicit need to credit the South. In this process, it was necessary for slavery protection to be disregarded as the reason for secession

[21]Stampp, *Imperiled Union*, 268.

[22]Robert F. Durden, *The Gray and the Black* (Baton Rouge: Louisiana State University Press, 1972), 3.

[23]James L. Roark, *Masters without Slaves: Southern Planters in the Civil War and Reconstruction* (New York: Norton, 1977), 105.

because the truth about slavery's relationship to the war interjected a divisive element, a moral disagreement, into the reunification efforts of whites, North and South. The essential thrust of the reunification effort was that "both sides were right." If the war had concerned freedom, both sides could not have been right. Therefore, the involvement of freedom had to go.

And the North was willing to participate in the revising of history simply because of racism itself. In spite of the differences between Northern and Southern views of slavery, the two sections shared an intense antagonism toward black people. The Northern fear and dislike helped persuade the North that it surely would not have caused such a fuss about an insignificant thing like the circumstances of these black people. The South was right, after all; slavery had not been the source of conflict between the sections.

Racism therefore gave the North a reason to accept the South's rationalization of the cause of the war and the change in the image of the freedman. Racism was also perceived as a social value in itself. It was a common ground between the sections and was therefore a unifying force. Slavery was discounted as the source of difficulty between the sections; then, identified as essentially ignorant and comic bystanders or helpmates to their owners, blacks were dropped from the history of the war. That they had fled into the Federal lines, had performed invaluable service to Federal soldiers, had joined the Federal army in large numbers—as many as 180,000[24]—and had fought and died for the United States were simply dropped from history. This revisionism met the social needs of both sections and served the North's racist antagonism. It also helped to seal reunion and affirm Southern honor.

Because it struck at the basic truths of the war, the false treatment of slavery and black people had a significant effect on the establishment of the Civil War as legend. Removed from their real role as the issue, their actual participation in the fighting ignored, the blacks were characterized as historically irrelevant. Racism became a motivation and prominent characteristic of the legendary treatment of the war.

[24]Dudley Taylor Cornish, *The Sable Arm* (New York: Norton, 1966), 288. Cornish estimates that black soldiers made up between 9 and 10 percent of the total number of Federal soldiers.

The disregard of slavery and of the authentic black people carried a steep price in terms of historical meaning. The war was deprived of any high purpose or significance. The North was pictured as having for no significant reason acted in such a way within the prewar political process as to provoke secession. A void was substituted for antislavery sentiment as the source of disagreement between the sections. The revised account also meant that the North had then bloodily defeated secession simply for the purpose of forcing the Southerners to remain a part of the nation against their own will.

The disregard of slavery unhinged cause and effect in regard to the war. The void of cause and effect did not remain. The historians promptly came forward. An endless string of hypotheses about the origins of the war was put together. Thomas J. Pressly's *Americans Interpret Their Civil War* remains a comprehensive statement of account of this historiography.[25] Gaines Foster pointed out that in this accounting, Southern culture was frequently portrayed as superior, something "blessed," a world peopled by "cavalier aristocrats or martyrs" as well as by the happy darky. "Grace and gentility," according to Foster, were attributed to the prewar South, and Piston noted that there also "developed a romanticized stereotype of the Confederate soldier."[26] These changes in the facts supplemented and reinforced the melodrama that had been created to mask the terrible tragedy of the war. Margaret Mitchell's *Gone with the Wind* is an orthodox statement of the legend, the twentieth century's most well-known Civil War story. It idealizes the men and women of the planter class, pictures Southern manhood as having superior courage, finds gentility in the planter aristocracy in spite of slavery, exaggerates the material disadvantages of the South's armies, and portrays the Yankees as bushwhackers. The slaves are pictured as the simple, happy, and devoted companions of their owners. As indicated earlier, the legend also rationalized the Southern defeat in a military sense.

The sections' social justifications had profound consequences. Reunion was facilitated and Southern honor assured, but truth was lost in

[25]Thomas J. Pressly, *Americans Interpret Their Civil War* (Princeton: Princeton University Press, 1962).

[26]Foster, *Ghosts*, 198; Piston, *Lee's Tarnished Lieutenant*, 157.

the process, as were equal protection of the laws, a promise of the Fourteenth Amendment, and the Fifteenth Amendment's guarantee of suffrage for blacks.

The legend of the war, still prevailing, resulted from a combination of the war's actual contradictions and traumas and the postwar social rationalizations of the participants. Both elements contributed to the fictions that made the legend. They produced romance in place of realism and significant distortions of critical facts. The legend seems to exist "in our bones" and defeats the efforts of today's historians to set it straight.

The Warrior Hero

The legend of the Civil War persists. It is a tale of glory. Because the truth of the cause of the war—the slavery disagreement—has been muted, it is a story of military competition between brave people for no particular reason other than the honor of it all.

An invariable character of the literary form called the legend is the Warrior Hero, the great man of superior personality and skill, a superman, a savior. General Lee supplies this role in the Civil War legend. He is the personification of the American romance of the Civil War. I was drawn to wonder about the legend itself and about how and why it existed and about Lee as a character in the legend. Thomas L. Connelly and others have studied the construction of the Lee tradition. I decided to inquire into its merits—that is, to try to determine the extent to which the Lee tradition is historical.

Although Douglas Southall Freeman wrote the landmark book about Lee as the Warrior Hero, he was not the first romancer. Writing in 1868, Fanny Downing described Lee as "bathed in the white light which falls directly upon him from the smile of an approving and sustaining God."[27] By 1880 this process had advanced considerably. John W. Daniel of General Jubal A. Early's staff wrote, "The Divinity in [Lee's] bosom shown translucent through the man, and his spirit rose up the Godlike."[28] As especially related to the O'Faolain phenomenon, Sir Frederick Mau-

---

[27]Fanny Downing, "Perfect through Suffering," *The Land We Love* 4 (January 1868): 193–205.

[28]Rev. J. William Jones, *Army of Northern Virginia Memorial Volume* (Richmond: Randolph and English, 1880), 122.

rice called Lee a "stout Democrat,"[29] in spite of Lee's scorn of the "immigrants from abroad" and people "from the slums of the city" who had fought for the North.[30] Writing in 1912, Gamaliel Bradford asserted that "in fighting for the Confederacy, Lee was fighting for slavery, and he must have known perfectly well that if the South triumphed and maintained its independence, slavery would grow and flourish for another generation, if not for a century. . . . This man, fighting as he believed, for freedom, for independence, for democracy, was fighting also to rivet the shackles more firmly on millions of his fellow men." But on the very next page, Bradford also rhapsodized about Lee: "In Lee, no pride, but virtue all; not liberty for himself alone, but for others, for everyone."[31] The man who fought for an additional generation or perhaps one hundred years more of slavery was magically transformed into a man who wanted liberty for everyone.

And then of course there is Freeman. In addition to anonymous and unverifiable anecdotes about Lee the man, Freeman rationalized every blemish, always blamed Lee's subordinates for military failures, and emasculated documents that would mar his characterization. The most dramatic example of this documentary phenomenon is his selective quotation from Lee's January 11, 1865, letter about putting slaves into the Confederate army. To support his claim that Lee was an emancipationist, Freeman quotes that portion of the letter in which the general suggested emancipation to induce the slaves to fight for the Confederacy. But he omits Lee's statement in the same letter that slavery was "the best" relationship between the races and his comment on the "evil consequences to both races" from emancipation.[32] In the final analysis, Freeman was quite candid about the object of his writing. In *The South to Posterity,* Freeman set forth a critical bibliography of books about the war. He acknowledged that he was "interested to ascertain which were the books that seemed to have made new protagonists for the South." He sought to

[29]Sir Frederick Maurice, *Robert E. Lee the Soldier* (Boston: Houghton Mifflin, 1925), 17.

[30]Rev. John Leyburn, "An Interview with Gen. Robert E. Lee," *Century Illustrated Monthly Magazine* 30 (May 1885): 166–67.

[31]Gamaliel Bradford, *Lee the American* (Boston: Houghton Mifflin, 1912), 43–44.

[32]Douglas Southall Freeman, *R. E. Lee,* 4 vols. (New York: Charles Scribner's Sons, 1942–44), 3:544.

identify the books "that have brought a new generation of Americans to an understanding of the Southern point of view."[33] Freeman, whose biography of Lee is a standard reference book, clearly was writing as an advocate.

Lee Considered had a specific, limited purpose, to examine historically six particular characteristics attributed to Lee as the Warrior Hero: his antislavery views, the manner and circumstances of his decision to secede, his generalship, his alleged magnanimity toward the North, his continued fighting after he believed that defeat was inevitable, and his alleged role as a postwar conciliator.

With regard to the peculiar institution, American culture clearly would want a hero of its legend to have been antislavery, as has been widely proclaimed about Lee. In an 1856 letter he wrote that slavery was "a moral & political evil," but he also wrote that slavery was "necessary" for the slaves' "instruction as a race." Further, he trafficked in slaves, saw to the recapture of fugitive slaves from Arlington, identified the maintenance of slavery as a Confederate war aim, and, of course, fought vigorously for the Confederacy. Late in the war, as noted earlier, he wrote that slavery was "the best" relationship that can exist between the races. I concluded that Lee was not antislavery in any meaningful, practical sense.

Although he disapproved of secession, Lee decided early in the crisis that he would go south under certain circumstances and surely would follow Virginia. While he was in this conditional state of mind, on March 15, 1861, the Confederate government offered him a brigadier generalship, the highest commission authorized by the Confederacy, and he neither accepted nor rejected it. Then on March 30, 1861, he accepted a Federal commission as colonel. The Virginia Convention voted to secede on April 17, and one day later, Lee rejected a Federal command. On April 20, 1861, he posted his resignation from the U.S. Army, and, without waiting for its acceptance pursuant to army regulations, agreed at once to go to Richmond to see the Virginia governor. On April 22 he accepted a major generalship from Virginia and command of its forces. His correspondence at the time suggested to others that he sought a passive role in the conflict and did not acknowledge the com-

[33]Douglas Southall Freeman, *The South to Posterity* (New York: Charles Scribner's Sons, 1951), x, xi.

petition for his services in high command. He also did not suggest that he would accept such a significant role in the Confederacy. Thus, well aware of the competition for his services in high command, on the day of his resignation and two days before accepting the Virginia commission, he wrote to his sister that it was his "sincere hope that my poor services may never be needed." On the same day, he wrote to his brother telling of his resignation and classified himself as "a private citizen" with "no other ambition than to remain at home."[34] I concluded that Lee's ambiguity suggested a lack of candor and too fine a line between loyalty to the United States and to the Confederacy.

To Jefferson Davis, Lee stated his strategic grasp of the war: "If we can defeat or drive the armies of the enemy from the field, we shall have peace. All our efforts and energies should be devoted to that object." Thus, Lee relied on the unrealistic goal of military defeat of the North instead of seeking to win by not losing. Accordingly, in the words of J. F. C. Fuller, Lee "rushed forth to find a battlefield, to challenge a contest between himself and the North."[35]

Regarding his military leadership, especially during 1862 and 1863, Lee was much too aggressive and consequently suffered unnecessary, irreplaceable, and disproportionate casualties. He surely accomplished marked tactical successes, but the price of these victories, which could have been avoided by a more defensive strategy, progressively deprived his army of maneuverability and led it into a fatal siege. His admirers insist on remarking on his successes, one battle at a time, and do not evaluate the consequences of his aggressive approach to the war. One admiring biographer unwittingly made this point, noting that Lee went "from one victory that led nowhere to another" and referring to Lee's "glorious . . . campaign filled with victories that resulted in total defeat."[36]

The nationalistic legend needed a hero who was not bitter about the North. Accordingly, the legend insists that Lee felt only charitably toward the Northerners. But the open and notorious written record shows him referring to the Federals as "vandals," people who would

[34]Capt. Robert E. Lee, *Recollections and Letters of Gen. Robert E. Lee* (Garden City, N.Y.: Doubleday, Page, 1924), 25–27.

[35]Clifford Dowdey and Louis H. Manarin, eds., *The Wartime Papers of R. E. Lee* (Boston: Little, Brown, 1961), 816; J. F. C. Fuller, *The Generalship of U. S. Grant* (Bloomington: Indiana University Press, 1958), 377.

[36]Manfred Weidhorn, *Robert E. Lee* (New York: Atheneum, 1988), 105, 120.

carry off Southern women, people full of "malice & revenge." He wrote that they would persecute his wife and rejoice at the death of a Confederate soldier's wife; they were "cowardly persecutors," "unchristian & atrocious."[37]

It is apparent that Lee believed that the cause was lost perhaps as early as Gettysburg and Vicksburg and at the latest when Lincoln was reelected. Was fighting on in these circumstances necessarily heroic? In General Order No. 9, issued on April 10, 1865, Lee said that he had surrendered at Appomattox "to avoid the useless sacrifice" of his soldiers. In advising Davis of the surrender, after the fact, he relied on avoiding future deaths and stated, "I did not see how a surrender could have been avoided."[38] I pose two questions on this point: (1) Did Lee do the right thing on April 9, 1865, when he surrendered his army for the reasons he reported at the time? (2) If the answer to that question is in the affirmative, at what earlier time would his surrender have been appropriate?

After the war, Lee was occasionally conciliatory, but he was much more of a bitter sectional advocate with deep antagonism toward the Northerners and toward the freedmen. In May 1865 while visiting with his cousin, Thomas H. Carter, Lee advised Carter not to depend for labor on the ninety or so blacks who still lived on the Carter farm. According to Lee, the government would provide for the blacks, and Carter should employ white people.[39] On March 12, 1868, in a letter to his son, Robert, who had taken up farming, Lee advised, "You will never prosper with blacks, and it is abhorrent to a reflecting mind to be supporting and cherishing those who are plotting and working for your injury, and all of whose sympathies and associations are antagonistic to yours. . . . Our material, social and political interests are naturally with the whites."[40] In terms of his attitude toward the North, in 1868 he wrote a letter regarding the impeachment of President Andrew Johnson in which he said, "I grieve for posterity, for American principles and Amer-

---

[37]Dowdey and Manarin, eds., *Wartime Papers*, 91, 142, 559, 646, 829, 678. *The War of the Rebellion: A Compilation of the Official Records of the Union and Confederate Armies* (Washington, D.C.: U.S. Government Printing Office, 1880–1901), ser. 1, vol. 6, pp. 42–43.

[38]*War of the Rebellion*, ser. 1, vol. 46, pt. 3, p. 744; pt. 1, p. 1267.

[39]Lee, *Recollections and Letters*, 168.

[40]Ibid., 306.

ican liberty. Our boasted self Govt. is fast becoming the jeer and laughing-stock of the world."[41] And in 1870, the year of his death, he told his colleague William Preston Johnston of the "vindictiveness and malignity of the Yankees, of which he had no conception before the war."[42]

Conclusion

People who write seek an engagement with readers. Typically, except for friends and family, the readers whose reactions the writer is aware of are the reviewers. *Lee Considered* received its fair share of reviews, and the reviewers' reactions were remarkably diverse.

There were favorable reviews who recognized the point of the book, most notably Drew Gilpin Faust and William S. McFeely.[43] There

[41]Charles Bracelen Flood, *Lee: The Last Years* (Boston: Houghton Mifflin, 1981), 186.

[42]W. G. Bean, ed. "Memorandum of Conversations between Robert E. Lee and William Preston Johnson, May 7, 1868 and March 18, 1870," *Virginia Magazine of History and Biography* 73 (October 1965): 477.

[43]In the *New York Times Book Review,* July 7, 1991, Faust wrote, "Just as we have distorted the figure of Lee, so we as a nation have remembered the Civil War not as history but as legend. . . . The representation of a Christ-like Lee, free from blemish and uncontaminated by either positive sentiments about slavery or negative feelings about Yankees, provided a myth around which Americans could unite. This in turn became the foundation for a larger legend that discounted slavery as a cause of Southern secession, and led Americans to embrace a racist view of the war that relegated blacks to passive and irrelevant roles and 'deprived . . . the nation as a whole of any high purpose for the war.' "

In the *Journal of Interdisciplinary History* (23 [Summer 1992]: 205–6), McFeely wrote, "The key word in Nolan's book is 'consequence.' One needs to look at what was or would have been the result of a person's actions, particularly when facing a war in which 600,000 of that person's countrymen were killed. The pose of a valorous persona riding above responsibility may work in myth, but not in history. The consequence of successful secession and of fighting the North to a draw or to victory would have meant the preservation of slavery; the consequence of prolonging the war into April 1865 produced more and more deaths and destruction in the South; the consequence of a paternalistic call for conciliation led to the white-people-only reconciliation that did take place.

". . . To honor Lee was to embrace the amnesia with which a whole nation turned its back on the people the war was all about. . . . White America did not want to remember that their black countrymen had had any part in their own liberation. Nor did the nation choose to notice that slavery, for the eradication were also reviewers who did not like the book. Some simply denounced the book on its face. They, by God, just didn't like it. Others at least informed me of their concerns. The book asserted that the South had seceded to protect slavery and that slavery was therefore the cause of the war. Several contended that this was either an oversimplification or was not so. Some dissenters objected to the criticism of Lee as a military leader, citing his tactical brilliance at such places as Chancellorsville. The chapter concerning Lee's prolonging of the war was objectionable to some who pointed out that according to nineteenth-century mores there was no alternative to Lee's actions.

I did discover ruefully how disabling being a lawyer is. Almost invariably negative reviewers emphasized that I am a lawyer. Several referred to the book as a "lawyer's brief." To a lawyer, a brief is an argument based on the facts. This is not what the reviewers were suggesting.

Piston has remarked on the difficulty of overturning cultural roles in history. I recognize this problem, but I think that history would be served if the romance, the glorification, was removed from what is presented as Civil War history. I would like for the legend to give way to the harsh facts of the matter: the war was all about slavery, resulted from a failure of American politics, and was, as Warren says, "a crime of monstrous inhumanity." It did not resolve the American racial conflict. The South and the North simply adopted a different form of alienation of black people.

In terms of Lee's personal characteristics, Lee writers tend to outdo each other in describing his virtues and heroism, frequently by using hyperbole and comparisons of Lee to sublime standards or well-identified, sublime personages. A random sample of these techniques is informative. I noted Downing's and Daniel's descriptions of Lee. Maurice assured us that Lee was "a stout Democrat." Marshall Fishwick described Lee as "Apollo on horseback," "the general on the beautiful white horse, fighting bravely as did the knights of old." Fishwick also saw Lee as "St. George slaying dragons" *and* St. Francis of Assisi because "literally everything and everybody loved him."[44] Charles Bracelen

---

of which African Americans were supposed to be eternally and quietly grateful, had been replaced by suppression."

[44]Marshall W. Fishwick, *Lee after the War* (New York: Dodd, Mead, 1963), 104, 105, 228.

Flood wrote that Lee was a "confederate Santa Claus."[45] Freeman sprinkled his narrative with winsome anecdotes: Lee rescued a baby bird under enemy fire; Lee succored a wounded Federal soldier; Lee carried a child from a burning building; Lee played with children during the war; Lee stopped to pray with his soldiers in the face of Federal artillery fire. On the last page of his four-volume biography, Freeman pictured Lee as an imitation of Christ in a scene in which a young mother brought her baby for him to bless. Clifford Dowdey also frequently described Lee in christological terms, the war as passion play with Lee as Christ.

The problem is that the elaborate praising of Lee pertains not only to the general himself. It also extends to the context of his life and the causes, conduct, and consequences of the Civil War. It defines the character of Lee's contemporaries and his Federal adversaries. Adulation of Lee may not be history, but it could be harmless. It is not harmless because in the apotheosis process the issues of the war and other people of the war are misrepresented or diminished. The trivialization of slavery as the reason for secession and the establishment of the Confederacy is an example. It is in part a consequence of the creation of the stainless Lee who could not appear in the legend as leading slavery's army. The diminution of Grant and, to an even greater extent, of Lee's lieutenants—Longstreet, Richard B. Ewell of Gettysburg, and J. E. B. Stuart of Gettysburg—are examples. Justifying Lee required the diminution of these generals. Thus, history would be served if the stained glass writing about Lee was eliminated.

As long as the legend persists, Lee's role will not change. He will remain the Warrior Hero of the legend. But if history replaces the legend, Lee will become a historical character of human proportions, and Civil War history will be more accurate.

[45]Flood, *Lee,* 200.

Historians' Perspectives on Lee

In 1991, the University of North Carolina Press published my book *Lee Considered: General Robert E. Lee and Civil War History*.[1] I was prompted to write the book by what I perceived as a conflict between the commonly asserted views of General Robert E. Lee—what I called the Lee tradition—and the facts of his life and career. I used "considered" in the title because it seemed that with very few exceptions Lee had not been considered by his biographers. Instead, they had simply reiterated a series of heroic statements about the general without having researched the relevant facts of his life or adverting to the possibility of an alternative view.

In the book I identified six almost uniformly asserted characteristics attributed to Lee that I concluded did not hold up under factual scrutiny. Specifically, I examined the historicity of the assertions of the Lee canon that (1) he was anti-slavery; (2) his siding with the South took place with complete propriety; (3) his generalship was flawless; (4) he was magnanimous toward the North during the war; (5) his dogged pursuit of the war after he believed it was lost was glorious and admirable; and (6) he was a conciliator between former foes after the war.

In regard to the slavery issue, I pointed out that Lee owned slaves, trafficked in slaves, and expressly embraced the protection of slavery as a war aim of the Confederacy. Further, I noted his letter to Andrew Hunter dated January 11, 1865, in which he said that he believed "the relation of master and slave ... was the best that can exist between the

[1] Alan T. Nolan, *Lee Considered: General Robert E. Lee and Civil War History* (Chapel Hill: The University of North Carolina Press, 1991).

white and black races ... in this country.[2] In reference to his generalship, I acknowledged the criticisms of Lee by the twentieth-century English general and military historian J. F. C. Fuller and by the nineteenth-
century American Colonel George A. Bruce. I quoted with approval
Fuller's comment that Lee "rushed forth to find a battlefield to challenge
a contest between himself and the North."[3] I contended that Lee's penchant for offensive warfare caused disproportionate and irreplaceable
casualties for his outnumbered army and that this ultimately led to his
being trapped in a siege at Petersburg that even he had predicted would
be fatal.

Lee's own statements provided the majority of the evidence I used
to examine the six issues mentioned above. I, of course, paid my respects
to Thomas Connelly's *The Marble Man* as a book that had given me the
courage to undertake my inquiry.[4] Acknowledging this debt, I insisted
that my effort was nevertheless quite different from Connelly's. *The Marble Man* is an intellectual history of the apotheosis of Lee and traces his
development into a heroic figure. Connelly provides a psychohistory of
Lee, an explanation of the man in terms of his life experiences. I was
concerned, on the other hand, with the merits—the truth or falsity—of
the major elements of the Lee tradition.

I write now to examine Lee scholarship since the publication of *Lee
Considered*. I believe that during the 1990s a change has occurred regarding how historians look at Lee. Writers no longer simply reiterate
the canons of the Lee tradition; instead they question and frequently reject perceived truths.

This new treatment of Lee is evident in nine books published since
1991: *Robert E. Lee: A Biography*, by Emory M. Thomas; *Uncertain Glory:
Lee's Generalship Reexamined*, by John D. Mackenzie; *Davis and Lee at
War*, by Steven E. Woodworth; *Lee Moves North*, by Michael A. Palmer;

[2]Ibid., 21; Letter, Robert E. Lee to Andrew Hunter, January 11, 1865, United
States War Department, *The War of the Rebellion: A Compilation of the Official
Records of the Union and Confederate Armies*. ser. 4, vol. 3 (Washington, D.C.: Gov-
ernment Printing Office, 1880–1901), 1007–9.

[3]Nolan, *Lee Considered: General Robert. E. Lee and Civil War History*, 104;
J. F. C. Fuller, *The Generalship of Ulysses S. Grant* (London: 1929), 377.

[4]Thomas L. Connelly, *The Marble Man: Robert E. Lee and His Image in American Society* (New York: Alfred A. Knopf, 1977).

The Warrior Generals, by Thomas B. Buell; *Lee the Soldier,* edited by Gary
W. Gallagher; *The Confederate War,* by Gary W. Gallagher; *How Robert E.
Lee Lost The Civil War,* by Edward H. Bonekemper III; and *Robert E. Lee's
Civil War,* by Bevin Alexander.

Among the authors I have listed above, Emory Thomas in particular
condemned my book at length in his preface and again in his bibliography. Curiously, despite his criticism, he does not disagree with my conclusions regarding any of the six characteristics of the general. With respect to slavery, Thomas states that "Lee's views on slavery continued to
be enlightened within very severe limits." He bases this assertion on a
letter Lee wrote to his wife in 1856. I also quoted this communication in
which Lee expressed negative feelings about slavery while still stating
that the institution was necessary.[5]

Thomas acknowledges that Lee owned slaves and was highly critical of those who were intolerant of what he called the "spiritual liberty"
of the slave owners. Thomas also noted that Lee trafficked in slaves and
cited an 1858 letter in which the general wrote of an incident in which
three of his slaves had rebelled against his authority and claimed to be
free. Lee recounted his success in "capturing them, tying them and lodg-
ing them in jail. They resisted until overpowered." But, Thomas assured
readers, physical repression was merely a form of punishment within the
slave system, and "Lee likely lacked the stomach to resort to torture." According to Thomas, "Lee dealt with assertive slaves by not dealing with
them; he got rid of them, rented them elsewhere." Thomas did not cite
Lee's letter to Andrew Hunter about slavery, but, like me, he seems to
have discovered that Lee was not opposed to slavery in any meaningful
sense.[6]

On the subject of Lee's generalship, Thomas also appears to agree
with my findings. He remarks in his book that Lee had become enam-
ored with offensive operations during the Mexican War and came to
consider such strategy universally valid. Thomas contends that this was
a "precept that [Lee] would have been wise to forget." Lee and his officers, continues Thomas, failed to realize that the conditions that prevailed
in Mexico—"the poor state of Santa Anna's army and the use of muskets

---

[5]Emory M. Thomas, *Robert E. Lee: A Biography* (New York: W. W. Norton &
Company, 1995), 173.
[6]Ibid., 173, 177, 183–4.

as the primary infantry weapons"—did not replicate themselves on the battlefields of the Civil War.[7]

On the question of strategy, Thomas notes that Confederate President Jefferson Davis had hoped to win the war "by not losing and outlasting his ememies' commitment to conquest." Although Thomas clearly states that "Lee never openly disputed Davis' version of victory," he does admit that the general "attempted to bend the President, to secure the authority and resources to win the war a different way"—by offensive strategy. Thomas also concludes that Lee's conduct of the Maryland and Gettysburg campaigns was flawed. At Antietam, says Thomas, Lee "should not have offered battle . . . he very nearly lost his army and the war."[8]

With respect to Lee's postwar attitudes, Thomas and I both discuss his bitterness toward the Union and his participation in the White Sulphur Letter. Written at the White Sulphur Springs resort and printed in newspapers across the country, the letter was a failed effort to ensure that Democrat Horatio Seymour triumphed over Republican Ulysses S. Grant in the 1868 presidential election by reassuring Northern voters of the South's loyalty to the union. In that letter, Lee dissembled as to his own and Southerners' mixed feelings about the freedmen. Elsewhere in his narrative, Thomas—an unabashed admirer of Lee biographer Douglas Southall Freeman, the Lost Cause's most distinguished spokesman—accepts Lee lore of highly questionable authenticity, including the unlikely story of Lee going to the communion rail with a black man in a Richmond church after the war.[9]

Thomas also provides us with an interesting analysis of Lee's candor: "To understand Robert E. Lee it was often important to look beyond his words and watch what he did rather than listen to or read what he said. Lee's actions often modified his words and sometimes the deeds contradicted the words." To Jefferson Davis, he often understated enormously the goals of his projected campaigns. For example, while Davis assumed that Lee invaded Pennsylvania to draw an enemy army out of Virginia, "Lee risked his army and his country in search of a decisive battle to win the war."[10]

[7]Ibid., 141.
[8]Ibid., 256, 262.
[9]Ibid., 390-1.
[10]Ibid., 413.

In my study, I had been puzzled by these characteristics, which suggest a lack of honesty. I concluded that Lee had a gift for self-delusion, which sometimes involved beguiling others. Thomas apparently had the same reaction. It seems Thomas and I agreed about those issues that our books commonly addressed: Lee and slavery, his generalship, and his postwar attitude toward reconciliation with the North.

In *Uncertain Glory*, John Mackenzie presents a thoughtful review of Confederate and Federal military affairs and pays close attention to Lee's conduct of his campaigns. He finds Lee seriously deficient in strategic vision and accuses him of losing a war that he could have won. Mackenzie's indictment echoes mine when he argues that Lee "preferred to use offensive strategy and tactics, areas in which he did not exhibit much expertise." Mackenzie also notes, "The South held to a misguided offensive strategy, while there is very persuasive evidence that a more defensive Confederate posture would have worn down the North's resolve to continue the war and led to a political settlement favorable to the South." Mackenzie writes, "throughout the war, Lee failed to see what was necessary for the Confederacy to win with logistics or the most suitable strategies and tactics. Lee spent the lives of his men too liberally, lost their loyalty and failed his country."[11]

Another detailed review of Lee's generalship appears in Steven Woodworth's *Davis and Lee at War*. The Battle of Malvern Hill, he writes, "was a horrible fiasco; ... the demonstration of the overwhelming Union firepower ... should have precluded the infantry ever going forward at all, but so muddled and sloppily written were the orders to the division and brigade commanders that they felt compelled to march the men out of the woods and up the open slope into the meat grinder of massed Federal artillery and musketry." At Antietam, says Woodworth: "the gritty Federals came within a hair's breadth of extracting from Lee the gravest penalty for his audacity. For the Confederates, it was a desperate struggle. . . . Never again until Appomattox would Lee's army be this close to destruction."[12]

Woodworth bluntly asserts that Lee failed at Gettysburg. Stymied by his Federal opponents during the fight, Lee continually "pressed as-

[11]John D. Mackenzie, *Uncertain Glory: Lee's Generalship Reexamined* (New York: Hippocrene Books, Inc., 1997), 28, 349–50.

[12]Steven E. Woodworth, *Davis and Lee at War* (Lawrence: University Press of Kansas, 1995), 169–70, 192.

saults far beyond the point at which reason would have demanded that he cut his losses and withdraw. Lee had always been combative, but this was extreme. . . . [His] actions were an unhappy caricature of the most unfortunate aspects of his tactics."[13] Yet despite these observations, and after having discussed the differences between Davis and Lee regarding the wisdom of a defensive or offensive strategy, Woodworth believes that the latter was not a foolish grand strategy.

Like Mackenzie, Woodworth also emphasizes that Lee lost the loyalty of his soldiers—an assertion supported by the fact that the troops of the Army of Northern Virginia, worn out by rigorous campaigning and benumbed by the horrors of war, began to desert in ever-larger numbers after Gettysburg. Woodworth claims that the problem of waning enthusiasm was endemic in the South and that the "morale of the whole Confederate people was beginning to crack. The realization began to creep through the hearts and minds of Southerners after July 1863 that they might lose this war."[14]

Woodworth also touches on my thesis that Lee's efforts to prolong the war were not heroic or worthy of glorification. He writes that "Lee had believed that defeat was only a matter of time since the beginning of the siege [of Petersburg], an immediate certainty after the reelection of Lincoln. He had fought on because he considered it his duty as a soldier, and for the same reason he probably did not fully communicate his misgivings to Davis."[15]

Michael Palmer's *Lee Moves North* refines my criticism of Lee's aggressiveness and his penchant for offensive strategy. Concentrating on the Maryland, Gettysburg, and Bristoe Station campaigns, Palmer notes that "all three were strategic offensives, and the only strategic offensives that Lee undertook as commander of the Army of the Northern Virginia." All were defeats for Lee. Palmer asserts that "the relationship between the strategic offensives and Lee's defeats, was, in fact, one of causation. Lee's approach to command, one that enabled him to achieve marked successes when his army fought on the strategic defensive, failed him miserably when he adopted the strategic offensive." Palmer then notes that "the differing strategic concepts embraced by Lee and

[13]Ibid., 245.
[14]Ibid., 253.
[15]Ibid., 327.

President Jefferson Davis, Lee's penchant for offensive tactics, his dislike of the details of staff work, his decentralized approach to command and control, and his strategic parochialism" all combined to lead to failure.[16]

Palmer also makes a passing comment on Lee's capacity for self-delusion, which, I said, extended sometimes to his beguiling others. Palmer describes a letter written by General Lee to Davis on September 4, 1862, as "a remarkable and disingenuous document. Here we have the commander of one of the most important of the Confederate armies about to undertake a risky invasion of northern territory on its own initiative. . . . Lee knew that it was physically impossible for Davis to even receive let alone reply to the letter before the army was across the Potomac and into Maryland." Palmer claims: "The facts remain, in shaping national strategy on the march, Lee exceeded his responsibilities as army commander. Lee was neither timely nor forthright in his communications with Jefferson Davis." Such letters state that Lee's intent was "feeding his army," and "harassing the Federals," to give the army "a few days' rest" in western Maryland, to recruit among the Marylanders, to forestall a Federal move into Virginia—there is no mention of intention for a battle. However, as Lee later acknowledged, "he entered Maryland in early September 1862 fully prepared to fight." In 1868, Lee said in an interview at Washington College, "I intended then to attack McClellan."[17]

Palmer observes that Lee's decision to cross the Potomac into Maryland was probably the worst decision he ever made as a general. He was about to lead a major offensive operation into Federal territory—the military and political ramifications of which were enormous—without discussing the matter, or at least the timing, with President Davis. Despite the extraordinary nature of the undertaking, no logistical forethought had been given to the expedition; there was no plan of operations, except for whatever existed in Lee's and Maj. Gen. Thomas J. Jackson's heads. Of the army's major commanders, only Jackson fully understood Lee's thoughts. "Lee's original plan," states Palmer, "[was] based on an assumption that weeks would pass before the Federals would make any substantive response." Union Maj. Gen. George B. McClellan, however,

---

[16]Michael A. Palmer, *Lee Moves North* (New York: John Wiley and Sons, 1998), xi–xii.

[17]Ibid., 17–22.

moved his army quickly even before the famous "Lost Order" was found, and this "earlier than expected reaction had checked Lee's original plan of campaign long before September 13." After McClellan's army had battled its way through the gaps in South Mountain, says Palmer: "Lee found himself facing disaster. With his army divided and weakened by desertion, its strength unknown even to its commander, Lee ordered a reconcentration at Sharpsburg, from where he could escape across the Potomac to Virginia, and safety."[18]

Once Lee learned from Jackson of the impending capitulation of Harpers Ferry, his aggressive nature returned, notes Palmer, and "Lee reversed himself, there would be no retreat . . . heavily outnumbered, his force still divided, and with his back to the river [Lee] had decided to fight . . . because it was battle that Lee had sought when he first crossed the Potomac." While McClellan made numerous tactical blunders, "it was Lee," accuses Palmer, "who committed the major strategic and operational errors . . . and who at Sharpsburg presented McClellan an opportunity to perhaps win the war in an afternoon."[19]

Palmer then questions what lessons Lee had learned from the Antietam failure:

> Would Lee henceforth eschew hastily planned, similarly half-cocked offensive operations? Would future offensive operations be approved ahead of time by the president, provided with appropriate available support—manpower and logistical—by the Confederate government and be well planned and staffed by Lee in cooperation with his principal subordinates? Would Lee continue to overestimate the fighting power of his own army, and underestimate that of the Army of the Potomac? In short, would Lee recognize the Maryland campaign for the fiasco and near-disaster that it was, and draw the proper conclusions from his experience? Unfortunately for the Confederacy, Robert E. Lee refused to consider the campaign a failure. . . . In fact [he] longed for the opportunity to strike north again and to engage the enemy in battle. [Despite the condition of his] poorly clad, barefooted patriots, [he] refused to resign himself to defensive

[18]Ibid., 22, 27, 29.
[19]Ibid., 29–31, 35.

operations. When the opportunity to move north presented itself again, Lee was prepared to strike, and to strike quickly, in much the same fashion as he had in early September 1862.[20]

According to Palmer, the next opportunity to observe if Lee had changed his behavior after his failure at Antietam was the Gettysburg campaign. Lee's second invasion of the North was motivated in part by his desire to avoid the transfer of some of his army to the West, as Davis and Secretary of War James A. Seddon were considering. Palmer notes that correspondence from Lee to Richmond prior to the start of the campaign was similar in tone to Lee's letters to Davis at the start of the Maryland campaign, suggesting "that the principal aim of the commander of the Army of Northern Virginia was not secrecy but obfuscation." He says that Lee's June 23 letter "is an interesting, and in some ways puzzling, document." Why, he asks, "at this late date, was he still unwilling to inform Davis that the Army of Northern Virginia had crossed the Potomac . . . why refrain from even mentioning that the army had already passed the river?" Palmer then states, "As he had the previous summer when the army entered Maryland, Lee assumed that he would be able to roam about the northern countryside for quite some time before being challenged by the slow reacting, and laggardly moving Army of the Potomac." Palmer is also struck by a "remarkable dispatch" written by Lee on June 25, wherein "The commander of the Army of Northern Virginia declared himself incommunicado [he would not write Davis again until after the battle of Gettysburg] and further lowered the president's expectations for a successful campaign."[21]

"The Gettysburg campaign," Palmer writes, "was, in its details, a campaign of improvisation, with Lee determining his future course of action from the saddle. Questions involving the timing of the crossing and strength of the forces sent over to the north bank of the Potomac were settled only as the campaign unfolded. . . . He shared few, if any, of his thoughts with his staff, his principal subordinates—[Lieutenant Generals James] Longstreet, [Richard] Ewell and [A.P.] Hill—or even the president of the Confederacy."[22]

Palmer goes on to say:

[20]Ibid., 36–7.
[21]Ibid., 58–60.
[22]Ibid., 64.

Pitfalls [were] inherent in [Lee's] fairly secretive, personally compartmentalized, and ad hoc approach to an offensive operation. If Lee possessed a clearly defined objective for the campaign, he never communicated that goal to anyone. [Or perhaps it would be more accurate to say that he communicated different objectives to different people, at different times.] Military historians consider a clearly defined objective one of the most universally accepted principles of war. But what was Lee's objective? Was it to seek out and defeat the Army of the Potomac? Was it to threaten Baltimore, Philadelphia and Washington? Was it to gather supplies for the army? Was it to force the Federals to withdraw troops from the West? Was it some or all of the above? ... Only once, during the Maryland campaign, had Lee undertaken an operation without a clearly defined and broadly understood objective. That campaign ended in near disaster at Sharpsburg. In the summer of 1863, a similar fate awaited the Army of Northern Virginia in Pennsylvania at a small town named Gettysburg.[23]

General Lee, Palmer asserts, deserves criticism for his failure to develop and communicate his campaign plan to his subordinates, and for his "very decentralized approach to command and control." It is Palmer's contention that a decentralized command structure needs "well-motivated and confident subordinates ... [who] understand the primary goals of a campaign" and that "Lee's unwillingness to share his concept of the campaign with his principal subordinates undermined the very system that he depended upon to win the victory he sought.... Lee's secretiveness and silence would become a critically important factor affecting the fighting power of the Army of Northern Virginia," affirms Palmer.[24]

Palmer also examines the celebrated cases of alleged failure among Lee's subordinates during the Gettysburg campaign and blames Lee for Maj. Gen. J. E. B. Stuart's seemingly errant conduct. He states: "Nine months [after Sharpsburg] Lee marched North again, expecting to operate in Pennsylvania throughout the summer before returning to Virginia in the fall. Sixteen days after Ewell's van crossed the river, the

[23]Ibid., 64–5.
[24]Ibid., 65–7.

Army of Northern Virginia found itself engaged in an epic battle at Gettysburg. The fault was not Jeb Stuart's." The alleged failures of Ewell and Longstreet he attributes to "Lee's unwillingness . . . to take charge of the battle." Palmer sees Pickett's Charge as "a senseless, even suicidal assault . . . the last of a series of decisions stretching back to early April 1863."[25]

After his retreat into Virginia, Palmer writes that Lee "chose to ignore [the lessons] of the Gettysburg campaign. He downplayed, to an incredible degree, the significance of his failures, and not just in the official reports." In a July 12 missive to his wife, "Lee displayed his well developed talent for understatement, writing 'You will have learned . . . that our success at Gettysburg was not as great as reported. In fact, we failed to drive the enemy from his position & our army withdrew to the Potomac.' " Palmer notes that though the campaign had ended poorly for the South, the experience in no way allayed "Lee's desire to resume the offensive."[26]

Palmer's analysis of Lee's Bristoe Station strategic offensive is especially useful because this effort is not as well known as Antietam or Gettysburg. Nevertheless, many facets of Lee's planning and behavior during the Bristoe campaign repeated the characteristics he exhibited during his forays into Maryland and Pennsylvania. This campaign appears to have been another of Lee's efforts to protect his army from suffering further detachments after two divisions of Longstreet's First Corps were sent to the western theater of operations. Having learned that the Army of the Potomac's Eleventh and Twelfth Corps had been sent to the Army of the Cumberland, Lee apparently decided to go on the offensive. "From Lee's official correspondence," writes Palmer, "it is unclear whether he sought to keep [Maj. Gen. George G.] Meade busy to prevent further detachments being sent to the west, to drive Meade out of Virginia, or to bring on a battle." In the midst of the campaign, "Lee offered several reasons for his march north, although he never mentioned engaging Meade's army until after the battle of Bristoe Station on October 14."[27]

On October 13, Lee wrote Secretary Seddon that the army was on the move "with the view of throwing Meade further back toward Wash-

[25]Ibid., 73–4, 86.
[26]Ibid., 87–8.
[27]Ibid., 95.

ington." Two days after Bristoe Station, he wrote to Seddon informing him that he had maneuvered "with the view of turning the right flank of the enemy and intercepting his line of retreat." In an October 17 letter to President Davis, completed as the Army of Northern Virginia retreated back to the Rappahannock River after its Bristoe failure, Lee wrote that he had moved north "with the view of bringing on an engagement with the army of General Meade." This was consistent with his prior strategic offensives.[28]

Palmer goes on to state that Lee's worn army was unprepared for a fall offensive: "Lee's health was poor. . . . The units of the Army of Northern Virginia were understrength, undersupplied, and unpaid, and the horses were in poor shape." After the defeat, Lee wrote Seddon on October 19, claiming, "Nothing prevented my continuing in his front, but the destitute condition of the men, thousands of whom are barefooted, a greater number partially shod, and nearly all without blankets, or warm clothing." Palmer notes that these facts were also true before Lee began his move north and adds that the Confederate commander's "penchant for hastily planned, unannounced offensives" did not allow Southern Quartermaster General Alexander R. Lawton "any advanced warning that the Army of Northern Virginia was about to strike North."[29]

After summarizing Lee's defeat at Bristoe Station, Palmer concludes that: "Once again, one of the Army of Northern Virginia's offensives had miscarried; once again, one of Lee's corps commanders had failed . . . Lt. Gen. Ambrose Powell Hill [was] too quick to press the assault at Bristoe Station. Despite the fact that Lee's army held the field, he knew that he had failed and had to retreat." In an October 23 report, Lee noted that Hill's attack had been "repulsed with some loss, and five pieces of artillery, with a number of prisoners, captured." Despite Hill's culpability for the Bristoe setback, Palmer indicates that "[Lee] must bear some of the responsibility. . . . Once again he had used his cavalry as rear guard and led the advance northward with his infantry. . . . The cavalry failed . . . to scout ahead of Hill's advance. . . . Neither Powell Hill nor [Maj. Gen.] Harry Heth was responsible for the absence of cavalry on the road to Bristoe Station."[30]

---

[28]Ibid., 95–6.
[29]Ibid., 100.
[30]Ibid., 114–15.

Finally, Palmer states: "The Bristoe Station campaign demonstrates that despite the disaster at Gettysburg, Lee remained wedded to the offensive. He could easily have remained on the defensive and allowed Meade to attack across the Rapidan." As J. F. C. Fuller said, "Lee's offensive distributions were frequently faulty, seldom well organized and generally badly staffed. . . . For Lee to attack an army twice the size of his in October was absurd. He marched north with nothing more than a hope that he might win some kind of meaningful, if only symbolic victory, but with the conviction that an offensive was the surest way to forestall further detachments from his own army."[31]

Thomas Buell's *Warrior Generals* is a review of the military history of the war. Referring, as does Emory Thomas, to Lee's Mexican War experience, Buell notes that during the Peninsula campaign in 1862 Lee had forgotten or dismissed a key aspect of that experience—reconnaissance. As an example of this oversight, Buell points out that Lee had not ordered topographical surveys or had maps made before the campaign's onset. Further, Lee's orders initiating the Peninsula assaults were marked by "ambiguity and omissions [that] would wreck Lee's plan even before the first gun had been fired."[32]

At Gaines' Mill on June 27, Buell asserts that "of five divisions at his disposal, Lee had gotten one in motion and had flung it against the whole of [Brig. Gen. Fitz-John] Porter's Corps." The Confederates lost eight thousand men while the Federal losses were half that number. "Lee . . . had but a slight understanding of conditions on Malvern Hill—trees in the valley limited his field of vision and he made no attempt to reconnoiter the terrain," points out Buell. The author also reaches the conclusion that Lee's "limited knowledge about artillery" led him to send "more and more regiments" in piecemeal attacks against Malvern Hill where, "like all that had gone before, they too were consumed" by the deadly Federal barrage. In Buell's opinion, "McClellan . . . survived [the Peninsula] . . . because of inept leadership within the Confederate high command, inferior staff, faulty tactics, and mediocre matériel." Even

[31]Ibid., 119; J. F. C. Fuller, *Grant and Lee: A Study in Personality and Generalship* (London: Eyre and Spottiswoode, 1933), 263.
[32]Thomas B. Buell, *The Warrior Generals* (New York: Crown Publishers, Inc., 1997), 70, 75.

Confederate officers like Maj. Gen. Daniel Harvey Hill, writes Buell, complained about the "blundering management of the battle."[33]

After Second Manassas, according to Buell, "It was altogether a time to think clearly about the future in concert with other minds, to refit the Army of Northern Virginia, to restore interior lines of communication, and to conserve the most precious resource of the Confederacy: its emaciated, ill-clothed, bone-weary infantry soldiers." Instead, says Buell, "Compelled by the certainty of his views, Lee chose to preempt Richmond and move so swiftly that Davis would be overtaken by events and forced to go along."[34]

Buell adds:

> Lee's Maryland campaign was a calamity for the Confederacy that would forever cripple its war aims. Civil war battles are ultimately fought for political objectives. No good reason existed to warrant an invasion of Maryland at that time, and under those circumstances. Lee's soldiers certainly knew this, for they abandoned the army in wholesale numbers. His assumption that the people of Maryland would support him was correspondingly fallacious, but he clung to it even after the debacle. "I regret that the stay of the army in Maryland," he wrote duplicitously to the secretary of war on September 20 "was so short as to prevent our receiving the aid I had expected from that State."[35]

Buell writes further that "Antietam reduced the Army of Northern Virginia to a mob of vandals. Defeated and disheartened, its officers and men had lost confidence in Lee's leadership and judgment. Thousands of deserters and stragglers, in growing numbers, roamed at will, and officers no longer exercised military order and discipline." Regarding September 18, 1862, the day after the Battle of Antietam, Buell makes a pregnant observation: "The fact was that Lee did not want to fight if he could avoid it, a drastic departure from his principle of fighting for the sake of fighting." He makes a similar observation that on May 5 at Chancellorsville, Lee wanted "to renew his assault against Hooker as on the

[33]Ibid., 79, 85–7, 95.
[34]Ibid., 105–6.
[35]Ibid., 122.

morning of the Sixth, but Hooker . . . withdrew across the river. . . . Lee's army [was] fortunate. Lee had reverted to his practice of fighting for the sake of fighting, but there was little to fight with." In Buell's judgment, further Rebel attacks would have done little to endanger "Hooker's entrenched forces."[36]

Turning to Gettysburg, Buell notes that in the interest of security "Lee wrote neither a plan nor orders" before this "extraordinary gamble" of a campaign, and the author wonders, why Lee even "attempt[ed] an invasion?"

> The Army of Northern Virginia was shaky, at best, in its readiness to fight. Lee had completed reorganizing just four days earlier. He had no plan, no real objectives; other than to react fatalistically to developments as his scattered army meandered on country roads . . . they had no destination, no timetable. By marching slowly, wear and tear on man and beast was lessened, and time was given to forage. . . . Eventually, of course, he knew that he would have to fight, for the Federal Government would not allow him a free hand indefinitely. . . . Lee did not know where the Federal Army was, for his chronically shaky intelligence system had collapsed. Stuart would misinterpret Lee's ambiguous orders . . . and [not] report on enemy whereabouts.[37]

Buell also compellingly addresses the issue of Lee in regard to the prolonging of the war. He starts by describing Lee's army at Petersburg:

> The Army of Northern Virginia crouched in agony behind its Petersburg ramparts. During the winter of 1864–65, the siege had degenerated into trench warfare of the most desolate kind. The Confederate soldiers lived in squalor and misery, neither fed nor clothed nor sheltered while Federal artillery and sharpshooters fired on anyone who moved. The army's leadership had collapsed. Generals contrived excuses to abandon their commands. Captains neglected their men. Lee with dismay read the December inspection report for Longstreet's corps, a dole-

---

[36]Ibid., 126, 131, 216.
[37]Ibid., 222–23.

ful indictment of the apathy of its officers. Lee angrily scratched out a letter to Longstreet . . . but spilling ink on paper could not impede the disintegration. In the absence of leadership, the sick, starving, dispirited enlisted men had incentive neither to drill nor to fight. Thousands deserted.[38]

Despite such a situation, Lee wrote to his wife "that he would do his duty & fight to the last." "To what and to whom Lee's sense of duty applied is unclear," comments Buell, "but it was neither to his soldiers nor the people of Virginia. In his "fight to the last" he would prolong a devastating war for no purpose whatever." Buell also comments that in such circumstances Lee's March request to Union Lt. Gen. Ulysses S. Grant for a military convention was preposterous.[39]

Gary Gallagher has also examined Lee. In *The Confederate War,* Gallagher promptly disposes of the issue of Lee's sentiments regarding the peculiar institution and refers to Lee's wartime letter to Hunter in which he discussed slavery. Gallagher is also deeply concerned with the issue of Lee's generalship and sets forth an extensive analysis of previous scholarship on this issue. Gallagher examines the idea that Lee's aggressive strategy and tactics, and the losses incurred as a result of pursuing such tactics, led directly to Confederate defeat. Gallagher also edited and contributed to *Lee The Soldier.* In his essay in that volume, Gallagher responds vigorously to those writers like myself who have criticized Lee and concludes his *Lee the Soldier* essay with the statement, "Without Lee and that famous field command, the Confederate experiment in rebellion almost certainly would have ended much sooner."[40]

In 1997, Edward Bonekemper wrote *How Robert E. Lee Lost the Civil War.* As the title suggests, he does not mince words. Lee was a failure, according to Bonekemper, from first to last. In western Virginia in 1861, Lee failed to take charge of his battles and issued complex and ineffective combat orders, characteristics that continued through the "slaughter on the Peninsula" to the end of the war. Overall, Bonekemper believes that Lee's generalship had a "lethal effect on the Army of

[38]Ibid., 414.

[39]Ibid., 414–15.

[40]Gary W. Gallagher, *The Confederate War* (Cambridge: Harvard University Press, 1997), 46–7; Gary W. Gallagher, ed., *Lee the Soldier* (Lincoln: University of Nebraska Press, 1996), 286.

Northern Virginia," and he points out that despite the devastating potential of modern weapons, Lee continuously relied on frontal attacks. Each battle, win or lose, was a failure, even Chancellorsville, where "the Confederates decimated themselves in a series of frontal attacks" on the Union's defensive perimeter to produce "a victory that wasn't."[41]

Bonekemper believes that Gettysburg was likely the nadir of Lee's efforts and finds Lee at fault for the actions of all the familiar scapegoats—Stuart, Ewell, and Longstreet. "Lee was either fighting the wrong war or fighting on the wrong side," is Bonekemper's scathing indictment of Lee's abilities. Bonekemper argues the Confederate defeat in the West is also Lee's responsibility because of his refusal to part with troops for this critical theater and his lack of exertion in preventing the incompetent Lt. Gen. John B. Hood's appointment to command of the Army of Tennessee. In the 1864 Overland campaign, Bonekemper believes that Lee played directly into Grant's hands by constantly attacking the Union army. Bonekemper concludes with this quote from military historian John Keegan: "The only cult general in the English-speaking world—Robert E. Lee—was the paladin of its only component community to suffer military catastrophe." Lee was responsible for that catastrophe. Bonekemper also quotes J. F. C. Fuller, "The more we inquire into the generalship of Lee, the more we discover that Lee, or rather the popular conception of him, is a myth."[42]

It is to be noted that Bonekemper is especially critical of Lee for continuing the war after the onset of the Petersburg siege. He writes, for example: "On December 31, 1864, less than half of the Confederate soldiers were present with their units. Therefore, 1865 should have witnessed no fighting. But Lee had yet to call a halt to the bloody proceedings. The thousands of deaths that year were a macabre tribute to his chivalry and sense of honor and duty."[43]

The thesis of Bevin Alexander's *Robert E. Lee's Civil War* is the general ineptitude of Lee, principally his relentless offensive strategy and tactics from the Peninsula to the war's very end, which destroyed his army and brought about the Confederacy's defeat. Alexander virtually

[41]Edward H. Bonekemper, III, *How Robert E. Lee Lost the Civil War* (Fredericksburg: Sergeant Kirkland's Press, 1997), 53, 79, 96–7.
[42]Ibid., 143, 147, 193, 214.
[43]Ibid., 181.

summarizes my book's thesis: "The key to understanding Lee as a commander is that he sought from first to last to fight an offensive war—that is, a war of battle and marches against the armies of the North. This offensive war, though it produced many spectacular clashes and campaigns that arouse fascination to this day, ultimately failed because Lee's methods and strategies were insufficient to overcome the South's weakness in arms and manpower."[44]

Alexander posits that the South should have used its two major armies to prevent "Northern movements into the South" and permit "the Confederacy to pursue a long war preserving its other, more limited resources, especially its manpower. In time the North might have become weary of its inability to end the war and stop losses." Alexander believes Lee "never understood the revolution that the Minie bullet had brought to battle tactics" and concludes that the general's "tendency to move to direct confrontation, regardless of the prospect or the losses that would be sustained, guaranteed Lee's failure as an offensive commander."[45]

The point of the foregoing discussion is not that these books agree or disagree with my analysis and conclusions about the Lee tradition. The point is not whether I agree with all of these writers' conclusions. The point is that these scholars acknowledge questions about Lee akin to those that I raised; they inquire into them, research the data, and discuss the pros and cons of the issues. In short, they "consider" Lee. These works represent a sea of change in Lee scholarship since *Lee Considered* appeared. The Lee advocates, who for a hundred years have insisted that every knee must bend at his name, may continue in their beliefs, but the rest of us can now consider Lee the mortal.

---

[44]Bevin Alexander, *Robert E. Lee's Civil War* (Holbrook: Adams Media Corporation, 1998), ix.

[45]Ibid., ix–x, xii.

Ex parte Milligan: A Curb of Executive and Military Power

Ex parte Milligan, the 1866 decision of the United States Supreme Court, is a chapter in the long story of the American Civil War. The response of the United States to the Southern rebellion took place within the general context of the legal system and without a suspension of the conventional political process. But there were impositions on the legal system and the political process, and the prosecution of Lambdin P. Milligan was such an imposition.

To state the case of Ex parte Milligan in a lawyer-like way is a relatively simple task, but the political context of the case is essential to an appreciation of its significance. A consideration of the political context also permits an inquiry into the question of Indiana's role in the Civil War.

Abraham Lincoln

On March 4, 1861, Abraham Lincoln stood on a temporary platform on the east front of the unfinished Capitol in Washington. Following an introduction by his friend Sen. Edward D. Baker of Oregon, the president-elect delivered his inaugural address. He was then sworn in by Chief Justice of the United States Roger Brooke Taney, author of the Dred Scott decision.

Directed in large part to the Southern states, seven of which had seceded and established the Confederate States of America, the inaugural address was a closely reasoned plea for the Union. Approaching a conclusion, Lincoln said:

You have no oath registered in Heaven to destroy the government, while I shall have the most solemn one to "preserve, protect and defend" it.[1]

As is well known, Lincoln was personally an intensely complicated man. I suggest that as president he was quite uncomplicated. Having taken an oath to preserve, protect, and defend the United States, he proposed to do just that. From the beginning, all men and all measures were determined by a single standard: the capacity to help or hurt the defeat of the rebellion.

Sandburg's Lincoln, the mythic hero, was folksy, sweet, and kind, a wholly sympathetic character. These were surely aspects of the man. But as Stephen B. Oates has recently pointed out, Lincoln was "a tough wartime President, flexing his executive muscles and expanding his war powers whenever necessity demanded."[2] He had taken an oath. He was dead in earnest and resolute.

Article II of the Constitution of the United States is almost quaint in the brevity of its description of the powers of the president. It says that "the Executive power shall be vested in" him. Section 2 states that he "shall be commander-in-chief of the army and navy." But until the Lincoln years, with the possible exception of the tenure of Andrew Jackson, the government of the United States was essentially a congressional government. Confronted with the unprecedented crisis and without significant precedent in terms of the role and power of his office, Lincoln proceeded as commander-in-chief to create the modern presidency, an office of great political power.

In the midst of the secession crisis, Lincoln authorized military commanders to declare martial law and thereby sanctioned arbitrary arrest and trial and conviction by military commission instead of the conventional courts. He also authorized the suspension of the writ of habeas corpus.[3] It is worthwhile at the outset briefly to discuss the significance

[1]Roy P. Basler, ed., *The Collected Works of Abraham Lincoln* 9 vols. (New Brunswick, N.J.: Rutgers University Press, 1953), 4:271. This source is hereinafter cited as *Collected Works.*

[2]Stephen B. Oates, *Abraham Lincoln, the Man Behind the Myths* (New York: Harper & Row Publishers, 1984), 120.

[3]See, for example, Lincoln to Gen. Winfield Scott, April 25 and 27, 1861, in *Collected Works,* 4:344, 347, and Lincoln's proclamation of May 10, 1861, concerning

of arbitrary arrest, military commission trials, and suspension of habeas corpus.

According to the American legal system, one may not be lawfully arrested unless he is suspected of committing a specific act that is proscribed by generally applicable law. The person arrested must be promptly brought before a conventional court and charged with the act. An arbitrary arrest has no such requirements. One may be seized at will and either charged with an offense known or unknown to the generally applicable law or, as was sometimes the case during the Civil War, retained in prison and never charged at all.

Jurisdiction is a lawyer's word, the kind of word that causes lay persons to dislike lawyers. It means *power*. In the law, an authority with jurisdiction over us has the legal power to force our obedience. Thus, the conventional courts may subpoena us, and the police authorities will seize us if we do not comply with the subpoena. The conventional court can sentence us to jail, and the police authorities will take us there and hold us. These conventional jurisdictions are, of course, subject to the Constitution and statutes that restrict and condition their power. They may only act according to due process, according to law. If the government sets up a collateral jurisdiction, that is, an agency with the *power* of the courts but without the constitutional and statutory restrictions and conditions of that power, a profound change in our status has occurred. A military commission is an example of such a collateral jurisdiction.

The writ of habeas corpus is a direction from the conventional court to an agency that is detaining someone. The writ commands the agency to produce the person in court and to justify the detention. If the detention cannot be justified, the prisoner is released by the court. The writ tests the legality of the detention, not the guilt or innocence of the

---

the state of Florida in ibid., 4:364–65. See also Lincoln's proclamation of September 24, 1862, suspending the writ, establishing martial law, and authorizing trial and punishment by military commission with respect to "all Rebels and Insurgents, their aiders and abettors within the United States, and all persons discouraging volunteer enlistments, resisting military drafts, or guilty of any disloyal practice, affording aid and comfort to the Rebels. . . ." Ibid., 5:436–37. See also William W. Winthrop, *Military Law and Precedents* (Washington, D.C.: Government Printing Office, 1920), 833–34.

prisoner. Article I of the Constitution, the article concerning the Congress, authorizes the suspension of the writ of habeas corpus "when in cases of rebellion or invasion the public safety may require it." It seems plain that the Lincoln program of arbitrary arrest and military commission jurisdiction was dependent on the unavailability of the writ. If habeas corpus had been available to a prisoner, a court would have released him because of the arbitrary character of the arrest or the unconventional military trial.

This then was the Lincoln administration's program for coping with the problem of dissent. Lincoln was sensitive to the anomaly of his situation. He addressed this issue in his message of July 4, 1861, to the Special Session of the Congress. Referring to the fact that he had authorized the military "to arrest, and detain, without resort to the ordinary processes and forms of law," he acknowledged that "the legality and propriety of what has been done" were questioned, and "the attention of the country has been called to the proposition that one who is sworn to 'take care that the laws be faithfully executed' should not himself violate them." Lincoln then described the crisis of the Union and stated his rationale, essentially that of necessity. Rhetorically, he asked: "Are all the laws, *but one,* to go unexecuted, and the government itself go to pieces, lest that one be violated?"[4]

A more detailed statement of Lincoln's position appears in his remarkable letter of June 12, 1863, to Erastus Corning. In this letter Lincoln responded to resolutions of May 16, 1863, made by New York Democrats meeting in Albany.[5] Referring to Clement L. Vallandingham of Ohio, a prominent Democratic politician and an articulate and intemperate critic of Lincoln and the war effort whose arrest had prompted the Albany resolutions, Lincoln stated his often-quoted epigram: "Must I shoot a simple-minded soldier boy who deserts, while I must not touch a hair of a wiley agitator who induces him to desert?" The popularity of this statement has, it seems to me, distracted us from a more careful consideration of the Corning letter.

Abe Lincoln was not a careless man. He was a highly competent, technical lawyer. As is well known, he also had an uncommon facility

---

[4] *Collected Works,* 4:429–30.
[5] All quotations from Corning letter are in ibid., 6:260–69.

with the language. When he set forth his views in a letter that he expected to be made public, I think that we may assume that the letter unambiguously reflected his state of mind. Setting aside its plainly political aspects, I read the Corning letter as Lincoln's brief on the issue of the propriety of his administration's treatment of dissent by means of arbitrary arrest, military trial, and the suspension of the writ of habeas corpus. One should read the letter to grasp it fully, but I will briefly describe it.

At the outset, Lincoln asserted his conclusion that the unusual proceedings that the New York Democrats complained of were *not* unconstitutional. They were, he said, within "the exceptions of the constitution, and . . . indispensable to the public safety." He then presented his arguments to support this conclusion.

Beginning as a good lawyer should with a statement of the facts, Lincoln contended that, at the time that he took office, persons sympathetic to secession had "pervaded all departments of the government, and nearly all communities of the people," and that the South relied on this fact and the ability of these sympathizers to subvert the government under the "cover" [Lincoln's word] of free speech, free press, and habeas corpus. Continuing with his factual premises, Lincoln then discussed the conventional civil courts. They were, he said, organized to try individuals or small groups of people, in quiet times, on "charges of crimes well defined in the law"; they were not competent to deal with massive groups of disloyal people in the loyal states whose acts damaged the war effort but did not constitute a "defined crime."

Lincoln then turned to the law. Referring to Section 9 of Article I of the Constitution, that is, the provision permitting the suspension of habeas corpus "when in cases of Rebellion or Invasion, the public Safety may require it," he contended that this language authorized not only the suspension of the writ but also arbitrary arrest, military commission trial, and the remaining aspects of his program. Specifically, he relied on this language of the Constitution in regard to the arrest and holding of persons "who can not be proved to be guilty of defined crime." Such arrests, he conceded, were not for what had been done by a defendant, but "for what probably would be done." Thus, in Lincoln's words, such arrests were "preventive," so as "to silence the agitator." With reference to Vallandingham, Lincoln stated his understanding that Vallandingham had been speaking to prevent the raising of troops. This, he said, was "warring upon the military; and this gave the military constitutional jurisdiction to lay hands on him."

The president concluded with a reassurance. He expressed confidence that the "right of public discussion, the liberty of speech and the press, the law of evidence, trial by jury, and Habeas corpus" would return once the rebellion was defeated.

Three aspects of the president's analysis seem to me to be noteworthy. In the first place, there is the letter's candid acknowledgment that arbitrary arrest, the military commissions, and suspension of habeas corpus imposed on the traditional American constitutional framework in fundamental ways. Preventive detention, instead of arrest for the commission of a generally prohibited act, freedom of speech, freedom of the press, trial by jury, and the law of evidence were also at stake. In addition, Lincoln's analysis of the Vallandingham arrest suggests that the military establishment had some independent status and autonomy, so that it was free to make and enforce its own laws in reference to people who interfered with it. Finally, there was Lincoln's confidence that the traditional rights would return when the war was over. Surely he hoped that this would happen, but history did not and does not support his optimism.

The Vallandingham Decision

It was the Vallandingham arrest that led to the United States Supreme Court's first opportunity to consider Lincoln's thesis. On April 13, 1863, Maj. Gen. Ambrose Burnside, commanding the Military Department of Ohio, issued General Order No. 38, declaring that thereafter all persons found within his lines "who shall commit acts for the benefit of the enemies of the country, shall be tried as spies or traitors, and if convicted shall suffer death."[6] Among the acts prohibited was declaring

---

[6] *Ex parte In the Matter of Clement L. Vallandingham, Petitioner,* February 15, 1864, 68 U.S. (1 Wall.) 243, 17 L. Ed. 589. The facts of the Vallandingham case are taken from the Supreme Court report. The case is described and discussed by numerous authorities, including Frank L. Klement, *Dark Lanterns—Secret Political Societies, Conspiracies, and Treason Trials in the Civil War* (Baton Rouge and London: Louisiana State University Press, 1984); J. G. Randall, *Lincoln, the President* (New York: Dodd, Mead & Co., 1952), vol. 3; and Frank L. Klement, *The Limits*

sympathy for the enemy. Significantly, the order also referred to punishing violators by sending them into the lines of the enemy. A few days after this order, Burnside issued Special Order No. 135, establishing a military commission to meet in Cincinnati for the trial of persons who might be brought before it. A detail of officers and a judge-advocate were appointed.

On May 1, 1863, at Mount Vernon, Ohio, Vallandingham addressed a political meeting at which he denounced the war as not for the purpose of restoring the Union, but for purposes of establishing a despotism that would free the blacks and enslave the whites. At length and bitterly, the speech attacked Lincoln and the military, including specifically General Burnside's General Order No. 38. On May 5 Vallandingham was arrested at his home by a military detail and taken to Cincinnati and imprisoned. On the following day he was arraigned before the military commission "on a charge of having expressed sympathies for those in arms against the Government . . . and for having uttered in a speech in a public meeting, disloyal sentiments and opinions, with the object and purpose of weakening the power of the government in its efforts for the suppression of an unlawful rebellion."[7]

The defendant challenged the jurisdiction of the military commission and refused to plead. A plea of not guilty was entered by the judge-advocate in his behalf. He was permitted to have counsel and to cross-examine witnesses and call witnesses in his behalf. After an exchange of statements between Vallandingham and the judge-advocate concerning the propriety and constitutionality of the proceeding, the military commission found the defendant guilty, except with reference to one portion of the speech attributed to him, and sentenced him to prison for the duration of the war. The finding and sentence were approved by General Burnside. On May 19, 1863, in commutation of the sentence, President Lincoln ordered that Vallandingham be delivered to a place outside the federal military lines.[8]

---

of Dissent: Clement L. Vallandingham & the Civil War (Lexington: University of Kentucky Press, 1970).

[7] *Ex parte Vallandingham*, 17 L. Ed. 589, 590.

[8] As is well known, Vallandingham was delivered to the Confederate lines in Tennessee. He went to Richmond, ran the blockade, and moved to Canada. In 1864 he was nominated for governor by the Ohio Democrats. Running his campaign from Canada, he was defeated. He returned illegally to Ohio in 1865. Mark

Vallandingham's lawyers then petitioned the Supreme Court of the United States for a writ of certiorari, that is, they requested the court to require the judge-advocate general of the army to send the proceedings of the military commission to the court for its review. They contended that the military commission had no jurisdiction to try the defendant. More specifically, Vallandingham argued that he was a civilian and was entitled to trial by jury pursuant to the third section of Article III of the Constitution. He also contended that the offense charged against him was not defined as a crime by the laws of the United States.

As a result of the Congress having "packed" the court in 1863, the Supreme Court to which Vallandingham applied was composed of ten justices. Taney was still the chief justice. Four of the justices were Lincoln appointees: Noah H. Swayne, Samuel F. Miller, David Davis, and Stephen J. Field. Neither Taney nor Justice Miller participated in the Vallandingham deliberations.[9]

Issued February 15, 1864, the opinion in *Ex parte Vallandingham* was written by Justice James M. Wayne, a Georgia Jacksonian. Appointed to the court by Jackson, Wayne had long been an outspoken adherent of the idea of the Federal Union. He wrote for six of the participating justices. Justice Samuel Nelson, a Tyler appointee from New York, concurred in the result but filed no separate opinion.[10]

Wayne's opinion focused on the issue of the Supreme Court's jurisdiction to review the actions of a military commission. It found that its appellate jurisdiction had its source in Article III of the Constitution, pursuant to "such regulations as the Congress shall make." Referring to the acts of Congress, the Court declared that such legislation provided for its jurisdiction to review the rulings of inferior federal courts, but did not extend that jurisdiction to review the decisions of military commissions. It thus denied Vallandingham's petition without an examination of the merits of his claims. Although perhaps defensible on narrow technical grounds, the decision effectively closed the conventional courts to the victims of the administration's program. Had the case been pursued

---

E. Neeley, Jr., *The Abraham Lincoln Encyclopedia* (New York: McGraw-Hill Book Co., 1982), 317–18.

[9]David M. Silver, *Lincoln's Supreme Court* (Urbana: University of Illinois Press, 1957), 84–85, 57.

[10]Ibid., 16–18, 20–22.

in a different legal form, or had the aged Taney been on hand, it is surely possible that the Court would have had to extend itself further in order to reach its result. The *Detroit Free Press* stated one public reaction: "The Supreme Court has no jurisdiction in matters of individual liberty, unless the party claiming redress can prove he was ravaged according to the law."[11]

Ex parte Milligan

We may now turn to the Milligan prosecution, but that case must be examined within its peculiar context. Indiana Civil War politics have been the subject of three exceptional studies by three able professional historians: Kenneth M. Stampp, Emma Lou Thornbrough, and Gilbert R. Tredway.[12] I must briefly state the facts that their books examine in detail. I concede that I do so with a broad brush.

Oliver P. Morton succeeded to the governorship in January of 1861 on Henry S. Lane's election to the United States Senate by the legislature at its regular session. That session and a special session convened by Morton in April were controlled by the victorious Republicans. The politicians of both parties promptly signaled that the war was not to mute the vigor of their disagreements. My own analysis suggests that there were three common denominators to the political conflict. The issues concerned *principle, personalities,* and *patronage.*

The issue of principle involved opinions as to the purpose of the war: was it to maintain the Union, or did it also involve the institution of slavery? A majority of the Democrats rejected the idea of a war against slavery. Perhaps a majority of the Republicans, a new party with many factions, agreed. Morton himself was initially conservative on this ques-

---

[11]*Detroit Free Press,* February 26, 1864.

[12]Kenneth M. Stampp, *Indiana Politics during the Civil War* (Indianapolis: Indiana Historical Bureau, 1949); Emma Lou Thornbrough, *Indiana in the Civil War Era* (Indianapolis: Indiana Historical Bureau and the Indiana Historical Society, 1965); and Gilbert R. Tredway, *Democratic Opposition to the Lincoln Administration in Indiana* (Indianapolis: Indiana Historical Bureau, 1973). These books are the principal sources on which this paper's statements about Indiana politics are based. They are specifically cited only when deemed necessary. See also John D. Barnhart, "The Impact of the Civil War on Indiana," *Indiana Magazine of History* 57 (September 1961):185–224.

tion. But there was a significant vocal minority of Republicans, of whom Congressman George W. Julian of the Fifth District was the most prominent, who insisted from the outset that there could be no permanent peace without abolition.[13] This, then, was the first issue, the relationship between slavery and the war, and for a long time the politicians maneuvered around it like medieval churchmen.

In terms of personalities, there were, of course, many, but Morton was *the* personality. According to Kenneth M. Stampp, and any reading of the press or the legislative history of the period surely supports him, "Governor Morton . . . was . . . frequently the central figure in these renewed political conflicts." Stampp asserts that "to a considerable extent this was caused by the Governor's own personality and ambition. Morton was an exceptionally able executive, but he was blunt, pugnacious, ruthless, and completely lacking in a sense of humor." Wholly intolerant of disagreement, his approach toward those who opposed him, in and out of his party, was to harass them and impugn their motives and their character. Both the Democrats and such Republican leaders as Julian and the president of the Indiana senate and speaker of the Indiana house were heavily at odds with Morton.[14]

And then there was patronage, in those days crude and unpretentious. Politicians and their followers were always sensitive to it and willing to fight about it. The very fact of the war significantly enlarged the scope of patronage, and the conflict about it increased in proportion. Not the least of the new subjects of patronage was power to appoint regimental and company officers for Indiana regiments. During the war, 18,884 such commissions were issued to Hoosiers.[15] The governor's control of this power was the subject of much political and legislative activity.

The factional and partisan bickering reached its first crescendo as the 1862 elections approached. It is only fair to the antagonists to acknowledge that additional issues of principle had emerged and were very real. Arbitrary arrest, suspension of the writ of habeas corpus, emancipation, the power of the presidency, tariff increases, the additional calls for volunteers, and the proposal of a military draft were easy

[13] *Centerville Indiana True Republican,* May 17, 23, 1861.
[14] Stampp, *Indiana Politics,* 82, 84.
[15] W. H. H. Terrell, *Report of the Adjutant General of the State of Indiana* (Indianapolis: Alexander H. Conner, state printer, 1869), 1:88.

to get excited about. And the war was killing a lot of Indiana soldiers and was going badly. The summer of 1862 saw McClellan's withdrawal from the Peninsula, the defeat at Second Bull Run, the invasion of Kentucky, and Lee's movement into Maryland. Kenneth Stampp fairly describes the Republican response to the Democrats' political exploitation of the state of the war. It was, he writes, "fierce and partisan . . . raising the cry of treason and identifying any sort of criticism with that term. Only traitors, they inferred, would denounce President Lincoln or Governor Morton while rebels were trying to destroy the nation."[16] George W. Julian was later to admit that "loyalty to Republicanism was . . . accepted as the best evidence of loyalty to the country."[17]

In his keynote speech to the 1862 Republican state convention, Morton spoke darkly of the Northwest Conspiracy, which he described as a Democratic scheme to take Kentucky and the states of the Old Northwest out of the Union and to ally them with the South. He told of secret treasonable societies in Indiana and warned that they would be suppressed.[18] In August, with Morton's involvement, a federal grand jury in Indianapolis issued an exposé of the Knights of the Golden Circle, allegedly a secret Democratic treasonable society. The report was widely used by the Republicans in the 1862 canvass.[19]

On October 14, 1862, the Democrats carried the state by 9,000 votes. The governorship was not at issue, but the Democrats took control of the rest of the statehouse and both houses of the General Assembly. Having studied the campaign and the activities of the Democrats in detail, Stampp concludes that "the Indiana Democracy of 1862 was eminently loyal. While it criticized methods, it campaigned as a war party and demanded suppression of the rebellion by force of arms."[20] Frank L.

[16]Stampp, *Indiana Politics,* 94.

[17]George W. Julian, *Political Recollections, 1840–1872* (Chicago: Jansen, McClurg & Co., 1884), 244.

[18]Stampp, *Indiana Politics,* 136; *Indianapolis Daily Journal,* June 19, 20, 21, 23, 1862.

[19]Terrell, *Report of the Adjutant General,* 1:295. Generally discredited by historians, the grand jury's report states that there were 15,000 members of the Knights of the Golden Circle in Indiana.

[20]Stampp, *Indiana Politics,* 151–52. There is an earlier and contrary thesis regarding the dissenting Democrats in 1862 and, for that matter, throughout the war. This thesis contends that the Northern Democrats and dissenters were, in the main, disloyal and committed to the success of the rebellion. See, for example, Leonard Kenworthy, *The Tall Sycamore of the Wabash: Daniel Wolsey Voorhees*

Klement of Marquette University, also a keen student of dissent during the war, agrees with Stampp, but he accurately observes that the Indiana Democrats "played partisan politics viciously while the nation's life was at stake."[21]

Having approached the brink of political destructiveness during the 1862 campaign, the parties proceeded in the 1863 legislature to go over the brink. Never one to assume a defensive posture, Morton fired the first shots. On January 3, as the legislators arrived in Indianapolis, the governor wired Secretary Stanton that he had been "advised that it is the intent of the Legislature . . . to pass a joint resolution to acknowledge the Southern Confederacy and urge the Northwest to dissolve all constitutional relations with the New England States."[22] Although there were many issues and side shows, three Democratic legislative plans, all blatantly political, seem to have created the ultimate impasse: reapportionment of the legislature and congressional districts; the establishment of an executive council, composed of the Democratic secretary of state, auditor, treasurer, and attorney general, to whom the governor was to be required to defer; and a military bill drafted so as to limit the governor's power over the large state military establishment. Alleging that these were treasonable proposals, on February 26, 1863, all but four Republicans in the House of Representatives withdrew and traveled to Madison so as to cross the river if the sergeant-at-arms came to bring them back. The legislature was deprived of a constitutional quorum and came to a standstill. Since no appropriation bills had been passed, each party assumed that the other would make the political concessions necessary to reconstitute the legislature, but these concessions were not made. The legislature adjourned without appropriating funds to conduct the state for the ensuing two years.[23]

(Boston: B. Humphries, 1936); Wood Gray, *The Hidden Civil War: The Story of the Copperheads* (New York: Viking Press, 1942); and George Fort Milton, *Abraham Lincoln and the Fifth Column* (New York: Vanguard Press, 1942). This paper rejects this thesis because those who assert it seem unable to support it with other than Republican allegations.

[21]Klement, *Dark Lanterns*, 152.

[22]Telegrams Received File, Vol. 4, Part 2, 759, War Department Records, National Archives, Washington, D.C.

[23]Ariel and William H. Draper, comps., *Brevier Legislative Reports* (South Bend, 1863), vol. 6. The previously noted books by Stampp, Thornbrough, and Tredway contain good descriptions of the legislative maneuvering. See also

The redoubtable Morton proceeded to conduct the state government by other means: War Department funding, loans from various counties on the basis of the governor's personal receipts, and loans from a New York banking firm. The state financial officers, the treasurer and auditor, were ignored. The funds were kept in a guarded safe in the governor's office under the administration of a Morton creation, the Bureau of Finance, headed by his military secretary, William Henry Harrison Terrell.[24]

The bitterness and partisanship that marked the 1862 election and the 1863 legislative breakdown continued unabated into 1864, as did the war itself. The 1864 state election in Indiana was scheduled for October 11, to be followed by the federal election on November 8. This time Governor Morton himself was running for reelection as the nominee of the Republicans, for the time being identified as the Union party. The war was two years older. All of the real issues of 1862 were there. More lives had been lost, and the final, bloody Virginia Campaign had begun in May. The loyalty issue was as vigorous as ever. Morton and his allies approached the campaign with the renewed claim that the Democrats supported the South and were in fact treasonable.[25]

Gen. Alvin P. Hovey, a native Hoosier and former colonel of the Twenty-fourth Indiana Volunteers, had been a prewar Democrat. A combat veteran, in 1864 he was the Commander of the Military District of Indiana. He shared Governor Morton's view that Morton's political foes were disloyal.[26] In the midst of the heated political campaign, with Morton's complicity, Hovey on September 17, 1864, issued Special Or-

---

Lorna Lutes Sylvester, "Oliver P. Morton and the Indiana Legislature of 1863," in *Their Infinite Variety: Essays on Indiana Politicians* (Indianapolis: Indiana Historical Bureau, 1981), 123–54.

[24]Sylvester, "Oliver P. Morton," 123–54; Stampp, *Indiana Politics*, 179ff. For a biographical sketch of Terrell, see "Editorial Note," *Indiana in the War of the Rebellion, Report of the Adjutant General* (Indianapolis: Indiana Historical Bureau, 1960). This volume is a reprint of volume 1 of the eight-volume report prepared by W. H. H. Terrell and published in 1869.

[25]Klement, *Dark Lanterns,* chap. 4; Stampp, *Indiana Politics,* chap. 10; Frank L. Klement, "The Indianapolis Treason Trials and Ex Parte Milligan," in *American Political Trials,* ed. Michael Belknap (Westport, Ct.: Greenwood Press, 1981), 107–110.

[26]Tredway, *Democratic Opposition,* 225.

ders No. 129 authorizing a military commission "to meet at the United States Court Rooms in the City of Indianapolis on the nineteenth day of September, 1864, . . . for the trial of . . . such . . . prisoners as may be brought before it."[27] General Hovey had already undertaken within the period prior to the elections a series of military arrests which involved numerous Indiana citizens, including eight men prominently connected with the Democratic party: William M. Harrison, secretary of the Democratic Club of Marion County; Harrison H. Dodd; William A. Bowles, a delegate to the 1864 Indiana Democratic Convention; Joseph J. Bingham, editor of the *Indianapolis Daily State Sentinel* and chairman of the Democratic State Central Committee; Horace Heffren, editor of the *Washington Democrat* of Salem, Indiana, formerly a state legislator and officer in Indiana volunteer regiments; Stephen Horsey; Andrew Humphreys, a leading Democrat from the Greene and Sullivan County area; and Lambdin P. Milligan, a Huntington lawyer. Milligan, who gave his name to the later decision of the Supreme Court of the United States, was a harsh and angry critic of Lincoln and Morton. He hated the fact of the war, concentrating his fire on the threat to constitutional government that he believed the war represented. Not a mainstream Democrat, he had unsuccessfully sought the Democratic gubernatorial nomination in 1864. Two more Democratic leaders, David T. Yeakel and James B. Wilson, were arrested after the state election but before the national election.[28]

---

[27] *Special Orders No. 129, September 17, 1864,* General Courts Martial, Records of the Office of the Judge Advocate General, National Archives, Washington, D.C. At the time of Hovey's appointment, Assistant Adjutant General E. D. Townsend, identifying Secretary Stanton as his authority, told Hovey that he was authorized to make "military arrests" and to organize "courts-martial." Letter of Townsend to Hovey, September 14, 1864, Hovey Manuscripts, Lilly Library, Indiana University, Bloomington. In notes that he wrote in approximately 1882 to be used in his obituary, Hovey credited himself with having "crushed a fearful rebellion" in Indiana by his arrests. Hovey Manuscripts, Lilly Library, Indiana University, Bloomington.

[28] The arrests and the individuals arrested are described in Tredway, *Democratic Opposition,* 218–19, and in Klement, "The Indianapolis Treason Trials," 101–27. David T. Yeakel and James B. Wilson were seized on November 5, 1864. Milligan is described in Darwin Kelley, *Milligan's Fight against Lincoln* (New York: Exposition Press, 1973). He is also characterized and discussed in Tredway, *Democratic Opposition,* 155–56, 156–59.

The arrests and the later trials were preceded and accompanied by vigorous and partisan publicity. This aspect of the matter originated with an exposé of a secret society, the Sons of Liberty, published in the *Indianapolis Daily Journal* on June 29, 1864, and continued with unusual intensity in the same organ after its acquisition on August 28, 1864, by William R. Holloway, Governor Morton's brother-in-law and private secretary.[29] The War Department in Washington cooperated. On October 8, 1864, Judge Advocate General Holt issued a lengthy report on the Order of the American Knights, "alias The Sons of Liberty." The report identified several of the defendants, including Dodd and Milligan, as officers of the society in Indiana and alleged that it was planning an armed insurrection and had 75,000 to 125,000 members in the state. A Northwestern Confederacy, in alliance with the South, was identified by Holt as a goal of the Sons of Liberty.[30]

General Hovey's military commission was initially composed of seven Indiana military officers. Maj. Henry L. Burnett of Ohio was the judge-advocate. It is the opinion of professional historians who have studied the events that several members of the commission were biased and partisan and had accepted Governor Morton's premise that disagreement and dissent were tantamount to disloyalty and treason.[31] Col. Benjamin Spooner had declared publicly that all persons not voting the straight Republican ticket were "traitors."[32] Four of the commissioners, including Spooner, delivered rousing speeches to Republican rallies while the trials were in progress.[33]

The first of the defendants to be tried was Harrison H. Dodd. The specifications involving Dodd alleged that he did "conspire against the Government . . . joining and organizing a subversive society for that purpose." He was also charged with a plan "to seize by force the United States arsenals . . . to release rebel prisoners at Camp Douglas, Camp Morton, Camp Chase, and Johnson's Island, to arm said prisoners, and

[29]Klement, *Dark Lanterns,* 152; Klement, "The Indianapolis Treason Trials," 109.

[30]Terrell, *Report of the Adjutant General,* 1:360. This report also appears in *Official Records of the Union and Confederate Armies* (Washington, D.C.: Government Printing Office, 1882–1900), series 2, 7:930–53.

[31]Tredway, *Democratic Opposition,* 225.

[32]*Lawrenceburg Democratic Register,* February 19, 27, 1863; April 15, 1864.

[33]*Indianapolis Daily Journal,* October 5, November 3, 16, 1864.

then march into Kentucky to cooperate with the rebels." Finally, it was alleged that Dodd had aroused "hostility to the Government" through public addresses and secretly arming subversive society members "for the purpose of resisting the laws of the United States."[34] Like the later trial of Milligan, this one featured the Sons of Liberty and the Northwest Conspiracy. The principal witness was a government private detective, Felix G. Stidger, who had infiltrated Dodd's group, befriended Dodd, and now testified at length concerning the alleged plots. Before the trial was completed, Dodd escaped from imprisonment and fled to Canada. On October 10, 1864, the military commission found Dodd guilty of each charge and specification and sentenced him to be hanged, which decision was approved by the War Department.[35]

On the day following Dodd's conviction *in absentia,* the Republicans swept the Indiana state elections with substantial majorities.[36] But the national election was still to come, and Milligan and the other prominent prisoners were still to be dealt with. In the skirmishing on the eve of the trial, the charges against Joseph J. Bingham, William M. Harrison, David T. Yeakel, and James B. Wilson were dismissed. Horace Heffren was released after the trial began. He and Harrison and Wilson were to appear as prosecution witnesses, presumably in consideration of the dismissal. This left Milligan, Horsey, Bowles, and Humphreys. On October 21, with the national elections looming, the military commission convened. To the original detail of the seven officers five additional colonels had been added to the commission.[37] There were five charges:

1. Conspiracy against the government of the United States;
2. Affording aid and comfort to the rebels against the authority of the United States;
3. Inciting insurrection;

[34]Record Group NN2716, Records of the Office of the Judge Advocate General's Office, General Courts' Martial, 1812–1939.

[35]Dodd's trial and escape are described and discussed in Tredway, *Democratic Opposition,* 225–26; Stampp, *Indiana Politics,* 247–49; Klement, *Dark Lanterns,* 173–77; Klement, "The Indianapolis Treason Trials," 108–10. See also Report of Judge Advocate General Holt to "The Secretary of War for the President," December 14, 1864, in *Official Records of the Union and Confederate Armies,* series 2, 7:1214–17.

[36]Stampp, *Indiana Politics,* 253.

[37]Tredway, *Democratic Opposition,* 224–25, 227. Benn Pitman, *The Trials for Treason* (Cincinnati, Ohio: Moore, Wilsatch & Baldwin, 1865), 73.

4. Disloyal practices; and
5. Violations of the laws of war.[38]

It was more specifically alleged that the defendants had established a secret military organization and planned to seize arsenals, release Confederate prisoners, raise an armed force, join with the Confederate forces to invade Indiana, Illinois, and Kentucky, and make war on the United States. Because of the prosecution's conspiracy theory, the acts of any one of the defendants could be imputed to them all. And because the already convicted escapee Dodd was a member of the conspiracy, his acts were included in the imputation.[39]

Each of the defendants was represented by counsel. Milligan's lawyer was John R. Coffroth, a Huntington Democrat, who braved the hostility of the judge-advocate and some of the members of the commission, as well as the prosecution's occasional efforts to implicate him in the alleged conspiracy.[40] Coffroth and the other defendants' counsel unsuccessfully raised the issue of the military commission's jurisdiction, and the trial ensued. Because this paper is concerned with the *legal* issue of jurisdiction, the evidence is beyond its scope, but some flavor of the proceeding may be gathered from this colloquy in which the judge-advocate questioned the newly cooperative Horace Heffren about the allegedly treasonable Sons of Liberty:

Q. Of what political faith were the majority of the men comprising the organization?
A. They were all Democrats.
Q. State whether any other class of men were admitted, or was it a *sine qua non* that a man must be a Democrat?
A. I do not think anyone would have got in unless he professed to be a Democrat.[41]

---

[38]General Court Martial Orders, October 15, 1864, Adjutant General's Papers, Records of the Office of the Judge Advocate General, National Archives, Washington, D.C.

[39]The specifications appear in the United States Supreme Court's report of the Milligan case. *Ex parte In the Matter of Lambdin P. Milligan, Petitioner,* December 17, 1866, 71 U.S. (4 Wall.) 2, 18 L. Ed. 281.

[40]Tredway, *Democratic Opposition,* 244–45.

[41]Testimony of Heffren, Record Group NN3409, Records of the Office of the Judge Advocate General's Office, General Courts' Martial, 1812–1939, MS No. 11:402–403.

The Republicans carried Indiana in the national elections on November 8, and the military commission on December 10, 1864, reached its decision. Milligan, Bowles, and Horsey were found guilty and sentenced to be hanged. Humphreys was also convicted and sentenced to imprisonment at hard labor for the duration of the war. With President Lincoln's approval, General Hovey promptly modified Humphreys's sentence. Humphreys was released providing he did not take part in any acts opposing the war and did not leave two specified townships in Greene County.[42]

One of the several curiosities of the Milligan case is the effort made to obtain clemency for the three men who were to be hanged. This is a story in itself, but this paper must briefly allude to it. Col. William E. McLean, one of the commissioners, wrote to Lincoln in behalf of Milligan. Disclosing that he had dissented from the commission's findings, McLean stated that "the evidence adduced wholly failed to sustain the charge of conspiracy" against Milligan. According to the colonel's letter, Milligan's outright release was called for by "common justice and the popular sentiment of the people of Indiana."[43] Joseph E. McDonald, the Indiana Democratic nominee for governor in 1864 and a political foe of Milligan, now acting with Coffroth as counsel for Milligan, urged Lincoln to pardon all three of the men.[44] But most surprising were Morton's efforts in behalf of the defendants.

With Lincoln's death, the issue of clemency passed to Andrew Johnson. On May 16, 1865, three days before the execution date, Johnson commuted Horsey's sentence to life imprisonment and postponed the execution of Milligan and Bowles to June 2.[45] On May 24, 1865, Morton

[42]Record Group NN3409, Records of the Office of the Judge Advocate General's Office, General Courts' Martial, 1812–1939; Klement, "The Indianapolis Treason Trials," 114; Tredway, *Democratic Opposition*, 249; Kenneth M. Stampp, "The Milligan Case and the Election of 1864 in Indiana," *Mississippi Valley Historical Review* 31 (1944–45):41.

[43]*Huntington Democrat*, June 7, 1866. See Kelley, *Milligan's Fight against Lincoln*, 95–96. Col. Reuben Williams, another commissioner, later recalled that "the testimony . . . was so convincing that there was not a dissenting vote on the first ballot. . . ." *Warsaw Times*, quoted in *Indianapolis Daily Journal*, January 8, 1900.

[44]Kelley, *Milligan's Fight against Lincoln*, 96. Kelley quotes a letter from Justice David Davis to William H. Herndon citing McDonald's intervention.

[45]President Andrew Johnson to General Hovey, May 16, 1865, *Official Records of the Union and Confederate Armies*, series 2, 8:587.

dispatched former Congressman John U. Pettit to see the president with directions "most earnestly to plead for the commutation of their punishment to life imprisonment."[46] On May 30, 1865, the president acted to commute the sentences to life imprisonment.[47]

In the midst of the clemency activity, on May 10, 1865, Milligan's lawyers filed a petition for writ of habeas corpus in the circuit court of the United States for the district of Indiana, sitting in Indianapolis.[48] Similar proceedings were instituted in behalf of Horsey and Bowles. Pursuant to the procedure, the application was considered by two judges, Justice David Davis of the United States Supreme Court, who was also a judge of the federal circuit that included Indiana, and Judge Thomas Drummond, a circuit judge. The procedure further provided that if these two judges disagreed, the questions at issue were to be certified to the Supreme Court of the United States.

Milligan's petition was based on an act of Congress that was intended to moot the question of whether the president or the Congress had the constitutional right to suspend the writ of habeas corpus as authorized by Section 9 of Article I of the Constitution. This issue had been active throughout the war. The legislation also responded to other aspects of the Lincoln administration's program to cope with dissent. Effective on March 3, 1863, it was identified as "An Act Relating to Habeas Corpus and Regulating Judicial Proceedings in Certain Cases."[49] It authorized the president to suspend the writ of habeas corpus when in his judgment the public safety required it. Referring to the statute, Lincoln had issued a proclamation accordingly on September 15, 1863. The statute further directed the secretaries of state and war to furnish to

---

[46]Governor Morton to President Johnson, May 24, 1865, Record Group NN3409, Records of the Judge Advocate General, General Courts' Martial, 1812–1839, Box 1164; William D. Foulke, *Life of Oliver P. Morton: Including His Important Speeches* (2 vols. Indianapolis-Kansas City: Bowen-Merrill Co., 1899), 1:428–31.

[47]Secretary Stanton to General Hovey, May 30, 1865, *Official Records of the Union and Confederate Armies,* series 2, 8:583–84, 637.

[48]The facts regarding this proceeding are taken from the United States Supreme Court report of the Milligan case, *Ex parte In the Matter of Lambdin P. Milligan, Petitioner,* December 17, 1866, 71 U.S. (4 Wall.) 2, 18 L. Ed. 281.

[49]This legislation is set forth in the United States Supreme Court's report. Lincoln's proclamation appears in *Collected Works,* 6:451.

the federal judges in states where the courts were operating the names of all persons held there in custody. It also stipulated that if a grand jury met after the list was furnished and did not indict the prisoner, he was entitled to be discharged. Finally, to avoid frustration of the statute by the failure of the cabinet officers to submit the list, the act provided that if the list was not furnished and twenty days had elapsed from the time of the arrest and termination of the session of the grand jury, the prisoner was entitled to a discharge. Milligan alleged, and it was a fact, that a federal grand jury had met in Indianapolis during January of 1865 and had not indicted him.

It may be noted that Vallandingham did not pursue this procedure or rely on this statute. It seems likely that a federal grand jury had met in his district, and it is known that he was not indicted. But he proceeded in 1863 by the certiorari route. I do not suggest that the decision in the case would have been any different had Vallandingham invoked the Milligan procedure—the war was in full cry at the time that the Supreme Court considered the Vallandingham case—but the speculation is an interesting one.

In the circuit court sitting in Indianapolis, Justice Davis and Judge Drummond were unable to agree on the issues presented by Milligan's petition. Accordingly, three issues were certified to the Supreme Court:

1st.   On the facts stated in said petition and exhibits, ought a writ of habeas corpus to be issued?

2nd.   On the facts stated in said petition and exhibits, ought the said Lambdin P. Milligan to be discharged from custody as in said petition prayed?

3rd.   Whether, upon the facts stated in said petition and exhibits, the Military Commission mentioned therein had jurisdiction legally to try and sentence said Milligan in manner and form as in said petition and exhibits is stated.[50]

It should be understood that the Supreme Court was not considering the charges against Milligan; it did not evaluate or consider the evidence adduced before the military commission. It was concerned entirely with questions of law. In short, regardless of the charges and

[50] *Ex parte Milligan*, 18 L. Ed. 281, 291.

evidence, the issues were whether the military commission proceedings were constitutional and whether Milligan was entitled to be discharged.

The case was argued on March 5 and 13, 1866, approximately a year after Appomattox and Lincoln's death. The Court was the same one that had heard Vallandingham's petition for certiorari except that Salmon P. Chase, appointed by Lincoln in December of 1864, had replaced Taney as the Chief Justice.[51]

Distinguished lawyers represented the parties. In addition to Coffroth and J. E. McDonald, Milligan's lawyers were A. L. Roache, David Dudley Field, James A. Garfield, and Jeremiah S. Black. Field, who was the brother of Justice Stephen Field of the Supreme Court, was a well-known New Yorker associated with efforts to reform the legal system of that state. Garfield, of course, was a member of Congress from Ohio and a future president. Black, who practiced frequently before the Supreme Court, had been Buchanan's attorney general and secretary of state. Although fewer in number, the United States surely had adequate counsel in Attorney General James Speed, Henry Stanbery, and the colorful and controversial Benjamin F. Butler. Butler had been a prewar Massachusetts politician, a political major general during the war, and was later to be a congressman and governor of Massachusetts.[52]

On April 3, 1866, the chief justice announced the order of the Court: a writ of habeas corpus was to be issued; Milligan was entitled to be discharged, a decision expressly based on the March 3, 1863, act of Congress; and the military commission had no jurisdiction to try and sentence Milligan. The same order was entered in the Bowles and Horsey companion cases. The chief justice announced that the opinion of the Court and any dissents would be read at the next term of the Court.

On December 17, 1866, Justice David Davis delivered the majority opinion, writing for himself and five of the other members of the Court. The opinion at first disposed of two procedural issues raised by the government.[53] Then it turned to the merits. Noting that Milligan was a civil-

---

[51]Silver, *Lincoln's Supreme Court,* 203, 205.

[52]*Encyclopedia Brittanica,* s.v. "Field, David Dudley," "Garfield, James A.," "Black, Jeremiah S.," and "Butler, Benjamin F."

[53]The first concerned the authority of the circuit court in Indianapolis to certify the three questions. If the circuit court had no such authority, the Supreme Court would not have had the jurisdiction to hear and decide the three questions. The opinion rejected this defense. The government then argued that the case was moot, that is, that it was no longer pending for decision because the

ian and a resident of a state in which the civil courts were functioning, Davis stated that "it is the birthright of every American citizen when charged with [a] crime to be tried and punished according to law." Davis then identified the constitutional provisions affecting the administration of criminal justice: trial by jury (Article III, Section 2); security against unreasonable search and seizure and the requirement of a judicial warrant, based on probable cause, before arrest (Fourth Amendment); grand jury indictment and due process (Fifth Amendment); and speedy and public trial by jury (Sixth Amendment). These, according to the opinion, had not been available to Milligan. The opinion then states:

> Every trial involves the exercise of judicial power; and from what source did the Military Commission . . . derive their authority? Certainly no part of the judicial power of the country was conferred on them; because the Constitution expressly vests it 'in one Supreme Court and such inferior courts as the Congress may from time to time ordain and establish'. . . .

The government had presented numerous grounds for the propriety of the military commission. The manner in which the opinion met several of them concerns the significance of the case.

Responding to a contention that the laws and usages of war supported the jurisdiction of the military commander, Justice Davis wrote: "Congress could grant no such power; and to the honor of our national legislature be it said, it has never been provoked . . . even to attempt its exercise." To the argument that martial law gave a military commander the power to suspend civilian rights and subject civilians and soldiers to his will, Davis responded: ". . . if true, republican government is a failure, and there is an end of liberty regulated by law." In any event, according to the opinion, "Martial rule can never exist where the courts are open. . . ." Thus, martial law would be confined to "the theatre of actual military operations, where war really prevails" and "there is a necessity to furnish a substitute for the civil authority, thus overthrown. . . ." As if responding to Lincoln's contention in his letter to Corning about exceptions to the Constitution during the Civil War, Davis adverted to the

---

record did not show that Milligan was still alive and it was legally presumed that he had been hanged. The opinion rather crisply rejected this contention. All quotations from the following opinions can be found in *Ex parte Milligan*, 18 L. Ed. 281, 295–302.

risk of evil or unwise leaders, unlike Lincoln, and wrote: "No doctrine, involving more pernicious consequences, was ever invented by the wit of man than that any of its provisions can be suspended during any of the great exigencies of government." Finally, it will be recalled that Lincoln had relied on the language of the Constitution's authorization of the suspension of the writ of habeas corpus "when in cases of rebellion . . . the public safety may require it" to justify suspension of the writ as well as his other acts: arbitrary arrest, military commission jurisdiction, and limitations on freedom of speech, assembly, and press. Davis rejected this rationale. Referring generally to the Constitution's restrictions on governmental power, Davis said: "Not one of these safeguards can the President or Congress or the Judiciary disturb, except the one concerning the writ of habeas corpus."

The chief justice and Justices Miller, Swayne, and Wayne filed a separate opinion authored by the chief justice. It is a somewhat curious document. It agrees with the majority on each of the three certified questions but disagrees with several of the dicta of the majority. Thus, Chase wrote that although the Congress had not authorized the military commission that tried Milligan, the minority believed that Congress had the power to do so. Regarding the writ of habeas corpus, Chase stated that when the writ is suspended, the Executive is authorized to arrest as well as detain and that "there are cases in which, the privilege of the writ being suspended, trial and punishment by military commission, in states where the civil courts are open, may be authorized by Congress, as well as arrest and detention." It appears therefore that the minority might have accepted the Lincoln program regarding dissent, although not necessarily in Milligan's case, had it been enacted by the Congress. The minority concluded with this reassurance: "We have no apprehension that this power, under our American system of government, in which all official authority is derived from the people, and exercised under direct responsibility to the people, is more likely to be abused than the power to regulate commerce or the power to borrow money."

Lambdin P. Milligan returned to Huntington and his law practice. In 1868 he filed suit for false arrest and false imprisonment in the Huntington Circuit Court against Morton, General Hovey, several members of the military commission, certain witnesses before the commission, and others whom Milligan believed were implicated. The case was removed to the Federal Circuit Court in Indianapolis and, after much delay, came to a jury trial in 1871. Again a distinguished battery of lawyers was involved. Milligan's counsel included Thomas A. Hendricks, former United States Senator from Indiana, later to be Tilden's running mate in 1876 and Grover Cleveland's vice-president.[54] Benjamin Harrison was chief counsel for the defendants. Although Milligan sought thousands of dollars in damages, state and federal indemnity statutes limited his claim to $5.00, plus the costs of the litigation.

It must again be emphasized that Milligan's guilt or innocence of the allegations before the 1864 military commission were not directly at issue. The issue in a legal sense was whether he had been arrested and held unlawfully in view of the Supreme Court decision. It nevertheless appears that many of the 1864 witnesses appeared and that the trial was rife with the political overtones of the military commission proceeding. At length the jury found for Milligan and awarded him the permissible $5.00 and costs estimated at $1,200.[55] It was the view of Governor Morton's allies that the small damage award somehow vindicated Morton and the military commission proceedings. In view of the statutory limitation on damages this seems to me an unwarranted conclusion.

Commentary

So much for *Ex parte Milligan* as a legal proposition. What of the facts? Was Milligan guilty of the charges against him?

The circumstances of Milligan's trial before the military commission suggest to me that although he was a bitter and sometimes irresponsible critic of Lincoln, Morton, and the Republican party, the judge-advocate did not prove him guilty of the offenses with which he was charged. That, of course, was the prosecution's burden. Kenneth M. Stampp, Gilbert R. Tredway, and Frank L. Klement, all of whom have studied the proceedings from the standpoint of guilt or innocence, are unconvinced

---

[54]Ralph D. Gray, ed , *Gentlemen from Indiana* (Indianapolis: Indiana Historical Bureau, 1977), 119–39. Gray wrote the essay concerning Hendricks.

[55]The file of this case, variously captioned as *Lambdin P. Milligan v. James R. Slack and Others* and *Lambdin P. Milligan v. Alvin P. Hovey and Others,* is identified as Case No. 142, Federal Records Center, Chicago. It is discussed in Tredway, *Democratic Opposition,* 257–62, and Klement, "The Indianapolis Treason Trials and Ex Parte Milligan," in *American Political Trials,* ed. Michael Belknap, chap. 5:119.

of his guilt.[56] As a lawyer, I believe that a trial prompted by political motives, before politically biased military officers, without the rules of evidence, with questionable informers as witnesses, and surrounded by lurid publicity is, in effect, a nullity. What is customarily identified as due process involves not simply a question of fairness to the accused. It is the only kind of forum in which there is a practical chance of establishing the truth.

There are, of course, other questions. Were there Indiana secret societies acting in behalf of secession? Was there a Northwest Conspiracy? There were indeed several secret societies, including the Knights of the Golden Circle, the Order of American Knights, and the Sons of Liberty. They were composed of dissenters, typically embittered Democrats who were out of the mainstream of their party. Some of them, including H. H. Dodd, were in contact with Confederate agents and discussed the release of Confederate prisoners and acts of war. Recent scholarship suggests that the membership of the secret societies was extremely small and that they did not have the will, the influence, or the means of interfering with the prosecution of the war. The Northwest Conspiracy also existed in the minds of Confederate agents and a small group of midwestern and Kentucky dissenters, again probably including H. H. Dodd, but it, too, was never a significant threat. Both the size and influence of the secret societies and the significance of the Northwest Conspiracy were inflated by Morton and the Republicans for partisan and personal political purposes.[57]

And there is, at last, the ultimate question. There is, conceptually, a difference between, on the one hand, disagreement about the war or with the Lincoln administration's means of prosecuting the war and support of the Southern bid for independence on the other. The latter,

---

[56]Stampp, *Indiana Politics during the Civil War;* Klement, *Dark Lanterns;* Klement, "The Indianapolis Treason Trials and Ex Parte Milligan," in *American Political Trials,* ed. Michael Belknap, chap. 5; Frank L. Klement, *The Copperheads in the Middle West* (Chicago: University of Chicago Press, 1960), 192–99.

[57]Stampp and Klement discuss the societies and the Northwest Conspiracy, but Tredway's examination in *Democratic Opposition,* chaps. 7, 8, 9, and 10, is the most comprehensive. For an excellent survey of the literature and scholarship about "Copperheads," see Richard O. Curry, "The Union as It Was: A Critique of Recent Interpretations of the Copperheads," *Civil War History* 13 (March 1967):25.

it would seem, is appropriately called "disloyalty." The ultimate question, therefore, is whether or not there was significant or widespread disloyalty in Indiana. Were Hoosiers, in the main, for the Union, or were they willing to see it sundered?

In 1869 the state published the eight-volume *Report of the Adjutant General of the State of Indiana.* The adjutant general was W. H. H. Terrell, Morton's friend and appointee. In volume I the report describes "Internal State Troubles," concerning the entire course of Indiana politics during the war, including the conspiracies, secret societies, and military commission trials. It is, of course, the Morton view of these events.

At the outset, Terrell states his premises. The rebel states "relied upon a greater power than their own in their attempt to displace the old Government by a new confederacy. . . . That power was the spirit of dissension, of faction, of treason in the North." This "disloyal feeling" "was extensive enough, and malignant enough" to accomplish the success of the rebellion. The report then states that this feeling was "strong enough to take Indiana out of loyal hands in 1862, and leave her nothing but the iron will and unfailing sagacity of her Governor to prevent her own soil being made the scene of endless and ruinous local wars." Terrell ultimately contends that it was the South's knowledge of the extent of treason and disloyalty in the North that caused the South to begin the war.[58]

These extravagant claims plainly suggest that Indiana was disloyal, that it teetered on the brink of secession, and that it was held to the Union cause by Governor Morton. These beliefs have long been part of the folk tradition of Indiana. Indeed, it was taught as history in Indiana schools in the 1930s and 1940s when some of us were in school. It lingers among us today. It is, of course, an extension of the politics of the war. It may incidentally be noted that the postwar politics of the Gilded Age, the days of "the Bloody Shirt," essentially embraced this proposition.

Certain statistics seem to me to answer the Morton tradition. At the same time, these statistics support the conclusion that the secret societies and conspiracies were not significant in numbers or influence.

The Indiana election returns of 1860 gave the four candidates the following totals:

---

[58]Terrell, *Report of the Adjutant General of the State of Indiana,* 1:231, 232, 233.

Lincoln, the Republican—139,000
Douglas, the Democrat—116,000
Bell, Constitutional Union—5,000
Breckinridge, Southern Democrat—12,000[59]

Breckinridge was the outright Southern candidate. Notwithstanding the usual fog of politics, it is plain that all of the others were firmly Union candidates. Thus less than 5 percent of the 1860 Indiana voters supported the Southern position.

Of more significance are the data assembled by William F. Fox in his work *Regimental Losses in the American Civil War.* According to Fox, 74.3 percent of Indiana's military population was enrolled in the federal armies, second only to Delaware, which furnished 74.8 percent. According to Fox, "it appears that the States of Delaware and Indiana were preeminently loyal, contributing more largely in proportion to their military population than any of their sister states."[60] According to Terrell, these soldiers were overwhelmingly volunteers.[61]

Finally, Gilbert R. Tredway has made an analysis of Indiana's volunteers by congressional district. The three banner Democratic districts were the first, second, and seventh. All three went Democratic in 1860, 1862, and 1864. Their Republican counterparts, the "safe" Republican districts, were the fifth, sixth, eighth, and ninth. Military quotas were established by congressional district according to population. Men were drafted in a district only to the extent that sufficient men did not volunteer to meet the district's quota. The Democratic districts consistently furnished more volunteers in proportion to their population than did the Republican districts until the last call of the war in December of 1864. Only then did the Republican districts surpass the Democratic dis-

---

[59] *The Statistical History of the United States, from Colonial Times to the Present* (Stamford, Ct.: Fairfield Publishers, Inc., 1965), 688.

[60] William F. Fox, *Regimental Losses in the American Civil War* (Albany: Albany Publishing Co., 1889), 532–36. Fox also made a complex adjustment to exclude black troops and certain others and to convert the data to the standard of a three-year enlistment. On this basis he ranked Kansas first and Indiana second in terms of the participation of the percentage of military population.

[61] Terrell, *Report of the Adjutant General of the State of Indiana,* 1:248. Terrell states that only 17,899 men were drafted in Indiana throughout the war.

tricts in volunteers. This was true in spite of the fact that the Democratic districts consistently paid smaller bounties to stimulate volunteers.[62]

In the majority opinion in *Ex parte Milligan,* Justice Davis, perhaps generally aware of these facts, discussed the status of the federal court in Indianapolis. "It needed no bayonets to protect it, and required no military aide to execute its judgements. It was held in a state, eminently distinguished for patriotism. . . ."[63]

Conclusion

The Lincoln administration's program to cope with dissent and those who disagreed with the administration presented a classic confrontation between government power and personal liberty, as that liberty is defined in the American political and legal process. It was a confrontation occurring in an authentic crisis. *Ex parte Milligan* stands on the side of personal liberty. The decision is a rebuke to those who would forego liberty in the interest of security.

It occurs to me that many of us today do not really comprehend what the personal liberty provisions of the Constitution are all about. In a given conflict between the popular will and the Constitution, many of us seem to miss the constitutional point and react instead on the basis of our response to the merits of the proposal of the popular will. But the point is that the Constitution is essentially a statement of limitations on the popular will and on the government as the agent of the popular will. The heart of any civil liberties case, therefore, concerns not whether the people approve of the act of government but a more fundamental question: should the government have this power? Inevitably, this question requires a consideration of whether or not the power at issue is subject to abuse. In an obscenity case, for example, the issue is not how one

---

[62]Tredway, *Democratic Opposition,* 60–62, and congressional district map facing page 225. The first district included the "pocket" counties, Vanderburgh and the southwest corner of the state; the second included Clark and Floyd counties and the southeast corner; and the seventh centered around Vigo and Sullivan counties.

[63]18 L. Ed. 296.

feels about allegedly obscene materials. The issue is whether government should have the power to limit what we read, in the light of the fact
that governments have historically abused the power to censor.

In *Ex parte Milligan,* the Supreme Court was unwilling to accord the
Lincoln administration the power of military commission jurisdiction.
An express reason for this denial of power was the risk of abuse by other
presidents or in other circumstances. It seems clear to me that the
Supreme Court was correct.

II

Gettysburg

Three Flags at Gettysburg

The soldier set forth his recollection:

> I got one of the band men to help me and, hanging on to the
> hand rail of the stairs, I climbed to the cupola. Looking over to-
> wards the right of the town, I saw what appeared like the whole
> rebel army in a chunk starting for our lines with their infernal
> squealing yell. It seemed as if everything stood still inside of me
> for a second or two and then I began to pray . . . that they
> would catch hell and they did. It seemed as if the fire from our
> lines doubled and doubled again and we could see long streaks
> of light through the rebel columns. But they went forward and
> I was afraid they would capture our guns, but all at once they
> seemed to melt away when our infantry opened on them. Then
> we could hear the northern cheer and we knew that . . . the old
> army of the Potomac was victorious . . .
>
> There were ten or fifteen of us in the observatory and they
> were wild with joy—some cried, others shook hands and all
> joined in the best cheer we could get up. I forgot all about my
> wound and was forcibly reminded about it when I went to
> shout as I had to sit down to keep from falling . . . Afterwards
> we could see it was all up with the Johnnies. Their wagons
> began to hustle off and the cattle were driven before them. The
> streets were filled with wounded and stragglers from the front
> and everything indicated that Lee had been badly beaten.[1]

[1] *Milwaukee Sunday Telegraph,* 27 January 1884.

The place was Gettysburg, more specifically the tower of the town courthouse. The time was July 3, 1863. The event was the Pickett-Pettigrew charge. The writer was James P. Sullivan of Company K of the Sixth Wisconsin Volunteers of the Iron Brigade, the First Brigade of the First Division of the First Corps of the Army of the Potomac. Known to his comrades as "Mickey" Sullivan, while witnessing the denouement of the three day battle the young Irishman was a prisoner of war, the result of his having been wounded and taken prisoner on July 1, the first day. Because of the way the battle began on July 1, it seems appropriate for a representative of the First Division of the First Corps to have witnessed its conclusion on July 3.

Major General John F. Reynolds, the commander of the First Corps, arrived at McPherson's Ridge west of Gettysburg at approximately 10:00 A.M. on July 1. There he joined Brigadier General John Buford whose cavalrymen had been dueling since early morning along the Chambersburg Pike with elements of Major General Henry Heth's division of A. P. Hill's Corps. A half mile east of McPherson's Ridge—the intervening low ground was mostly open meadow—was Seminary Ridge. Further to the east and to the south was other defensible high ground, the now well-known eminences of Cemetery Hill, Culp's Hill, Cemetery Ridge and the Round Tops. Having consulted with Buford, Reynolds decided to defend McPherson's Ridge and the town of Gettysburg. With the benefit of hindsight, it may be said that the marches and maneuvers of the two armies committed them to Gettysburg as the site of their great collision. But it was A. P. Hill, John Buford, and John F. Reynolds who made the express decision to fight there. Lee and Meade simply accepted that decision after the fact.[2]

To carry out his decision, Reynolds was initially to be dependent on the closest infantry, the First Division of his corps. Having camped the night before along the Emmitsburg Road, south of Gettysburg and near Marsh Creek, that division was marching up the road at the time their corps commander and John Buford met on McPherson's Ridge. Reynolds had reason to feel comfortable in relying on the First Division. Commanded by Brigadier General James S. Wadsworth and composed in addition to artillery of Brigadier General Solomon Meredith's First

[2]Edwin B. Coddington, *The Gettysburg Campaign* (reprint ed., Dayton: Press of Morningside Bookshop, 1979), p. 263.

Brigade and Brigadier General Lysander Cutler's Second Brigade, the 3500 soldiers were veterans. Meredith's First Brigade, the western men, wearing their distinctive, high-crowned regular army dress hats, were well known members of the corps. This was the Iron Brigade, the Nineteenth Indiana, Twenty-fourth Michigan, and the Second, Sixth and Seventh Wisconsin.[3]

Cutler's Brigade and the Second Maine Battery led the First Division onto the field. Because the Confederate pressure on the cavalry was intensifying, they left the Emmitsburg Road at the Codori Farm and hurried north to Seminary Ridge. Behind Cutler, following his general route from the road, the Iron Brigade came forward. As the Federal infantry arrived east of McPherson's Ridge, Heth's Confederates were committed: Davis' Brigade of Mississippi and North Carolina soldiers moved eastward north of the Chambersburg Pike and Archer's Brigade of Tennessee and Alabama regiments advanced south of the Pike up McPherson's Ridge toward the woods that crowned McPherson's Ridge. Having directed the Second Maine Battery to a dangerous position north of the pike, between it and an unfinished railroad cut that ran north of and roughly parallel to the pike, Reynolds sent Cutler's regiments forward on both sides of the pike. With the Sixth Wisconsin and the brigade guard, twenty men from each of the regiments from the brigade, posted in reserve at the seminary, the rest of the Iron Brigade faced left at the seminary. Responding to the command "Forward into line," they formed line of battle from line of march and, with the Second Wisconsin on the right, advanced en echelon south of the pike toward the west and McPherson's Woods.

Striking Archer head on, but also overlapping his right, despite heavy casualties the Iron Brigade overpowered Archer, capturing the general and a substantial number of his men, killing and wounding others and driving the rest off the field toward the west. But elsewhere along McPherson's Ridge, the initial action was going against the Federals. John F. Reynolds had been killed, to be succeeded by Major General Abner Doubleday, and Cutler's men who had started the infantry fight had been badly handled. On the right flank Cutler's regiments

[3]O.R., Series I, Vol. XXVII, Part I, p. 144; Alan T. Nolan, *The Iron Brigade* (reprint ed., Berrien Springs, Michigan, Hardscrabble Books, 1983), p. 230; Coddington, *Gettysburg Campaign*, p. 267.

north of the railroad cut had been driven by Davis' regiments. The Federals had then been ordered to withdraw to Seminary Ridge, which uncovered the rest of the Federal line, from north to south the Maine cannoners north of the Pike, Cutler's left regiments south of the pike, and the Iron Brigade, still farther south, in McPherson's Woods. Tasting victory, Davis' Brigade pivoted toward the pike and the rear of the Federal line. The railroad cut, which created deep depressions where it passed through McPherson's and the ridges west of Gettysburg, seemed to create a convenient and protected route to the Federal rear.[4]

Disaster confronted the Federals. But there was the reserve, the Sixth Wisconsin and the brigade guard at the seminary with Lieutenant Colonel Rufus R. Dawes in command. On Doubleday's order, Dawes marched by the right flank at the double-quick, advancing north toward the right flank of Davis' line which was moving toward the east. Taking losses as they advanced, Dawes men reached and crossed the Chambersburg Pike and swept on. Wheeling toward their right to face Dawes, Davis' men took cover in the railroad cut and Dawes ordered his men to charge the cut. Cutler's regiments that had fought on the south side of the pike checked their backward movement and, forming on Dawes' left, moved with Dawes toward the enemy. The Federal charge was successful but costly. Among the Federal wounded was the Sixth Wisconsin's Mickey Sullivan whose account of the third day begins this article. For the Confederates the railroad cut was a redoubt but also a trap, and they were shot down or surrendered in large numbers.[5]

One incident stands out in the race by the Sixth Wisconsin and the brigade guard for the railroad cut. As with most such events there is conflict in the evidence in regard to the details, but the essentials are plain. As they approached the cut, the soldiers of the Sixth Wisconsin and the brigade guard spied the color of the Second Mississippi Infantry of Davis' Brigade, the burden of W. B. Murphy of Company A, the color-bearer of that regiment. Corporal Francis A. Wallar of Company I of the Sixth Wisconsin was one of several of the charging Federals seized with

---

[4]Nolan, *The Iron Brigade* pp. 236–9.
[5]Nolan, *The Iron Brigade* pp. 239–40; *Milwaukee Sunday Telegraph*, 20 January 1884; Rufus R. Dawes, *Service With the Sixth Wisconsin Volunteers* (Marietta, Ohio: E. R. Alderman & Sons, 1890), pp. 164–73.

the idea of capturing the color. There ensued a vicious struggle. Wallar was later to write, "I started straight for it, as did lots of others. Soon after I got the flag there were men from all of the companies there. I did take the flag out of the color-bearer's hand."[6] Color-bearer Murphy, who claimed that a dozen of the Federals were shot down in the effort to seize the flag, provided his own account: "We made a desperate struggle for our colors. My color guards were all killed and wounded in less than five minutes, and also my colors were shot more than a dozen times, and the flagstaff was shot and splintered two or three more times." It was, according to Murphy, "one of the most deadly struggles that was ever witnessed during any battle of the war . . . a large man made a rush for me and the flag. As I tore the flag from the staff he took hold of me and the color . . . the flag was taken from me."[7] In nominating Wallar for a Medal of Honor, General Meade briefly described Wallar's "gallantry":

> [He] captured the flag of the Second Mississippi Regiment near Gettysburg July 1, 1863. While the brigade was making a charge Corporal Waller [sic] advanced and captured the flag; he stood on it and fired three times before taking it up. The flag sent to First Army Corps Headquarters.[8]

This, then, is the first of the Three Flags.

Hurled back on both sides of the Chambersburg Pike by the First Division of the First Corps, the Confederates were forced to reorganize and both sides were reinforced. For the Confederates, the Divisions of Ewell's Second Army Corps arrived north of the town to the left of A. P. Hill's men, and Hill advanced Pender's Division to the support of Heth. Heth also brought out his fresh brigades, Pettigrew's and Brockenbrough's. For the Federals, the Second (Robinson's) and Third (Rowley's) Divisions of the First Corps arrived as did O. O. Howard's Eleventh Corps. By mid-afternoon, the two sides faced each other over

---

[6]Francis A. Wallar, *The Blackhat,* Issue No. 24 (Milwaukee: 1986), p. 2. Wallar's account appears in his letter dated May 10, 1883, and may be found at the State Historical Society of Wisconsin, Madison, in a scrapbook donated by Major F. L. Phillips.

[7]W. B. Murphy, *The Blackhat,* Issue No. 25 (Milwaukee: 1986) pp. 7–8. Murphy's account may be found in a letter dated June 29, 1900, from him to Dr. F. A. Dearborn in the Bragg Papers, State Historical Society of Wisconsin, Madison.

[8]*O.R.,* Series III, Vol. IV, p. 817.

a wide, semi-circular front running from the Fairfield Road west of the town to the Heidlersburg Road northeast of Gettysburg. The Iron Brigade held McPherson's Woods, with the Nineteenth Indiana on the left. The regimental commander was Colonel Samuel J. Williams. Lieutenant Colonel William W. Dudley was second-in-command. The acting Sergeant Major of the Nineteenth was Asa Blanchard.[9]

At approximately 3:00 P.M., the Confederate advance began all along the line. Outnumbering the Federals, they advanced two and three lines deep in the Iron Brigade's front, overlapping the Federal left. The Confederate numbers and the overlapping Confederate lines meant that ultimately the Federals would have to retire. Watching the Confederates advancing in their front, the Iron Brigade waited until the enemy reached Willoughby Run at the western edge of McPherson's Woods. Then the western rifles opened and the Confederates poured a telling converging fire into the woods. The Iron Brigade's front seemed impregnable, but the enemy's second line gradually moved around the Nineteenth's left. As the Hoosier line was gradually bent backwards the western men were ordered to withdraw to a line in the eastern edge of the woods, where they again stood to face the enemy. Then another withdrawal was ordered, this time to the low ground between McPherson's and Seminary Ridges, and again the enemy came on. Changing fronts between rounds so as to meet the flank assault as well as that from the front, the western soldiers held on.[10]

The Nineteenth Indiana's Lieutenant Colonel Dudley later described the action of Sergeant Major Blanchard during this part of the fighting:

> . . . our colors were shot down time and time again until all the color guard had been either killed or wounded; when, by . . . (Blanchard's) request, he was put in special charge of the duty of keeping them afloat, and as fast as the bearers were felled he detailed others to take them up.

At one point Dudley went personally to assist Blanchard and, while briefly holding the flag himself, he was shot down with a wound that

---

[9]Coddington, *Gettysburg Campaign* pp. 286–7 and map facing page 287.
[10]Nolan, *The Iron Brigade* pp. 243–45.

took his leg. In the midst of this melee Blanchard apologized to Dudley for not having prevented Dudley's brief possession of the flag, and detailed two slightly wounded soldiers to move Dudley out of the line of fire. Dudley's account continued:

> From where I lay I clearly saw him raise the flag. While he was holding it the order came for the line to retire to the top of the hill behind us; this it did slowly, forming a line and frequently facing about to deliver volleys at the advancing enemy until the crest was reached. Here a determined stand was made and I was carried to the Seminary and lost sight of the individuals of the Regiment and their actions but could see the line as it gallantly withstood the terrific front and flank fire from the enemy. I was told by others who witnessed it that on this line . . . (Blanchard), having seen that capture was imminent, had torn the flag from the staff and wrapped it around his body under his sword belt; and that while moving about, cheering and encouraging the men to stand fast, he received a musket ball in his groin severing the artery and causing his almost immediate death . . .
>
> Lieut. Macey carried the flag from this point to the rail pile on Seminary hill where the line was next reformed.[11]

The second flag was that of the Nineteenth Indiana Volunteers.

As the Federals had waited for the enemy's afternoon attack, the Twenty-fourth Michigan Volunteers held the position immediately to the right of the Nineteenth Indiana in McPherson's Woods. The Michigan regiment had lost one color-bearer during the morning fight. It lost another on the brigade's second line in McPherson's Woods during the Confederates' afternoon attack. Withdrawn then to the position between McPherson's and Seminary Ridges, a third color-bearer was killed. Colonel Henry A. Morrow's official report added further details regarding the Michigan flag as the regiment proceeded to its final line at the barricade on Seminary Ridge.

> By this time the ranks were so diminished that scarcely a fourth of the forces taken into action could be rallied. Corpl. Andrew

[11]Norma Fuller Hawkins, "Sergeant-Major Blanchard at Gettysburg," *Indiana Magazine of History*, XXXIV, No. 2 (June 1938): 215–16. Bloomington.

Wagner, Company F, one of the color guard, took the colors, and was ordered by me to plant them in a position to which I designed to rally the men. He was wounded in the breast and left on the field. I now took the flag from the ground . . . and was rallying the remnant of the regiment, when Private William Kelly, of Company E, took the colors from my hands, remarking . . . "The colonel of the Twenty-Fourth shall never carry the flag while I am alive." He was killed instantly. Private Lilburn A. Spaulding, of Company K, seized the colors and bore them for a time. Subsequently I took them from him to rally the men, and kept them until I was wounded.

Finally, inside the barricade of rails on the crest of Seminary Ridge between the Seminary building and the Chambersburg Pike, the Federals stood until withdrawn to Culp's Hill and Cemetery Hill. Wounded just before he reached the barricade, Colonel Morrow had left the field, but the acting regimental commander, Captain Albert M. Edwards, found "the colors in the hands of a wounded soldier, who had fallen on the east side of the barricade. He was reclining on his right side, and was holding the colors in his left hand . . . severely wounded . . . he is, therefore, probably among our dead."[12] This was the third of the Three Flags.

The point of this account of the Three Flags is not to recount further the blood and guts of the war. The Three Flags surely tell us something about the first day at Gettysburg. In 1961, I had this to say about July 1:

> But the storied fights at Culp's Hill, the Wheat Field, the Peach Orchard, Little Round Top, and "the little clump of trees" were to be but anticlimax to the men of the First Corps . . . (which) counted casualties of more than 6,000 of its 9,403 men. This was 2,000 more than the losses of the Eleventh Corps, 2,000 more than Sickles was to lose the next day in the Wheat Field and Peach Orchard, and 2,000 more than the Second Corps was to give up in defending the Federal center against Pickett's assault. Surely the veterans of the First Corps could be pardoned for feeling that too much emphasis was later placed on the last two

[12] *O.R.*, Series I, Vol. XXVII, Part I, pp. 268–69.

days of the battle, when the Federals had the edge in manpower and the advantage of the ground. . . .

(It) was the Iron Brigade and its First Corps comrades who had determined the matter, by their dogged, desperate fighting, which had permitted Federal possession of the key ground and had purchased the time for the Army of the Potomac to concentrate.[13]

It is still my view that the first day and its decisiveness in reference to the outcome of the battle are not sufficiently emphasized in much of the Gettysburg literature. This tendency includes careless writing in which expressions like "swept from the field," "collapsed" and "fled" are typically used to describe the defeat of the Eleventh and First Corps. In the Eleventh Corps the killed and wounded numbered almost 2,300, a statistic that suggests hard fighting prior to its retreat.[14] But terms like those noted are surely exaggerations as applied to the First Corps. It is plain that in the morning action on July 1, the brigades of Archer and Davis were defeated by the First Division brigades of Meredith and Cutler. With respect to the afternoon fight the question is whether the Federals were "swept away" or fought a good fight and were then withdrawn. Disregarding entirely the Federal descriptions of the First Corps' defense, it is appropriate to examine the Confederate reports.

Referring to the Iron Brigade's front, the commander of Pettigrew's Brigade reported on the Iron Brigade's second line in McPherson's Woods: "On this second line, the fighting was terrible—our men advancing, the enemy stubbornly resisting, until the two lines were pouring volleys into each other at a distance not greater than 20 paces. At last the enemy were compelled to give way. They again made a stand . . . and the third time they were driven from their position."[15] Division commander Heth reported that the Twenty-sixth North Carolina of Pettigrew's force "lost in this action more than half of its numbers in killed and wounded." Heth also wrote that "The number of . . . (Pettigrew's) own

---

[13]Nolan, *The Iron Brigade* pp. 255–56, 258–59.

[14]The Eleventh Corps casualties appear at *O.R.*, Series I, Vol. XXVII, Part I, p. 183. The return of casualties for the Army of the Potomac is at pp. 173–87 of this volume.

[15]*O.R.*, Series I, Vol. XXVII, Part II, p. 643.

gallant dead and wounded, as well as the large number of the enemy's dead and wounded left on the field over which it fought, attests . . . the gallant part it played on July 1" and that the Federal dead marked the place of the Federals' second line "with the accuracy of a line at a dress parade."[16] As they moved east up the west face of Seminary Ridge, the Confederates met further stout resistance in the First Corps' front. Colonel Joseph Newton Brown of Perrin's Brigade reported that the Federal barricade seemed "a sheet of fire and smoke, sending its leaden missiles . . . in the faces of men who had often, but never so terribly, met it before." A soldier of the Forty-seventh North Carolina, Pettigrew's Brigade, wrote that, "The earth just seemed to open and take in that line which five minutes ago was so perfect."[17]

The truth about the first day is that the First Corps was defeated but it did not quit the fight. Instead, it was withdrawn so as to position itself on advantageous ground in order to continue the battle. An incidental but significant error arising out of the careless writing about the Federal retreat on the first day involves that part of the Lee apology that faults Ewell for not having attacked Cemetery Hill late in the day. Lee's report acknowledged that the Confederates had no information concerning the location of the rest of the Federal army. He also stated that the four Con-federate divisions present were "already weakened and exhausted by a long and bloody struggle," which surely contradicts the conventional image of an enemy that was "swept away." Immediately following these admissions Lee remarked that "General Ewell was . . . instructed to carry the hill occupied by the enemy, if he found it practicable, but to avoid a general engagement until the arrival of the other divisions of the army."[18]

How Ewell was to attack Cemetery Hill while at the same time avoiding a general engagement has never been explained by the Lee apologists. And regarding Lee's first condition—if Ewell found it "practi-cable"—one may stand today at the Culp House below Cemetery Hill and Culp's Hill and look up at the precipitous and complex terrain. Hav-

[16] *O.R.,* Series I, Vol. XXVII, Part II, pp. 638–39.

[17] Varina D. Brown, *A Colonel at Gettysburg and Spottsylvania* (Columbia, S.C.: The State Publishing Company, 1931), p. 79; John H. Thorp, *Histories of the Several Regiments and Battalions from North Carolina,* Walter Clark, ed. (Raleigh, 1901) III: 89–90.

[18] *O.R.,* Series I, Vol. XXVII, Part II, pp. 317–18.

ing retreated through the town to Cemetery Hill, elements of the First Corps were dispatched to Culp's Hill. Other elements of the First and the Eleventh Corps were nearby on Cemetery Hill. Pfanz notes that these Federals had about forty guns and ample ammunition.[19] Without knowledge of the whereabouts of the remainder of the Federal army, with these formidable heights in fact manned by the Federals and with the Confederate divisions "weakened and exhausted" according to Lee, it appears that Ewell correctly decided that the fighting on the first day was ended. He did not share Lee's emotional and mistaken belief of the Confederates' invincibility. Lee made a different decision on the following two days in different circumstances. The consequences of Lee's decision surely do not contradict Ewell's conclusion on July 1.

[19]Coddington, *Gettysburg Campaign* map facing page 293; *O.R.*, Series I, Vol. XXVII, Part I, 266; Harry W. Pfanz, *Gettysburg, the Second Day* (Chapel Hill: The University of North Carolina Press, 1987), p. 39.

Reynolds of Gettysburg

G reat events are typically made up of a series of small incidents. This was certainly true of the titanic three days at Gettysburg in 1863. Some of these smaller incidents are significant in and of themselves in that they had critical impact on the course and outcome of the great event. The actions of Maj. Gen. John F. Reynolds on the first day of the battle were such significant and decisive incidents. It is appropriate to emphasize Reynolds' involvement, his last and finest hour. One may first identify him, to see him as a general officer.

In several ways, Reynolds was typical of the ranking generals of the Army of the Potomac. Thus he was politically conservative, a pre-war Democrat antagonistic to abolition. On the other hand, he was intensely committed to the Union, a patriot in a very real sense and angry about secession. His military philosophy was similarly conservative. Like McClellan, he believed that the war should have been in the hands of the military, free and clear of the political objectives and necessities of the government and uninhibited by civilian control. He perceived a nonexistent line between politics and war, and between the government and its military forces. Under this extra-constitutional view, the Washington administration should not have had the jurisdiction or the power to decide and direct the military establishment. Reynolds' inability to structure army command in this way caused him to reject the offer of command of the Army of the Potomac.

His concept of warfare was also traditional. He was initially skeptical of volunteer soldiers, was a strict disciplinarian, and believed in the protection of the private property of the enemy. Despite these characteristics, Reynolds was highly popular with his Washington superiors and his military peers and those he commanded, both officers and enlisted men. Unlike other major military figures of the Eastern theater, he was discreet with his politics and was not an intriguer. The commands of Burnside and Hooker had been marked by political intrigue and jockeying. Reynolds and Meade, who was junior to Reynolds, had long been friendly rivals. They cooperated on Meade's appointment to command and brought on a needed period of stability to the army.

Douglas Southall Freeman has written that Lee's "army . . . had been wrecked at Gettysburg." Without belaboring the classic issue of the decisiveness of that battle in terms of the war, it is surely fair to say that the Confederate defeat was highly damaging. It forever limited Lee's capacity to maneuver and thus predicted the ultimate siege which led to his surrender. There has been much careless writing about Gettysburg's first day. Confederate apologists sometimes speak of a Confederate victory on the first day, as if July 1 represented a battle in and of itself without reference to the succeeding two days and as if unmindful of what the stakes were on July 1. Other writers, referring to the Federals, use such words as "swept from the field," "collapsed," and "fled" to describe the action of the Eleventh and First Corps. The Federals were indeed defeated on the first day but their dogged and desperate fighting had permitted Federal possession of the key ground and had purchased the time for the Army of the Potomac to gather on that ground. Lee reported that the four Confederate divisions engaged on the first day were "weakened and exhausted by a long and bloody struggle," which surely contradicts the image of Federals that were "swept away."

The truth is that at stake on the first day of Gettysburg were two factors critical to the battle's outcome, *field position* and *time*. The key ground was the high ground south of the town: Cemetery Hill, Culp's Hill, Cemetery Ridge and the Round Tops. Possession of these heights—Porter Alexander called them "a position unique among all the battlefields of the war"—provided a significant Federal advantage. And time was essential so that the several missing corps of the Army of the Potomac could gather to defend this ground. These factors were what the first day of the battle was all about. The Federals held the ground and acquired the time. John F. Reynolds was the principal agent of these accomplishments.

Crediting Reynolds on the first day does not mitigate the contribution of Brig. Gen. John Buford. Screening the advance of the army's left wing, Buford initially established a cavalry line on July 1, west and north of Gettysburg as the divisions of Heth, Pender, Rodes, and Early moved toward town. The horsemen's skillful and tenacious defense afforded Reynolds his opportunity. Ordered by Meade to advance his First Corps to Gettysburg early on July 1, with the Eleventh Corps in support, it was Reynolds' decision to fight at McPherson's Ridge, and his bringing up the Eleventh Corps, that created the defense in depth of the high ground south of the town. This defense set up the ultimate battle site on that high ground.

It is only fair to note that Reynolds' decision was especially timely in the light of Meade's obvious uncertainty. Meade's order that sent the first corps to Gettysburg said that he would "assume position for offensive or defensive, as occasion requires, or rest to the troops." Uncertainty marked another of Meade's communications to Reynolds on July 1: "The commanding general cannot decide whether it is his best policy to move to attack until he learns something more definite of the point at which the enemy is concentrating . . . Meanwhile, he would like to have your views upon the subject." This communication proceeded to discuss whether or not Gettysburg was the appropriate place for a Federal concentration and again solicited Reynolds' "suggestions." It is generally believed that Reynolds did not receive this latter communication, or the more or less simultaneous Pipe Creek Circular, but his actions plainly established his views of the proper role and place for the Army of the Potomac.

Significantly, after Reynolds' death a series of commanders on the field ratified Reynolds' decision. Doubleday, Howard, and finally Hancock clung to McPherson's and Seminary Ridges until the Federals were withdrawn, and the Federal Corps then assembled on the "position unique" from which Lee was heavily defeated. Lost Cause writers and Lee apologists have tried to diminish the Federal accomplishments on the first day by reiterating the "Ewell card": only Ewell's wrong-headed failure to attack Cemetery Hill permitted the Federals to hold the advantageous field position. These commentators forget that Lee was on the field and did not order such an attack. He also justified Ewell in his official report.

John F. Reynolds' death at Gettysburg has guaranteed his status as a romantic hero of the war. It is well to remember that this supreme contribution was matched by his tactical judgement.

R. E. Lee and July 1
at Gettysburg

Although President Jefferson Davis approved of the Army of Northern Virginia's moving into Maryland and Pennsylvania in 1863, the Gettysburg campaign was General Robert E. Lee's idea. In 1914, Douglas Southall Freeman wrote that Lee's "army . . . had been wrecked at Gettysburg."[1] This catastrophic consequence was the result of leadership failures on the part of the army commander. The first of these was strategic; the second involved a series of errors in the execution of the campaign.

In regard to strategy, it is apparent that the drama of Gettysburg and the celebrated controversies associated with the battle have obscured the primary question about the campaign: Should it have been undertaken; should Lee have been in Pennsylvania in 1863? When questioning Lee's campaigns and battles, one is frequently confronted with the assertion that he had no alternative. Accordingly, before addressing the question of the wisdom of Lee's raid into Pennsylvania, one must consider whether he had an alternative.

On the eve of the campaign, during the period following Chancellorsville, Lee's army remained near Fredericksburg on the Rappahannock facing Joseph Hooker's Army of the Potomac, located on the north side of that river. In this situation, Lee had at least three possible options: to attack Hooker across the river, which surely would have been

---

[1]Douglas Southall Freeman, ed., *Lee's Dispatches: Unpublished Letters of General Robert E. Lee, C.S.A., to Jefferson Davis and the War Department of the Confederate States of America, 1862–1865* (1915; rev. ed., ed. Grady McWhiney, New York: G. P. Putnam's Sons, 1957), xxxvii.

problematical; to assume the defensive as he had at Fredericksburg in December 1862 and was to do again in 1864; or to undertake a raid into the North. The most likely of these choices was surely the middle course—to assume the defensive and force the Army of the Potomac to come after him. Lee apologists, committed to the "no alternative" thesis, would exorcise this option. The analysis of Colonel Charles Marshall, Lee's aide-de-camp and military secretary, is illustrative. In an effort to justify the campaign, Marshall carefully constructed the no alternative argument. He identified the same three choices for Lee set forth above. Rejecting the choice of Lee's attacking across the river, he eliminated the defensive option by the naked assertion that had Lee stood on the defensive south of the river he "was bound to assume . . . the enemy would abandon his effort to dislodge him from his position at Fredericksburg, and would move his army to Richmond by water." This, Marshall insisted, would have required Lee to retreat to defend Richmond. Based on this assumption, Marshall eliminated the defensive option and, as if by magic, concluded that there was no alternative to the Gettysburg raid. That the Federals would not have moved against Lee but would, instead, have proceeded directly to Richmond by water is simply Marshall's hypothesis. In fact, the evidence since the 1862 withdrawal from the Peninsula pointed to the North's commitment to the overland route.[2]

The Southern army's need for food is the premise of another no alternative justification for Lee's moving into Maryland and Pennsylvania. The South's supply problems were severe, as Robert K. Krick has graphically stated.[3] Collecting supplies and living off the Northern country was surely a motive for the campaign. But the Army of Northern Virginia was sustained in Virginia from July 1863 until April 1865, so it was not necessary to go North for food and forage. If supplying the army had really been the motive for the campaign, a raid by small, mobile forces

---

[2]Maj. Gen. Sir Frederick Maurice, ed., *An Aide-de-Camp of Lee, Being the Papers of Colonel Charles Marshall* (Boston: Little, Brown, 1927), 190. Although concerned with the overland campaign of 1864–65, Andrew A. Humphreys's discussion of the water route alternative illuminates the considerations affecting the choice of routes toward Richmond. See Humphreys, *The Virginia Campaign of '64 and '65: The Army of the Potomac and the Army of the James* (New York: Charles Scribner's Sons, 1883), 6–9.

[3]Robert K. Krick, "Why Lee Went North," in Morningside Bookshop, *Catalogue Number Twenty-Four* (Dayton, Ohio, 1988), 10.

rather than the entire army would have had considerably more promise and less risk.

Since there was an alternative, we may return to the primary question: Should Lee have undertaken the campaign at all? This question cannot be meaningfully considered in the abstract. It must be considered within the context of the larger question of the appropriate grand strategy of the war from the standpoint of the Confederacy. In this larger respect, the concern is not military strategy in the sense of a campaign or battle, that is, operational strategy. Rather, it is grand strategy, that is, to paraphrase Carl von Clausewitz, the art of employing military forces to attain the objects of war, to support the national policy of the government that raises the military forces. In evaluating a general's performance, the only significant inquiry is whether the general's actions related positively or negatively to the war objective and national policy of his government.

The statements of two Confederate leaders describe quite different theories of the South's grand strategy to win the war: E. Porter Alexander, chief of ordnance of the Army of Northern Virginia and later chief of artillery of Longstreet's First Corps, has described the South's appropriate grand strategy in this way:

> When the South entered upon war with a power so immensely her superior in men & money, & all the wealth of modern resources in machinery and transportation appliances by land & sea, she could entertain but one single hope of final success. That was, that the desperation of her resistance would finally exact from her adversary such a price in blood & treasure as to exhaust the enthusiasm of its population for the objects of the war. We could not hope to conquer her. Our one chance was to wear her out.[4]

This fairly describes a defensive grand stategy—to wear the North out instead of trying to defeat the North militarily.

The second view was Lee's. It may be found in two letters to President Davis. The first, written en route to Gettysburg, is dated June 25,

[4]Edward Porter Alexander, *Fighting for the Confederacy: The Personal Recollections of General Edward Porter Alexander*, ed. Gary W. Gallagher (Chapel Hill: Univ. of North Carolina Press, 1989), 415.

1863, at Williamsport, Maryland. Lee states: "It seems to me that we cannot afford to keep our troops awaiting possible movements of the enemy, but that our true policy is, as far as we can, so to employ our own forces as to give occupation to his at points of our selection." He further argues that "our concentration at any point compels that of the enemy." It is important that this letter was concerned with Confederate military forces on a wide range of fronts, including Virginia, North Carolina, and Kentucky. Since it contemplates drawing Federal armies to Confederate points of concentration to "give occupation" to the Federals, the letter is a prescription for military confrontation. It is therefore a statement of an offensive grand strategy, whether the confrontation at the "point of concentration" was to take the form of the tactical offensive or defensive on the part of the South. The second letter to Davis is dated July 6, 1864, shortly after the siege of Petersburg began. Lee wrote: "If we can defeat or drive the armies of the enemy from the field, we shall have peace. All our efforts and energies should be devoted to that object."[5]

This, then, was Lee's view of the way, as Clausewitz defined grand strategy, for the Confederacy "to attain the objects of [the] war." The South was to pursue the military defeat of the North. Lee's offensive grand strategic sense is reiterated again and again in his dispatches to Davis, the War Department, and his fellow general officers. These dispatches, in the *Official Records* and *The Wartime Papers of R. E. Lee,* bristle with offensive rhetoric and planning: "striking a blow," "driving the enemy," "crushing the enemy."[6]

Any doubt that Lee was committed to the offensive as the South's appropriate grand strategy is presumably eliminated when one considers the most obvious source for identifying his grand strategic thinking, the campaigns and battles of the Army of Northern Virginia. Consistent with the grand strategy that he said he believed in and repeatedly planned and advocated, Lee from the beginning embraced the offen-

---

[5]U.S. War Department, *The War of the Rebellion: A Compilation of the Official Records of the Union and Confederate Armies,* 128 vols., (Washington, D.C.: GPO, 1880–1901), ser. 1, vol. 27, pt. 3:932 (hereafter cited as *OR;* all references are to volumes in Series 1); Clifford Dowdey and Louis H. Manarin, eds., *The Wartime Papers of R. E. Lee* (Boston: Little, Brown, 1961), 816.

[6]*OR,* vol. 29, pt. 1:405; ibid., vol. 51, pt. 2:761; Dowdey and Manarin, eds., *Wartime Papers,* 675.

sive. Appointed to command the Army of Northern Virginia on June 1, 1862, he turned at once to the offensive, beginning with major engagements on the Peninsula—Mechanicsville, Gaines's Mill, Frayser's Farm, and Malvern Hill. Following on the heels of the Seven Days, the Second Bull Run campaign was strategically offensive in an operational sense although, except for Longstreet's counterattack on August 30, it may be classified as defensive from a tactical standpoint. At Antietam Lee stood on the defensive, but the Maryland campaign was strategically offensive; his moving into Maryland assured a major battle in that state. At Chancellorsville, he chose not to retreat when confronted by the Federal pincer movement. Instead, he repeatedly attacked, and the Federals retreated back across the river.

The point is not that each of these campaigns and battles represented an error by Lee. Driving the Federals away from Richmond in 1862, for example, may have been required to maintain Southern morale and to avoid the practical consequences of losing the capital. The point is that the offensive pattern is plain. Lee believed that the South's grand strategic role was offensive.

Lee's grand strategy of the offensive, to defeat the North militarily as distinguished from prolonging the contest until the North gave it up, created a profound problem. It was not feasible and, indeed, was counterproductive to the Confederacy's "objects of war." Curiously, that Lee's attack grand strategy was misplaced is suggested by his own awareness of factors that argued against it. The primary reason the attack grand strategy was counterproductive was numbers, and Lee was sensitive to the South's manpower disadvantage and its implications. A letter of January 10, 1863, to Secretary of War James A. Seddon, between his victory at Fredericksburg and Ambrose E. Burnside's abortive Mud March, reflects this awareness. "I have the honor to represent to you the absolute necessity that exists . . . to increase our armies, if we desire to oppose effectual resistance to the vast numbers that the enemy is now precipitating upon us," Lee wrote. "The great increase of the enemy's forces will augment the disparity of numbers to such a degree that victory, if attained, can only be achieved by a terrible expenditure of the most precious blood of the country."[7]

[7]Dowdey and Manarin, eds., *Wartime Papers*, 388–89.

Further recognition of the numbers problem appears in Lee's letter of June 10, 1863, to Davis, after Chancellorsville and at the outset of the Gettysburg campaign:

> While making the most we can of the means of resistance we possess . . . it is nevertheless the part of wisdom to carefully measure and husband our strength, and not to expect from it more than in the ordinary course of affairs it is capable of accomplishing. We should not therefore conceal from ourselves that our resources in men are constantly diminishing, and the disproportion in this respect between us and our enemies, if they continue united in their effort to subjugate us, is steadily augmenting. The decrease of the aggregate of this army as disclosed by the returns affords an illustration of this fact. Its effective strength varies from time to time, *but the falling off in its aggregate shows that its ranks are growing weaker and that its losses are not supplied by recruits* (emphasis added)[8].

The *Official Records* are full of Lee's analyses of his strength problems. These communications predict that unless his army was reinforced, "the consequences may be disastrous" and include such statements as "I cannot see how we are to escape the natural military consequences of the enemy's numerical superiority."[9]

Consciousness of his numerical disadvantage, of the ever-increasing Federal disproportion, did not mute Lee's commitment to the grand strategic offensive. Nor did that grand strategy permit his army to "husband our strength." During the Seven Days' battles on the Peninsula, George B. McClellan lost approximately 9,796 killed and wounded, 10.7 percent; Lee's casualties were 19,739 men, 20.7 percent of his army. Although Federal casualties in killed and wounded at Second Bull Run exceeded Lee's by approximately 1,000 men, the Army of Northern Virginia lost in excess of 9,000, almost 19 percent as compared to 13.3 percent for the Federals. In spite of McClellan's ineptitude, Lee lost almost 12,000 men, 22.6 percent, at Antietam, immediately following losses in excess of 1,800 at South Mountain on September 14. McClellan's Antietam casualties were 15.5 percent. At Chancellorsville, Lee lost almost

[8]Ibid., 508.
[9]Ibid., 843–44.

11,000 of 57,000 effectives, in excess of 18 percent, a much higher proportion than Joseph Hooker's 11.4 percent.[10]

These statistics show the serious attrition of Lee's limited numbers. In addition, Lee's losses were mostly irreplaceable, as he was aware. Finally, his losses also seriously affected his army's leadership. "The Confederates' ability to operate as they moved northward was affected by the loss of much mid-level command," Robert K. Krick has written. "The heart of the Confederate Army was starting to feel this difficulty for the first time just *before* Gettysburg. To the tremendous losses of the successful but costly campaign in the summer of 1862 . . . were added the victims of the dreadful bloodshed at Chancellorsville" (emphasis added).[11] Clearly, the Federals' increasingly disproportionate strength was the result of Northern reinforcements, but it was also exacerbated by Lee's heavy, disproportionate, and irreplaceable losses. Had Lee taken the defensive, the increasing Federal manpower advantage would have been slowed.

It is appropriate to contrast the alternative grand strategy of the defensive. In 1986, historians Richard E. Beringer, Herman Hattaway, Archer Jones, and William N. Still, Jr., noted that "no Confederate army lost a major engagement because of the lack of arms, munitions, or other essential supplies." These authors then summarized the case as follows:

> By remarkable and effective efforts the agrarian South did exploit and create an industrial base that proved adequate, with the aid of imports, to maintain suitably equipped forces in the field. Since the Confederate armies suffered no crippling deficiencies in weapons or supply, their principal handicap would be their numerical inferiority. But to offset this lack, Confederates, fighting the first major war in which both sides armed themselves with rifles, had the advantage of a temporary but very significant surge in the power of the tactical defensive. In addition, the difficulties of supply in a very large and relatively thinly settled region proved a powerful aid to strengthening the strategic defensive. Other things being equal, if Confederate

[10]These data are taken from Thomas L. Livermore, *Numbers and Losses in the Civil War in America, 1861–65* (1901; reprint, Dayton, Ohio: Morningside House, 1986), 86, 88–89, 92, 98.

[11]Krick, "Why Lee Went North," 11.

military leadership were competent and the Union did not display Napoleonic genius, the tactical and strategic power of the defense could offset northern numerical superiority and presumably give the Confederacy a measure of military victory adequate to maintain its independence.[12]

British observers sensed the feasibility of the grand strategy of the defensive as the war began. Harking back to their own experience in America, they did not see how the South could be conquered. The War of Independence analogy is not perfect, but it is illustrative. The military historian Colonel George A. Bruce has pointed out that George Washington "had a correct insight into the minds of his own people and that of the enemy, the strength of resolution of each to endure heavy burdens, looking forward with certainty to the time when the public sentiment of England, led by Chatham and Burke, would be ready to acknowledge the Colonies as an independent nation. With these views he carried on the war for seven years, all the way from Boston to Yorktown, on a generally defensive plan, the only one pointing to the final goal of independence"[13] (emphasis added). The Americans, on the grand strategic defensive, lost many battles and retreated many times, but they kept forces in the field to avoid being ultimately defeated, and they won because the British decided that the struggle was either hopeless or too burdensome to pursue.

A Confederate defensive grand strategy would have been premised on E. Porter Alexander's conservative principle "to wear her [the North] out," to "exact . . . such a price in blood & treasure as to exhaust the enthusiasm of its population." To contribute to this wearing out, it was essential for Lee to maintain the viability of his army, to keep it in the field as a genuine force. That viability depended on his retaining sufficient relative strength for mobility and maneuver so as to avoid a siege and also to undertake timely and promising operationally strategic offensives and the tactical offensive. Lee could have accomplished these things had

[12]Richard E. Beringer, Herman Hattaway, Archer Jones, and William N. Still, Jr., *Why the South Lost the Civil War* (Athens, Ga.: Univ. of Georgia Press, 1986), 9, 16.

[13]Lt. Col. George A. Bruce, "The Strategy of the Civil War," in *Papers of the Military Historical Society of Massachusetts,* 14 vols. and index (1895–1918; reprint, Wilmington, N.C.: Broadfoot Publishing Company, 1989–90), 13:469.

he pursued a defensive grand strategy. And despite Southern manpower disadvantages, this grand strategy was at the outset feasible because of the North's logistical task and the relative power that the rifled gun afforded the defense.

It is to be emphasized that the grand strategy of defense would not have required Southern armies always to be on the strategic operational or tactical defensive. As the British military historian Major General J. F. C. Fuller points out, "It is possible to develop an offensive tactics from a defensive strategy."[14] Thus, if Lee's grand strategic sense of the war had been defensive, he could nevertheless on appropriate occasions have pursued offensive campaigns and offensive tactics in the context of that defensive grand strategy. The Revolution again provides an illustration. Although pursuing a grand strategy of defense, the Americans were sometimes aggressive and offensive, for example, at Trenton, Saratoga, and Yorktown.

The Federal manpower superiority would also have been less significant had Lee assumed the defensive in 1862–63, as evidenced by what happened in the overland campaign in 1864–65. Despite his prior losses and the great Northern numerical superiority, Lee's defense in 1864, again in Alexander's words, exacted "a price in blood" that significantly affected "the enthusiasm of [the North's] population" for continuing the war.[15] Indeed, Lee demonstrated in 1864 the feasibility of the grand strategy of the defense. Had he adopted the defensive earlier he would have had available a reasonable portion of the more than one hundred thousand officers and men that he lost in the offensives in 1862 and 1863, including Gettysburg. With these larger numbers he could have maintained mobility and avoided a siege.

[14]Maj. Gen. J. F. C. Fuller, *The Generalship of Ulysses S. Grant* (1929; reprint, Bloomington: Indiana Univ. Press, 1958), 365.

[15]On the question of Northern morale in the early summer of 1864, see Lt. Col. Alfred H. Burne, *Lee, Grant and Sherman* (New York: Charles Scribner's Sons, 1939), 65, and William H. Swinton, *Campaigns of the Army of the Potomac: A Critical History of Operations in Virginia, Maryland and Pennsylvania, from the Commencement to the Close of the War, 1861–1865* (New York: Charles Scribner's Sons, 1882), 494–95. Swinton's perceptive study argued that after Cold Harbor the outlook in the North was so gloomy "that there was at this time great danger of a collapse of the war. The history of this conflict truthfully written will show this."

It is in the context of grand strategy that one must view the primary issue regarding Gettysburg, that is, whether Lee should have been there at all. The Gettysburg campaign, Lee's most audacious act, is the apogee of his grand strategy of the offensive. The numerous reasons for the campaign offered by Lee and the commentators are well known: the necessity to upset Federal offensive plans, avoidance of a siege of the Richmond defenses, alleviation of supply problems in unforaged country, encouragement of the peace movement in the North, drawing the Federal army north of the Potomac in order to maneuver, even the relief of Vicksburg. Some or all of these reasons may have contributed to the decision, but fighting a battle was plainly inherent in the campaign because of the foreseeable Federal reaction and because of Lee's intent regarding a battle.

In his outline report dated July 31, 1863, Lee stated that "It had not been intended to fight a general battle at such a distance from our base, unless attacked by the enemy." The foreseeable Federal reaction to Lee's presence in loyal states suggests that the "unless attacked" provision was meaningless. As Hattaway and Jones point out: "Lee could have been under no illusion that he could bring off such a protracted campaign without a battle. . . . If he raided enemy territory, it would be politically if not strategically imperative for the Union army to take the offensive."[16] And on June 8, 1863, in a letter to Secretary of War Seddon, he spoke of the "difficulty & hazard in taking the aggressive with so large an army in its front, entrenched behind a river where it cannot be advantageously attacked" and of drawing the enemy out into "a position to be assailed." In the outline report, the same report in which he stated that "it had not been intended to fight a general battle a such a distance from our base," he wrote of his intent to "transfer the scene of hostilities north of the Potomac": "It was thought that the corresponding movements on the part of the enemy to which those contemplated by us would probably give rise, might offer a fair opportunity to *strike a blow* at the army then commanded by General Hooker, and that in any event that army would be compelled to leave Virginia" (emphasis added).[17]

---

[16]*OR*, vol. 27, pt. 2:308; Herman Hattaway and Archer Jones, *How the North Won: A Military History of the Civil War* (Urbana: Univ. of Illinois Press, 1983), 398.

[17]Dowdey and Manarin, eds., *Wartime Papers*, 505; *OR*, vol. 27, pt. 2:305.

The point is that the Gettysburg campaign involved substantial and unacceptable risks for Lee's army. His northernmost base in Virginia was to be Winchester, after it was taken by Richard S. Ewell. Winchester was ninety miles from Staunton, the available rail terminus. For this reason, and simply because of the distances involved, the extended lines of communication, and the necessity to recross the Potomac, these risks extended to the loss of the Army of Northern Virginia. In any event, assuming victory, the Gettysburg campaign was bound to result in heavy Confederate casualties, as Lee surely knew because of his losses in previous victories and at Antietam. Such foreseeable losses at Gettysburg were bound to limit his army's capacity to maneuver, to contribute to the risk that his army would be fixed, and to increase the risk of his being driven into a siege in the Richmond defenses. Lee had repeatedly said that a siege would be fatal to his army.[18]

Colonel Charles Marshall, whose writings originated many of the still-current rationalizations of Lee's generalship, set forth what he called "Lee's Military Policy." Having identified the critical importance of the defense of Richmond, Marshall wrote that Lee sought "to employ the enemy at a distance and prevent his near approach to the city." The Maryland campaign and Gettysburg fit this purpose, according to Marshall. But having identified the Confederacy's inherent strength problem, Marshall states that Lee was "unwilling to incur the risks and losses of an aggressive war having for its object the destruction of the enemy." Indeed, wrote Marshall: "General Lee thought that to expose our armies to the sacrifices of great battles the object of which was only to disperse or destroy those of the enemy would soon bring the Confederacy to the verge of exhaustion. Even victory in such engagements might prove disastrous. The North could readily raise new armies, while the means of the South were so limited that a few bloody victories might leave it powerless to continue the struggle."[19]

These are fine words, a prescription for a defensive strategy, but surely they do not describe Lee's military policy. For an accurate description of Lee's leadership one may again consult Major General Fuller, who in 1929 characterized Lee's strategy: "He rushed forth to find a battlefield, to challenge a contest between himself and the

---

[18] *OR,* vol. 27, pt. 3:868–69; ibid., vol. 40, pt. 2:703.
[19] Maurice, ed., *Aide-de-Camp of Lee,* 73, 68.

North."[20] This is why Lee went north in 1863. It was a continuation of his offensive grand strategy, to "defeat or drive the armies of the enemy from the field." Win, lose, or draw, the Gettysburg campaign was a strategic mistake because of the inevitable casualties that the Army of Northern Virginia could not afford.

In regard to defective execution, it is plain that if an army commander is to undertake a high-risk, strategically offensive maneuver, he had better do it with great care, especially if he is moving into enemy territory with extended lines of communication and endemic relative manpower problems. The fact is that Lee proceeded at Gettysburg without essential control of his army in three crucial respects—reconnaissance, the onset of the battle, and the renewal of the battle on the afternoon of July 1.

In his detailed report of January 1864, Lee made the following statements relating to the reconnaissance: "It was expected that as soon as the Federal Army should cross the Potomac, General Stuart would give notice of its movements, and nothing having been heard from him since our entrance into Maryland, it was inferred that the enemy had not yet left Virginia." This report also recounts Lee's learning from a scout on the night of June 28 that the Army of the Potomac had crossed the river and was approaching South Mountain. Colonel Marshall, who drafted the relevant orders as well as Lee's reports, also states that Lee "had not heard from him [Stuart] since the army left Virginia, and was confident from that fact, in view of the positive orders that Stuart had received, that General Hooker had not yet crossed the Potomac."[21] The facts challenge both the candor of Lee's report and the assumption that Stuart's silence meant that the Army of the Potomac was not following Lee.

In the first place, Lee should have assumed that the Federal army would place itself between him and Washington, by that time a well-developed pattern in the Virginia theater. In addition, dictating the movements of the Army of the Potomac was one of the premises of Lee's movement north. In his outline report of July 31, 1863, Lee stated as an objective of the campaign "the transfer of the scene of hostilities north of the Potomac." He intended, he wrote, that his movement north would provoke "corresponding movements on the part of the enemy . . . and

---

[20]Fuller, *Generalship of Grant*, 377.
[21]*OR*, vol. 27, pt. 2:316; Maurice, ed., *Aide-de-Camp of Lee*, 217.

that in any event that army would be compelled to leave Virginia." Lee reiterated the substance of these expectations in his detailed report of January 1864.[22] And as he proceeded, Lee knew considerably more than he admitted in his January 1864 report.

On June 18, Lee advised Davis that "the enemy has been thrown back from the line of the Rappahannock, and is concentrating, as far as I can learn, in the vicinity of Centreville. The last reports from the scouts indicate that he is moving over toward the Upper Potomac." Centreville is about halfway to the Potomac from Fredericksburg. Thus Lee was aware that the Federals were on the move. On June 19, in another communication to Davis, Lee reported that "indications seem to be that his [the enemy's] main body is proceeding toward the Potomac, whether upon Harper's Ferry or to cross the river east of it, is not yet known." On the following day from Berryville, Virginia, having reported the location of the parts of his own army—Ewell was by this time across the river—Lee again reported what he knew of the Federals: "The movement of the main body . . . is still toward the Potomac, but its real destination is not yet discovered." Three days later, on June 23, another dispatch went to Davis: "Reports of movements of the enemy east of the Blue Ridge cause me to believe that he is preparing to cross the Potomac. A pontoon bridge is said to be laid at Edward's Ferry, and his army corps that he has advanced to Leesburg and the foot of the mountains, appear to be withdrawing." This letter also reported that Ewell was "in motion toward the Susquehanna" and that A. P. Hill's and James Longstreet's corps were nearing the Potomac.[23]

Two more dispatches bear on Lee's expectations. On June 22, in the first of his controversial dispatches to Stuart, he stated that "I fear he [the enemy] will steal a march on us, and get across the Potomac before we are aware." And on June 25, he advised Davis from opposite Williamsport, "I think I can throw General Hooker's Army across the Potomac."[24] From these statements it is apparent that Lee knew that his plan was working—the enemy was following him across the Potomac and out of Virginia. He would have the opportunity to "strike a blow."

On June 22 the much-debated issue of Stuart's orders arose. Lee's cavalry force included, in addition to horse artillery, six brigades under

[22] *OR,* vol. 27, pt. 2:313.
[23] Ibid., 295–97.
[24] Ibid., pt. 3:913, 931.

Stuart: Wade Hampton's, Beverly H. Robertson's, William E. "Grumble" Jones's, Fitzhugh Lee's, A. G. Jenkins's, and W. H. F. Lee's, the last-named temporarily commanded by Colonel John R. Chambliss, Jr. Jenkins moved with Ewell, screening the front of the advance, while Robertson and Jones were to guard the mountain passes behind the army. Hampton, Fitz Lee, and Chambliss were to ride with Stuart. Also with the Army of Northern Virginia was Brigadier General John D. Imboden's command of four regiments.[25]

Setting aside postwar recollections of conversations and concentrating on the contemporaneous written word, Lee's June 22 communication to Stuart is the first relevant document. This letter, written at Berryville, begins with a direct inquiry regarding the enemy: "Do you know where he is and what he is doing?" The letter then identifies specific assignments for the cavalry brigades with Stuart: "If you find that he [the enemy] is moving northward, and that two brigades can guard the Blue Ridge and take care of your rear, you can move with the other three into Maryland, and take position on General Ewell's right, place yourself in communication with him, guard his flank, keep him informed of the enemy's movements, and collect all the supplies you can for the use of the army."[26]

Lee's June 22 letter to Stuart was sent to General Longstreet for forwarding to Stuart. Lee's letter to Longstreet that accompanied it is lost, but Longstreet's letter of transmittal to Stuart, dated 7:00 P.M. on June 22, refers to Lee's writing of Stuart's "passing by the rear of the enemy" and included advice from Longstreet: "If you can get through by that route, I think that you will be less likely to indicate what our plans are than if you should cross by passing to our rear."[27]

On the following day, June 23, another directive went from Lee to Stuart. Written at 5:00 P.M., it contained the following relevant provisions:

> If General Hooker's army remains inactive, you can leave two
> brigades to watch him, and withdraw with the three others, but

---

[25]Edwin B. Coddington, *The Gettysburg Campaign: A Study in Command* (New York: Charles Scribner's Sons, 1968), 594–95.

[26]*OR*, vol. 27, pt. 3:913. Lee's orders to Stuart and Longstreet's transmittal letter are reproduced in the Appendix.

[27]*OR*, vol. 27, pt. 3:915.

should he not[28] appear to be moving northward I think you had better withdraw this side of the mountain tomorrow night, cross at Shepherdstown the next day, and move to Fredericktown.

You will, however, be able to judge whether you can pass around their army without hindrance, doing them all the damage you can, and cross the river east of the mountains.

In either case, after crossing the river, you must move on and feel the right of Ewell's troops, collecting information, provisions, etc.[29]

This order, like that of June 22, included the instruction to the cavalryman to feel Ewell's right and give Lee information. Since Lee knew his plan was working and the Federals were following him and were to cross the Potomac, information should have been his concern. In the circumstances, any commander in control of his army would have issued instructions to Stuart that were short, single-minded, and not discretionary. In the June 22 communication, Lee had asked a question regarding the enemy: "Do you know where he is and what he is doing?" He should have told Stuart that this question needed a prompt answer and that Stuart's one task was to keep him constantly informed of the enemy's movements. Lee did not do this, and taken together the orders contain the following problems:

1. No time sequences were specified; no deadlines were stated by which time Stuart was to perform his tasks or make reports.

[28]It is apparent that the word "not" was unintended. Read literally, the orders of June 23 set forth different movements for Stuart depending on the same facts: "if General Hooker's army remains inactive" and "should he [Hooker] not appear to be moving northward." This almost certainly represented a careless ambiguity, but it seems not to have been a critical one. In both of the orders printed in the *Official Records,* Stuart was to feel Ewell's right and give him information. Virtually all writers have ignored this seemingly misplaced "not" in Lee's instructions to Stuart. An exception is Coddington, who in *The Gettysburg Campaign,* 108, overlooks the possibility of a simple error and speculates that perhaps Lee "considered it possible that Hooker would move southward to threaten Richmond, in which case Stuart's occupation of Frederick, a town equidistant from Baltimore and Washington, would be an effective deterrent."

[29]*OR,* vol. 27, pt. 3:923.

2. Four missions for the brigades with Stuart were identified in the two orders—guarding Ewell's flank, keeping Ewell informed of the enemy's movements, collecting supplies for the army, and inflicting all possible damage on the Federals.

3. Stuart was to "judge whether you can pass around their army without hindrance." Even Colonel Marshall acknowledges that it was left to "Stuart to decide whether he can move around the Federal army."

4. The reference to Stuart's then "cross[ing] the river east of the mountains" is not specific as to location. Sir Frederick Maurice says that "Lee certainly meant that Stuart was to cross immediately east of the mountains, so as to be close to the right flank of the army," but that is not what the communication says.[30]

What fair and reasonable conclusions may be drawn in view of these problems with the orders? In the first place, the orders were ambiguous and uncertain with regard to such critical matters as the times and places of Stuart's movements. Second, contrary to the assertion of some writers, in riding around the Federal army Stuart was manifestly not acting on his own. That ride was expressly contemplated by Lee and was expressly left to Stuart's judgment. Third, regardless of other problems of interpretation, Stuart could not perform reconnaissance adequately with so many other tasks to perform. Two of these tasks indeed contradicted the reconnaissance function and minimized the likelihood of success in the performance of that function. Collecting provisions and doing damage to the enemy were sure to draw the cavalry away from the intelligence task and delay its progress, which they did. These collateral missions diminished the intelligence function and diluted the significance of that function. Their existence was bound to have contributed to Stuart's judgment that the ride around the Federals was a reasonable thing to do. Fourth, pushing east around the Union army was inconsistent with protecting the Confederate army's right. Stuart could not effectively protect Ewell's right and at the same time place eighty-five thousand Federals between himself and Ewell.

A fifth conclusion may be drawn regarding the orders to Stuart. Those orders are usually considered in the context of Lee's need for in-

---

[30]Maurice, ed., *Aide-de-Camp of Lee*, 208 n.

formation concerning the movements of the Federal army. They are not analyzed in reference to the movements of the Confederate army after the orders were issued to Stuart. Such an analysis is appropriate.

Lee's entire army was on the move in June 1863. The army commander moves an army and knows where all of its parts are or are supposed to be. The individual parts do not necessarily know where the rest of the army is. A commander in control of his army may not rationally leave the movement of a detached unit up to that unit's commander, in this case Stuart, and then proceed to move the rest of the army and hope that the detached unit will be able to find its way to the moved or moving main body. The army commander is responsible for keeping the detached unit informed. Lee made no plan or timely effort to do this. In his June 22 communication to Stuart, Lee told the cavalry leader that the army's advance, Ewell's corps, was to move toward the Susquehanna River via Emmitsburg and Chambersburg. The June 23 order stated that "the movements of Ewell's corps are as stated in my former letter. Hill's first division will reach the Potomac to-day, and Longstreet will follow tomorrow."

These messages were the last Stuart received from Lee before the cavalry moved out on the night of June 24 to begin the fateful ride around the Federals. Thus there was justice to Stuart's complaint in his defensive official report that when he started east he understood that the rest of the army was moving toward the Susquehanna. Accordingly, he stated that when he swung north he moved toward York to rendezvous, only to discover that the Confederates had left that area. His sole source of information regarding the Confederate army's location was Northern newspapers. Finally, on the night of July 1, he received a dispatch from Lee telling him that the army was at Gettysburg.

There is a final conclusion that may be drawn regarding reconnaissance. Stuart had been given the discretion to "pass around their army," with no time or distance limitations. Having in mind that Lee knew the Federal army was following him, a reconnaissance contingency plan was surely in order. There was also justification for Stuart's statement in his report that if cavalry "in advance of the army the first day of Gettysburg" was wanted, "it must be remembered that the cavalry [Jenkins's brigade] specially selected for advance guard to the army by the commanding general on account of its geographical location at the time, was available for this purpose." Kenneth P. Williams's observation is fair:

"There were still three cavalry brigades near at hand that he [Lee] could have called upon for mounted service: Imboden's operating toward the west, and those of B. H. Robertson and W. E. Jones guarding the passes below the Potomac that soon needed little or no guarding. There seems to be no excuse for Lee's finding himself at Chambersburg on the 28th without a single regiment of cavalry."[31]

This, then, was the Confederate reconnaissance failure as the armies moved toward July 1, 1863, and this failure was essentially Lee's.

The second leadership error in execution on July 1 concerns the onset of the battle. Coddington states that "to say that Stuart's late arrival was a major cause of Lee's defeat is a little too pat an answer to the question of why the Confederates lost the battle." There were other command failures. Colonel Marshall speaks of the Gettysburg campaign as involving the "risk [of] the battlefield which chance might bring us during a movement northward."[32] As it turned out, it was simply a chance battlefield.

In his July 31, 1863, outline report, part of which has been previously quoted, Lee states: "It had not been intended to fight a general battle at such a distance from our base, unless attacked by the enemy, but, finding ourselves unexpectedly confronted by the Federal Army, it became a matter of difficulty to withdraw through the mountains with our large trains. At the same time, the country was unfavorable for collecting supplies while in the presence of the enemy's main body.... A battle thus became in a measure unavoidable."[33]

In their essentials, these words bear little resemblance to what Lee in fact intended or what in fact occurred. In the same report, he stated that his movement was intended to require Hooker to move with him and that this "might offer a fair opportunity to strike a blow" at the Federals. With regard to the "unless attacked" condition of the report, Lee was not attacked. His forces initially attacked and were the aggressor for three days. As a result of the initial attack, a battle occurred on July 1, not by plan but by chance.

[31] *OR*, vol. 27, pt. 2:207–8; Kenneth P. Williams, *Lincoln Finds a General: A Military Study of the Civil War*, 5 vols. (New York: Macmillan, 1949–59), 2:666.
[32] Coddington, *Gettysburg Campaign*, 207; Maurice, ed., *Aide-de-Camp of Lee*, 191.
[33] *OR*, vol. 27, pt. 2:308.

Had Lee seriously intended to avoid a chance battle, he could have so instructed his corps commanders. The *Official Records* contain no such circular. Lee's reports do not say that he had issued any such order. Nor do the reports of Hill, Ewell, or Longstreet. Even after he learned on the night of June 28 that the Army of the Potomac had, as he expected, crossed the river, there is no evidence of warning orders. No such orders were forthcoming before July 1, and the battle and the battlefield were left to chance until it was too late because he had not asserted control over his army. This was his second failure of control.

Lee provided a laconic account of the start of the battle in his official report dated July 31, 1863. "The leading division of Hill met the enemy in advance of Gettysburg on the morning of July 1," he wrote. "Driving back these troops to within a short distance of the town, he there encountered a larger force, with which two of his divisions became engaged. Ewell, coming up with two of his divisions by Heidlersburg road, joined in the engagement." The battle thus began without Lee's knowing the location of other elements of the Federal army and without the Confederate army's being closed up. On June 30 Henry Heth had sent James J. Pettigrew's brigade from Cashtown to Gettysburg and discovered the enemy, principally cavalry, there. Lee was at Chambersburg. Hill's November 1863 report states: "A courier was then dispatched with this information to the general commanding . . .; also to General Ewell, informing him, and that I intended to advance the next morning and discover what was in my front." As Coddington notes, Hill's "announcement seemed not to have disturbed the commanding general."[34]

As that fateful July 1 began, conservative instincts came over Lee, and he briefly and belatedly asserted himself to control events. Thus Ewell's 1863 report of the campaign recites that at Heidlersburg on the night of June 30 he received Lee's order to proceed to Cashtown or Gettysburg "as circumstances might dictate," together with a note from Hill saying that he was at Cashtown. On July 1, Ewell reported that he started for Cashtown and Hunterstown. Receiving a note from Hill telling of his advance on Gettysburg, Ewell ordered Robert E. Rodes's and Jubal A. Early's divisions toward that place. Ewell notified Lee of these movements and was informed by Lee that, "in case we found the enemy's forces very large, he did not want a general engagement

[34]Ibid., 307, 607; Coddington, *Gettysburg Campaign*, 264.

brought on till the rest of the army came up." Ewell's report continued: "By the time this message reached me, General A. P. Hill had already been warmly engaged with a large body of the enemy in his front, and Carter's artillery battalion, of Rodes' division, had opened with fine effect on the flank of the same body, which was rapidly preparing to attack me, while fresh masses were moving into position in my front. It was too late to avoid an engagement without abandoning the position already taken up, and I determined to push the attack vigorously."[35] In short, Lee's attempt at control came too late because of his failure to react to Hill's June 30 communication and because of the onrush of events.

Lee's renewal of the battle on July 1 constitutes the third error in execution. He apparently did make a second effort at control when he became aware of the fighting at Gettysburg. This awareness, Coddington states, occurred while Lee rode from Chambersburg to Cashtown, where he and his party heard the sound of cannon fire to the east. Walter H. Taylor adds that at Cashtown Lee received a communication from Hill and that he then sent instructions to Heth to avoid a general engagement but to ascertain the enemy's force and report immediately. A. L. Long confirms the Cashtown report from Hill but states that it was a request for reinforcements and that Lee rushed Richard H. Anderson's division forward. General W. N. Pendleton, who was with Lee, mentions the sound of cannon fire. He reports further that the command party hastened toward Gettysburg and that, "arriving near the crest of an eminence more than a mile west of the town . . . we took positions overlooking the field. It was, perhaps, 2 o'clock, and the battle was raging with considerable violence. . . . Observing the course of events, the commanding general suggested whether positions on the right could not be found to enfilade the valley between our position and the town and the enemy's batteries next the town."[36]

Pendleton's account suggests that if Lee, aware of Heth's morning attack, instructed Heth to avoid a general engagement, he abandoned this caution when he reached the field. And Coddington, relying on

---

[35] *OR*, vol. 27, pt. 2:444.

[36] Coddington, *Gettysburg Campaign*, 280; Walter H. Taylor, *Four Years with General Lee* (1877; reprint, Bloomington: Indiana Univ. Press, 1962), 280; A. L. Long, *Memoirs of Robert E. Lee: His Military and Personal History* (New York: J. M. Stoddart, 1886), 275–76; *OR*, vol. 27, pt. 2:348–49.

Heth's postwar account, confirms Lee's decision to commit the Confederates to the afternoon attack. Coddington tells of Heth's observation of Rodes's becoming engaged and states: "[Heth] took the trouble to find Lee and seek his permission to attack in coordination with Rodes. Lee refused the request on the grounds that Longstreet was not up. Returning to his division, Heth saw the enemy shifting his weight to meet Rodes's attack. He again sought Lee's consent to give assistance, and this time received it. These meetings of the two generals occurred before the grand assault all along the Union line."[37]

Thus did Lee permit the renewal of the battle in the afternoon of July 1 in spite of his lack of knowledge of the Federal army's whereabouts and the absence of his own First Corps, which meant that he did it without having reason to believe that he had sufficient manpower to deprive the Federals of the high ground south of the town. Laxness with respect to reconnaissance and his lack of control of Hill's movements had caused him to stumble into a battle. The renewal of the battle represents Lee's third failure with respect to the events of July 1. It committed him to a major confrontation on this particular ground. The need for food and forage did not require his renewal of the battle on July 1 any more than they did on the days following July 1. Porter Alexander, referring to July 2 and the retreat to the Potomac, notes that the Confederates foraged successfully for more than a week in a restricted area of Pennsylvania. he also states that it was feasible for the Confederates to have abandoned Seminary Ridge on the night of July 1 or on July 2: "The onus of attack was upon Meade. . . . We could even have fallen back to Cashtown & held the mountain passes . . . & popular sentiment would have forced Meade to take the aggressive."[38] This was even more true in the early afternoon of July 1, when Lee authorized the all-out Confederate attack on Seminary Ridge, without sufficient troops of his own on hand to keep going and without knowledge of the whereabouts of the rest of the Federal army.

At the close of the day, the net effect of his command failure was that Lee was on the battlefield and in the battle that chance had brought him. As a consequence, he was significantly disadvantaged: he confronted an enemy that occupied what Porter Alexander called a "really

[37]Coddington, *Gettysburg Campaign*, 309.
[38]Alexander, *Fighting for the Confederacy*, 233–34.

wonderful position," with interior lines; Lee's line was a long exterior line, a difficult one from which to organize a coordinated attack; and four of his divisions, as Lee reported, were "weakened and exhausted by a long and bloody struggle."[39]

Committed to the Lee tradition, a number of commentators in the *Southern Historical Society Papers* and elsewhere have attempted to rationalize his command failures in regard to July 1. As has been indicated, Stuart's absence is a major thrust of these efforts. Blaming Hill, in spite of Lee's knowledge on June 30 of Hill's planned movements on July I, is another. Lee's advocates also attempt to moot the issue of his command failures by placing blame on Ewell. They argue that these failures would have been irrelevant if only Ewell had pushed on late on July I and seized Cemetery Hill or Culp's Hill. It is argued that this could have been readily accomplished. A number of Confederate officers said so—after the war and when the Lee tradition of invincibility was being formed.[40] A good lawyer may reasonably be skeptical of the *Southern Historical Society Papers* as evidence. Written after the facts during the creation of the Lost Cause tradition, their value as history is surely limited. Like the patriarchal stories of the Old Testament, such accounts have ideological rather than historical value. They nevertheless require a response.

An initial difficulty in regard to the controversy about Ewell's conduct concerns identification of the issue. The advocates on both sides insist on debating whether or not Ewell would have been successful. This is inevitably a hypothetical question and therefore inappropriate for historical inquiry. Properly framed, the issue historically can only be whether Ewell made a reasonable decision in the circumstances. There is a second problem. Those who criticize Ewell frequently resort to a contention that is also inappropriate: regardless of the facts, Ewell "should have tried." They forget that Ewell was not a Civil War student. He was a general officer responsible for the consequences of his acts

---

[39]Ibid., 234; *OR*, vol. 27, pt. 2:317.

[40]These postwar recollections by John B. Gordon, Henry Kyd Douglas, James Power Smith, Isaac R. Trimble, Jubal A. Early, Walter H. Taylor, and others are cited in Douglas Southall Freeman, *Lee's Lieutenants: A Study in Command,* 3 vols. (New York: Charles Scribner's Sons, 1942–44), 3:92–102.

and for the lives of his soldiers. Finally, the partisans frequently overlook the fact that there was more involved for the Confederates than simply getting on the heights. There was also the question of whether they would be able to stay if the Federals were to mount a prompt effort to drive them off.

With the foregoing considerations in mind, one may pursue the question of whether Ewell made a rational decision. This is a matter of the evidence with respect to four factors: the nature of the terrain, the Federal forces opposed, the manpower available to Ewell, and the orders given to Ewell by Lee.

The terrain confronting Ewell may be seen today looking up from the area of the Culp House and the low ground immediately to the west of that house. The heights are precipitous, irregular, and complex, marked by hollows and ravines. An attacking force would have been advancing uphill against defenders with ample places from which to effect an ambush.

In considering the Federal forces opposed—and the troops Ewell could have used—the identification of precise times of day is an impossible task. Any discussion of the issue is limited by inability to state exactly when either Federal or Confederate units were available. Nevertheless, Federals to oppose an attack were on the heights or very close by during the general time period in which Ewell was considering the question:

1. One brigade of Adolph von Steinwehr's division and Michael Wiedrich's battery had been on Cemetery Hill since the arrival of the Eleventh Corps.
2. The remnant of the Iron Brigade, approximately seven hundred men, had been sent from Cemetery to Culp's Hill and was entrenching there in a strong position.
3. The 7th Indiana of Lysander Cutler's brigade, five hundred rifles, which had not been engaged, had arrived and had been sent to Culp's Hill with the members of that brigade who had come through the day's fighting.
4. The remaining effectives from the First Corps and Eleventh Corps, "basically intact" according to Harry W. Pfanz, were present. There were skirmishers in the town at the base of Cemetery Hill.

5. The Federals had a total of forty guns and ample ammunition on the heights.
6. Henry W. Slocum's Twelfth Corps was close by, approximately one mile from the scene. John W. Geary's division was on the Federal left by approximately 5:00 P.M.; the first division was on the Federal right at about the same time.[41]

Confederate perceptions of this opposition are illuminating. In his 1863 report, Rodes stated that before "the completion of his defeat before the town, the enemy had begun to establish a line of battle on the heights back of the town, and by the time my line was in a condition to renew the attack, he displayed quite a formidable line of infantry and artillery immediately in my front, extending smartly to my right, and as far as I could see to my left, in front of Early." Ewell's 1863 report was similar: "The enemy had fallen back to a commanding position known as Cemetery Hill . . . and quickly showed a formidable front there. . . . I could not bring artillery to bear on it."[42] There were, in short, substantial forces opposed to Ewell, infantry and artillery, placed on imposing terrain.

With regard to the manpower available for the attack, each of the Confederate corps on hand was missing a division. In the case of Ewell, Edward "Allegheny" Johnson's division was not present. It arrived at a late hour. From Hill's corps, Anderson's division did not come up until after the day closed. Lee's detailed report describes the four divisions that had participated in the July 1 fight as "already weakened and exhausted by a long and bloody struggle." Hill reported that his two divisions were "exhausted by some six hours hard fighting [and that] prudence led me to be content with what had been gained, and not push forward troops exhausted and necessarily disordered, probably to encounter fresh troops of the enemy." Ewell's report similarly noted that "all the troops with me were jaded by twelve hours' marching and fighting."[43] And the Confederate reports uniformly state that the Southern units had lost formation at the conclusion of the movement that drove

---

[41] *OR*, vol. 27, pt. 1:721, 277, 283, 704, 758–59, 777, 825; Harry W. Pfanz, *Gettysburg—The Second Day* (Chapel Hill: Univ. of North Carolina Press, 1987), 38–39.

[42] *OR*, vol. 27, pt. 2:555, 445.

[43] Ibid., 470, 607, 445.

the Federals from Seminary Ridge. Ewell's task was not simply to continue an organized assault that was ongoing. He would have been required to marshal forces and undertake a new movement against the heights.

Douglas Southall Freeman, Lee's great advocate, is always anxious to rationalize Lee's failures at the expense of his lieutenants. In *Lee's Lieutenants,* he criticizes Ewell for not mooting Confederate problems on the first day by taking the heights. He describes in detail Ewell's communications at this hour and his efforts to organize the forces with which to attack. Having recounted Lee's advising Ewell that none of Hill's troops were available on Ewell's right, Freeman states: "All of this meant that if Cemetery Hill was to be taken, Ewell must do it with his own men." Noting then that Early had detached two brigades under John B. Gordon to operate on Ewell's left, Freeman says: "Still again, the force with which Ewell could attack immediately was small. . . . Two Brigades of Early, then, and the tired survivors of Rodes's confused charges—these were all Ewell had for the attack till Johnson arrived. Nor would this force . . . have any support from the right."[44] Even Freeman concedes that Ewell did not have significant numbers for the attack.

Finally, what were Ewell's orders? Lee's detailed report identifies them and also their logic:

> It was ascertained . . . that the remainder of that army [the Federal army] . . . was approaching Gettysburg. Without information as to its proximity, the strong position which the enemy had assumed could not be attacked without danger of exposing the four divisions present, already weakened and exhausted by a long and bloody struggle, to an overwhelming number of fresh troops. General Ewell was, therefore, instructed to carry the hill occupied by the enemy, if he found it practicable, but to avoid a general engagement until the arrival of the other divisions of the army. . . . He decided to await Johnson's division, which . . . did not reach Gettysburg until a late hour.[45]

In *Lee's Lieutenants,* Freeman covers this issue in a chapter titled "Ewell Cannot Reach a Decision."[46] Surely this is nonsense. Pursuant to

---

[44]Freeman, *Lee's Lieutenants,* 3:97–98.
[45]*OR,* vol. 27, pt. 2:317–18.
[46]Freeman, *Lee's Lieutenants,* 3:90–105.

Lee's order, Ewell decided that it was not "practicable" to attack. Lee was on Seminary Ridge and available. The plain fact is that he did not issue a peremptory order to Ewell for the reasons he states in his report: the Federal army was approaching, but its proximity was unknown; the "strong position" of the enemy; the worn condition of the Confederate forces available; the risk of the presence of overwhelming and fresh Federal troops; and the desire to avoid a general engagement.

It is unhistoric to conclude that Ewell was necessarily wrong in his judgment. His decision was reasonable in the circumstances, and that responds to the only historically appropriate question concerning Ewell's conduct.

One can only conclude that Lee's movement across the Potomac was a grave strategic error. In addition, in reference to the first day of the battle, there were significant command failures on Lee's part that were destructive to the Confederate chances of victory at Gettysburg.

The Railroad Cut
at Gettysburg

The great story of Gettysburg is well known to Civil War readers. That great story is made up of a number of "little stories," particular incidents that were unusually dramatic. A few of the particular, dramatic incidents were also decisive in terms of the outcome of the battle. One of these was the successful assault on the railroad cut by the Sixth Wisconsin Volunteers and the Iron Brigade Guard on the first day of the battle.

It is fair to say that this early action at the railroad cut preserved the First Corps' line along McPherson's Ridge at the outset of the three-day battle. The preservation of that line set up the rest of the fighting on the first day. Although defeated on that day, the First and Eleventh Corps punished the Confederates severely and delayed them so that the high ground south of the town was saved for the Union. It was from this high ground that the Federal army decisively defeated the Army of Northern Virginia on the second two days of the battle. Had the First Corps been driven from McPherson's Ridge on the morning of July 1, 1863, the events that afternoon and on July 2 and July 3 would surely have taken a different course, a course destructive to the Federals.

The early action at the railroad cut is therefore entitled to an in-depth description. Lance J. Herdegen and William J. K. Beaudot have carefully examined this action. Having researched the event with a depth and scope that is truly remarkable, and that includes the observations of a number of participants, they have put the story together in a detailed, fast-moving account. Excellently written, the book also tells us a great deal about what the Civil War was really like. It is a valuable contribution to our knowledge of Gettysburg and our understanding of the war as a whole.

III

The Iron Brigade

Virginia's Unwelcome Visitors

In the late summer of 1862, as is the case today, a good road ran in a generally north-easterly direction between Warrenton and Centreville. Known in 1862 as the Warrenton Turnpike, the road passed through New Baltimore, Buckland Mills, Gainesville, and Groveton. Continuing to the east, it ran past the Henry House Hill and crossed Bull Run at the Stone Bridge before it reached Centreville. South of this turnpike, running roughly parallel to it, were the tracks of the Orange and Alexandria Railroad. At Manassas Junction, almost due south of the Stone Bridge over Bull Run, the Orange and Alexandria Railroad joined the Manassas Gap Railroad, which then extended to the west, and passed through Thoroughfare Gap in the Bull Run Mountains. The countryside thereabouts is rolling with occasional ridges. In 1862, it was marked by patches of woods and marginal farms. One of these small farms, along the north side of the Warrenton Turnpike between Gainesville and Groveton, belonged to a man named John C. Brawner.

At the level of the turnpike, Brawner's farm presented an open field and a small woods. The woods occupied the eastern edge of the property along the turnpike. The open ground and the wooded ground ran north from the turnpike and rose gradually to a slight ridge, the crest of which was perhaps a quarter of a mile from the turnpike. Along the crest, west of the woods, were the Brawner farmhouse, a barn, and a small orchard.

North of the crest on which the Brawner buildings rested the Brawner property was unwooded, another open field. At the northern edge of this field, about a quarter of a mile north of the farm buildings, the ground rose again to the line of a second ridge and became densely wooded. Just inside this wooded area was an abandoned railroad embankment extending east and west, more or less parallel with the turnpike. This wooded ridge was known as Stony Ridge.

A distinguished Confederate general officer later characterized the Brawner Farm as simply "a farmhouse, an orchard, a few stacks of hay, and a rotten 'worm' fence." But, as the result of another of history's haunting coincidences, in August of 1862 this unprepossessing and unlikely place became intimately involved with the larger affairs of men.

The logistical situation in the Virginia theatre of the war was unusually complex during the late summer of 1862. Three armies, two Northern and one Southern, were on the move. One Federal army, John Pope's Army of Virginia, had been maneuvering in northern Virginia along the Rappahannock. General George B. McClellan's Army of the Potomac, having been withdrawn from its unsuccessful campaign on the Peninsula before Richmond, was en route to join Pope to the north. General Robert E. Lee's Army of Northern Virginia, no longer required to defend Richmond against McClellan's army, was moving north to attack Pope before McClellan's army could join him. As of August 20, Pope's Federals, in the process of being augmented by some of McClellan's divisions, occupied a line between Sulphur Springs and Kelly's Ford on the north bank of the Rappahannock. Lee's two army corps, Jackson's and Longstreet's, were on the south side of the river confronting the Federals. Having jockeyed for several days for a crossing of the river in front of the Federals, Lee decided on a new strategem.

On August 25, Jackson left the Confederate positions along the Rappahannock and marched rapidly west and north around the Federal army's right, passing through Amissville, Orlean, Salem, and Thoroughfare Gap en route to the rear of John Pope's army. On the night of August 26, Jackson's Corps descended on the Federal supply depot at Manassas Junction and destroyed the massive Federal stores there. But Jackson's maneuver was perilous. Separated from Longstreet's Corps, he was vulnerable. He had to avoid a confrontation with the Federal divisions until Longstreet's Corps could rejoin Jackson's. In order to protect himself from this vulnerability, Jackson sought a place to hide his approximately 25,000 soldiers until Longstreet could come up.

The Federal commanders were of course sensitive to Jackson's situation, and their strategy was precisely the opposite of the Confederates. They set out to find Jackson's Corps with the intention of attacking him before Longstreet could join him. Marked by command confusion and faulty reconnaissance, the Federal search for Jackson was inept. One of the Federal divisions in the search was King's Division of General McDowell's Third Army Corps, composed of four brigades, the first three of which were commanded, respectively, by Generals Hatch, Doubleday, and Patrick. The Fourth Brigade of the division was led by West Pointer John Gibbon of the regular army, a North Carolinian who had stayed with "the old flag," although he had three brothers in the Confederate Army.

Gibbon's Brigade was unusual in several ways. Brigaded on October 1, 1861, composed of the Nineteenth Indiana Volunteers and three Wisconsin regiments—the Second, Sixth, and Seventh—it was the only all-Western brigade in the Eastern armies of the Union. When appointed to command the brigade in May 1862, Gibbon had ordered new uniforms for his Western men. Most of the Federal soldiers were clad in the conventional uniform, a short dark blue sack coat, light blue trousers, and a dark blue kepi. Gibbon outfitted his Westerners in the dress uniform of the regular army: a dark blue single-breasted frock coat with light blue collar and cuff trim, reaching almost to the knees, light blue trousers and, most distinctive, the high crowned black felt Hardee hat, festooned with a black plume, its broad brim turned up on one side. White leggings, not worn by the regular army, were added to the outfit. Gibbon's soldiers wore the uniform all the time, for dress as well as fatigue.

An historic regular artillery unit, Battery B of the Fourth U.S. Artillery, was attached to Gibbon's Brigade. Armed with six brass smoothbore Napoleons, the battery had been commanded by Gibbon himself before his promotion to command of the infantry brigade. Although the battery was manned by a core of pre-war regulars, it had been understrength and had been heavily augmented by the detachment of volunteer infantry soldiers from the regiments of the division, including a number of Hoosiers and Badgers from the infantry regiments that Gibbon commanded on his promotion to brigade command.

Except for the Second Wisconsin Volunteers, Gibbon's Western soldiers were essentially untried in battle. The Second Wisconsin had fought at Bull Run in July 1861, but the other Wisconsin regiments and the Hoosiers of the Nineteenth Indiana had not been seriously engaged because King's Division had been withheld from McClellan's Peninsula Campaign.

On August 27, 1862, as Pope searched for Jackson, Gibbon's regiments marched with their division for Warrenton. On the night of the 27th, they camped along the Warrenton Turnpike near New Baltimore, west of Gainesville and the Brawner Farm. The next day, the 28th, they continued eastward on the pike, passing through Gainesville. Just beyond Gainesville, King's Division was ordered to leave the turnpike and to march on a country road to the southeast, toward Manassas Junction.

Shortly after beginning this movement, the soldiers were halted during the afternoon as Pope, realizing that Jackson was not at Manassas, reconsidered the concentration of Federal forces. In the late afternoon Pope decided that Jackson was at Centreville, eight miles east of Gainesville on the Warrenton Turnpike. King's Division was ordered to march at once for Centreville.

Returning to the turnpike, the division started east for Centreville. It was late afternoon, approximately 5 P.M., and the sun was beginning to set. Because of the confused marching and counter-marching of the Federal divisions, King was now beyond easy supporting distance of the other Federal forces. Ahead of Gibbon's untried Western soldiers was the Brawner Farm; just above the farm loomed Stony Ridge.

Wholly unknown to the Federals, Stony Ridge was the hiding place of Stonewall Jackson's Corps, 25,000 Confederate soldiers "packed like herring in a barrel," according to one of them. The naturally aggressive Jackson had personally observed the Federal traffic on the turnpike while hiding. There had already been slight skirmishing between his pickets and various Federal units on the turnpike. Jackson had seen King's Division leave the pike beyond Gainesville, when it was ordered to the southeast toward Manassas Junction. Now he saw the same Federals reappear on the turnpike and start east for Centreville. The apparently isolated division was to march across his front, past the Brawner Farm. At about the same time, Jackson heard from Lee. Longstreet had reached Thoroughfare Gap, was expected to force it and was within supporting distance. Jackson immediately disposed his troops to attack.

Hatch's Brigade, the leader of King's column, reconnoitered the Brawner Farm area ahead of Gibbon. A regiment of Hatch's infantry skirmished north of the turnpike, and his artillery shelled the woods to the north and east. The skirmishers exposed several mounted Confederates east of the Brawner Farm, toward Groveton, but these horsemen promptly withdrew and no alarm was felt. Hatch's Brigade marched on and passed out of sight over the hills to the east. Gibbon then put his column in motion, and behind Gibbon's Brigade the brigades of Doubleday and Patrick moved out. Since there was no expectation of battle, convenient marching intervals were established between the brigades. Gibbon's soldiers marched in column of fours, with arms at will, the Sixth Wisconsin in the lead, followed in order by the Second Wisconsin, Seventh Wisconsin and the Nineteenth Indiana. Battery B brought up the rear. According to one of the Federal officers, the Federals marched along "as unsuspectingly as if changing camps."

Gibbon's soldiers heard artillery as Hatch's artillery, ahead of them and out of sight, exchanged fire with distant Confederate guns. Suddenly, as the head of Gibbon's column emerged from the cover of the woods at the eastern edge of the Brawner property, a Confederate battery fired on it from a position north of the farm. Another battery, firing from the north and west of the farm, promptly opened on Doubleday's and Patrick's soldiers to the rear of Gibbon's men. Believing that the enemy guns were unsupported horse artillery, Gibbon ordered Battery B to the head of his column to respond to the eastern battery and directed the Second Wisconsin, his combat veterans, to silence the battery firing toward his rear.

Battery B drove rapidly up the turnpike, unlimbered and went into position on a knoll east of the Brawner woods and just north of the turnpike. As the Federal gunners commenced firing, the Second Wisconsin moved through the woods. Having formed in line of battle in the open field near the Brawner farm house and barn, they started forward. As they approached the crest of the ridge, the unsuspecting Federals were suddenly fired on from their right flank by skirmishers from Starke's Brigade of General William B. Taliaferro's Stonewall Division. In spite of their surprise, the Wisconsin men did not falter. Wheeling to their right, they returned Starke's fire. The flank companies of the Wisconsin regiment were sent forward as skirmishers, and Starke's men withdrew over the crest of the ridge, followed by the Wisconsin skirmishers. Within a few yards, the Federal skirmishers confronted a larger group of Confederates posted in a small grove of trees. Shots were exchanged as the other Wisconsin companies, moving with their skirmish line, reached the crest of the ridge. Looking north from the crest, the Western men at last knew the truth: thousands of Confederate infantry were filing out of wooded Stony Ridge and advancing toward the Brawner property. At once Baylor's Stonewall Brigade, also of Taliaferro's Division, opened fire on the Second Wisconsin. Rejoined by its skirmishers, the embattled Second Wisconsin returned this fire and held its ground.

At last aware of the force of the Confederate assault, having dispatched calls for help to division commander King and to the brigades of Doubleday and Patrick, Gibbon sent the Nineteenth Indiana to form on the left of Second Wisconsin, extending his line toward the Brawner farm buildings. The Seventh Wisconsin went in to the right of the Second. Gibbon committed the Sixth Wisconsin to the right of the Seventh, to a position in a field east of the Brawner woods. The ground there was lower than that in the woods and than the Brawner ridge. The men of the Sixth Wisconsin looked up to their left, to the higher ground, where their Western comrades were fighting. Behind the Sixth, the guns of Battery B were at work.

The battle was now joined. Gibbon's line was just south of the crest of the Brawner ridge. From left to right, it followed the ridge line, passed along the edge of the woods and extended into the field east of the woods. There was a large gap in the line between the positions of the Seventh and Sixth Wisconsin. Having driven off the Confederate battery that had begun the affair, Battery B now moved to a new position so that it could fire into this gap. Both of Gibbon's flanks were in the air and were overlapped by the larger Confederate forces, even before Confederate reserves entered the battle.

In addition to Starke's Brigade, the Confederate skirmishers that had surprised the Second Wisconsin, and to Baylor's Stonewall Brigade, Jackson now committed the brigade of Colonel A. G. Taliaferro from the same division. He also sent in the brigades of Generals Isaac R. Trimble and Alexander R. Lawton, from General Richard S. Ewell's Division, and additional artillery. Other Confederate brigades were ordered up but did not become seriously engaged. Although not ordered to do so, Doubleday finally sent the 76th New York and the 56th Pennsylvania from his brigade into the gap between the Seventh and Sixth Wisconsin. His remaining regiment, the 95th New York, moved to the support of Battery B. Battery D of the 1st Rhode Island Light Artillery of Doubleday's Brigade also joined the battle.

As is well known, precise numbers of opposing forces during the Civil War are difficult to establish because of the state of the reports. Of his superior numbers available, Jackson committed between 5,900 and 6,400 infantry. Even after reinforcement by Doubleday's regiments in the gap, Gibbon was able to field between 2,500 and 2,900 infantry. The two sides were relatively even in artillery engaged.

Because of the lateness of its onset and the rapidly descending darkness, the fight at Brawner Farm was *short.* From the first Confederate artillery fire to the last desultory infantry fire, it lasted for approximately three hours, perhaps two of which were intense. But it was far from *sweet.* According to General Taliaferro, "It was a stand-up combat, dogged and unflinching, in a field almost bare. There were no wounds from spent balls; the confronting lines looked into each other's faces at deadly range, less than one hundred yards apart, and they stood as immovable as the painted heroes in a battle-piece." There were some minor advances and retrograde movements by both lines, but essentially, the opposing forces simply planted themselves and blazed away. The Confederates held the farm house at the northern edge of the orchard; their line then extended opposite the Brawner Woods and into the low ground in the field east of the woods. The Federals clung to the farmyard, the southern edge of the orchard and the northern face of the woods, extending their line into the same low ground. Gibbon, who was to fight in many more battles, later said that it was "the most terrific musketry fire I . . . ever listened to." General William B. Taliaferro reported it as "one of the most terrific conflicts that can be conceived of." General Trimble's report stated that, "I have never known so terrible a fire as raged . . . on both sides." And Doubleday wrote that, "There have been few more unequal contests or better contested fields during the war." Perhaps General William B. Taliaferro provided the best summary description of the engagement at Brawner Farm. After the war, referring to the Federal as well as Confederate participants, he wrote: "Out in the sunlight, in the dying daylight, and under the stars, they stood, and although they could not advance, they would not retire. There was some discipline in this, but there was much more of true valor."

And of course, this kind of fighting exacted a fearful toll. Thirty-seven percent of Gibbon's Western men were casualties, including three of four regimental commanders, the lieutenant colonel of the Seventh Wisconsin, and the majors of three of the four regiments. Doubleday's regiments also lost heavily. On the Confederate side, the total losses exceeded those of the Federals, and the Federal rifles accounted for division commanders

William B. Taliaferro and Richard S. Ewell. Nine regimental commanders, including three in the Stonewall Brigade, were killed or wounded. Douglas Southall Freeman has written that the battle was one of Jackson's costliest in proportion to the numbers engaged.

Darkness and the tacit consent of the opposing commanders terminated the engagement. The surviving Federals returned to the turnpike and ultimately made a painful night march to Manassas. Jackson's men returned to their lair on Stony Ridge and the unfinished railroad embankment. Reporting that the Federal numbers were "greatly superior," General William B. Taliaferro reported that the Federals "withstood with great determination the terrible fire which our lines poured upon them." Stonewall Jackson struck a similar note, writing that the Federals "maintained their ground with obstinate determination."

And so the first fight was over for the "black-hatted fellows," as the Confederate prisoners of the battle called Gibbon's soldiers that night. Stonewall Jackson's admiring biographer, the Englishman G. F. R. Henderson, was later to write of Brawner Farm on August 28, 1862: "The men who faced each other that August evening fought with a gallantry that has seldom been surpassed. . . . The Federals, surprised and unsupported, bore away the honors. The Western Brigade, commanded by General Gibbon, displayed a coolness and steadfastness worthy of the soldiers of Albuera."

The fight at Brawner Farm was in fact the prophetic beginning of a storied career for the soldiers from the Old Northwest and for Battery B. They were engaged again on the following two days in the decisive Confederate victory at Second Bull Run, larger battles that have tended to obscure the fight on the Brawner Farm on August 28. Following Lee into Maryland, they fought a spectacular fight on September 14 at South Mountain, where the name "Black Hat Brigade" was changed to a new sobriquet, the "Iron Brigade," the name that they have carried into history. The famous and bloody cornfield on the Federal right, near Antietam's Dunker Church, was their next struggle. After Antietam, they were reinforced by the newly-raised Twenty-fourth Michigan Volunteers, thus maintaining their regional integrity. Because the Michigan men also turned out to be unusual fighters, the brigade also retained its iron reputation. Back in Virginia, the brigade fought in the Federal debacles at Fredericksburg and Chancellorsville.

And then there was Gettysburg in July 1863. As the First Brigade of the First Division of the First Corps—a designation that was simply a co-incidence of the Federal army's structure, but which the Western men naively claimed as an honor they had earned—the brigade fought on the first day west of the town, at McPherson's Woods along the Cashtown Pike and ultimately in the defense of Seminary Ridge. The Federals were outnumbered on that first day. It was the First Corps' dogged and des-perate fighting west of the town on that day that permitted Federal pos-session of the key ground—Cemetery Ridge, Culp's Hill and Little Round Top—and bought the time for the Army of the Potomac to con-centrate its superior strength. Surely these were the factors—superior numbers and position—that ultimately made the victory, and they were possible because of the soaring Federal effort on the first day. For the Iron Brigade, the cost of this effort was prohibitive. The Twenty-fourth Michigan, the newcomers, had casualties of 80 percent, the highest total loss of any Federal regiment for the three days of Gettysburg. The Iron Brigade led the casualty list for the entire army.

Reduced to 600 men, the brigade was reinforced after Gettysburg with various Eastern regiments and forever lost its Western identity, but the remnants of the Western regiments were nevertheless on hand for the final Virginia campaign. Beginning with the Wilderness in May 1864, a long list of equally haunting Virginia names was added to their battle honors and further reduced the regiments: Laurel Hill, Spottsylvania, the North Anna, Cold Harbor, Petersburg, Globe Tavern, Boydton Plank Road, Weldon Railroad, Hatcher's Run, and Five Forks. Along the way, part of the Second Wisconsin was mustered out and the remainder of that regiment merged with the Sixth Wisconsin. The Nineteenth Indiana was consolidated with the Twentieth Indiana, with the Twentieth as the survivor. The Twenty-fourth Michigan was withdrawn from the field in February 1865. In the stillness at Appomattox, only the Sixth Wisconsin and Seventh Wisconsin, and Battery B, were present in name, but the Sixth included veterans of the Second Wisconsin, and the veterans of the Nineteenth Indiana were on hand disguised as members of the Twentieth Indiana Volunteers.

In his landmark study *Regimental Losses in the American Civil War,* Colonel William F. Fox found that more men fell at the guns of Battery B of the Fourth U.S. Artillery, the Iron Brigade's kinsmen, than in any other field artillery battery in the Federal service. With respect to men

killed and mortally wounded in the regiments of the Iron Brigade, Fox
states: "In proportion to its numbers, this brigade sustained the heaviest
loss of any in the war." Significantly, the Second Wisconsin was *first* in
combat fatalities on the regimental list, and the Seventh Wisconsin was
sixth, for the entire Federal army. The Nineteenth Indiana ranked
eleventh. These statistics become meaningful when one adverts to a conclusion that Fox drew from his research: "A study of regimental actions
shows clearly that the battalions which faced musketry the steadiest,
longest and oftenest were the ones whose aggregate loss during the war
was the greatest."

It is Colonel Fox's conclusion that has led contemporary professional historians to state their opinions of the brigade. The eminent Virginia historian James I. Robertson, Jr., has stated that although the
North had a number of outstanding brigades, "by far the most famous
of them all was the Iron Brigade." And T. Harry Williams of Louisiana
State wrote that "It was probably the best fighting brigade in the army."

This, then, was the Iron Brigade, a distinguished but unwanted vis-
itor to Virginia during the Civil War.

How does one account for the superiority of the Iron Brigade? What
made these Western soldiers so headlong and courageous? Why
did they "face musketry the steadiest"? These are appropriate questions
for anyone interested in military history.

I suggest that Brawner Farm was a critical moment, more specifically
when the Second Wisconsin was surprised on both flanks and outnumbered at the outset of that engagement and stood its ground. There are
indications in the diaries and letters of the soldiers that the men of the
Second Wisconsin, the only combat veterans in the brigade, had boasted
of their prowess as veterans. With their Western companions close by,
the soldiers of the veteran regiment may have felt compelled to give a
good account of themselves. The Second's bragging may also have created an unconscious motivation in the other regiments of the brigade to
do as well as the Second when their time came. A later example of this
phenomenon took place at Fredericksburg in December 1862, when the
Twenty-fourth Michigan, newly assigned to the brigade, was first under
fire. By that time, of course, the Wisconsin and Indiana soldiers were
seasoned veterans. They had earned the title of Iron Brigade, and the
Michigan men were simply beneficiaries of that title. As the Iron Brigade

maneuvered to cross the river, a shell landed near the Twenty-fourth. Colonel Henry A. Morrow, the Virginia-born colonel of the Michigan regiment, enjoined his soldiers with, "Steady, men, those Wisconsin men are watching you." And the Michigan men *were* steady. In any event, I believe that the reaction of the Second at Brawner Farm and the reaction then of the other three regiments and Battery B established the basis for a tradition. But that reaction, and the brigade's ability to live up to the tradition, were not coincidences. *Something* caused the reaction and permitted the tradition. What was that something?

It was not, I suggest, some innate superiority of these soldiers, because they were from Indiana, Wisconsin, and Michigan. Perhaps because we today subconsciously regret the homogeneity of our society and the corresponding decline of state and regional identity, modern Americans tend to think of it in mythic terms. But the Iron Brigade cannot be fully explained this way. On both sides, the war was largely fought by the plain people, the ordinary men who left ordinary pursuits to be, for a time, soldiers. The truth is that in terms of their demographics and sociology, the soldiers of the Iron Brigade could not even claim deep roots in the states in which they enlisted. Two men reached the permanent rank of colonel in the Nineteenth Indiana, Solomon Meredith and Samuel J. Williams. Meredith was a native of North Carolina, and Williams was from Montgomery County, Virginia. They were newcomers to Indiana. A look at the 43 men who became officers of field grade—colonel, lieutenant colonel, major—in the five regiments of the brigade further demonstrates this phenomenon. Of those whose origins are traceable at all, three were natives of Virginia; two were North Carolinians; nine were born in New York State, and five were from Ohio. New England and Pennsylvania were the birthplaces of six more of these officers, and five were born abroad, in Ireland, England, Canada, Switzerland, and Hungary. The most distinguished commander of Battery B was also foreign-born. The men of the brigade, officers and enlisted men, were in fact of the Northern patchwork, an area of great mobility: some native-born, some not; some Northern-born, some not; some farmers, some not. Surely they were more rural and frontier than the Eastern regiments, but there is nothing to suggest that this created a critical difference between them.

It seems to me that three elements account for the superiority of these soldiers; leadership, training, and *esprit de corps*.

With respect to *leadership,* and first considering leadership at the regimental level, one may again look at the 43 field officers. Of those whose pre-war biographies are available, 30 had uprooted themselves from their places of origin, in the United States or abroad, and moved to the frontier. Almost a fourth had been elected to public office in their new Indiana, Wisconsin, and Michigan communities, evidence before the days of media control of the political process that they had the respect and confidence of their contemporaries. Almost all of them, although relatively young, had made career changes. Four had traveled to California. They were, in short, energetic men, restless and seeking, men who were accustomed to social and physical risk and to self-reliance. Most of them could boast that they had been acknowledged as leaders by their civilian contemporaries, and they had asserted this leadership by raising volunteers for their regiments when the war came.

At the brigade level, there was an even more obvious relative advantage. The first commander of the brigade was Rufus King, a West Pointer who, before moving to Wisconsin, had been adjutant general of New York when William H. Seward was Governor. King did not distinguish himself as a general officer, but he commanded the brigade for seven months before it was in combat, and the diaries and letters of the soldiers suggest that he was effective during the organizational period. King went on to division command before leaving the army in 1863. He was succeeded by John Gibbon. In Gibbon, the brigade had a great commander. In effect the architect of the Iron Brigade, Gibbon proceeded from command of Battery B to command of the Iron Brigade and then on to division and corps command.

Gibbon was everything a Civil War commander should have been. A regular from "the Point," he was "spit and polish" but intelligent, wise, and humane enough to know how to train and lead civilians in a democratic army and to avoid the rigidity and brutality characteristic of the regular army. He relied on incentives, pride, and psychological insight in pre-Freudian times. He recognized the brigade's regionalism and state pride and had the good sense to dress his soldiers distinctively. His professional background, which included service in the Mexican War and a keen knowledge of the uses of artillery, were a significant plus. He was, finally, a man of high physical courage; the soldiers invariably commented on this and sought to emulate his example.

Gibbon led the brigade at Brawner Farm, Second Bull Run, South Mountain, and Antietam, the period in which its proud name was acquired. When he was promoted on November 4, 1862, Solomon Meredith of the Nineteenth Indiana Volunteers became the brigade commander, a position he occupied until he was wounded on the first day of Gettysburg, the day on which the organizational integrity of the brigade was destroyed by casualties. Meredith's promotion gave the brigade its second successive commander from North Carolina. A pre-war Indiana politician, Meredith was not in Gibbon's league as a soldier, but the conduct of the brigade under his leadership was exceptional. The soldiers' letters and diaries are warmly admiring of Meredith. From Gettysburg to Appomattox, the brigades that included the remnants of the Western regiments were invariably commanded by men who had distinguished themselves as field officers of these regiments. It is plain that the Western men were unusually well-led and that this was a critical factor in their performance.

As has been said, the brigade was organized on October 1, 1861, and not seriously engaged until Brawner Farm. Thus they had the relative luxury of eleven months of *training*, and an opportunity to develop organizationally at both the regimental and brigade levels. This training was especially intense after Gibbon took over. A professional, he was a great believer in training. The diaries and letters of the men are replete with accounts of Gibbon's regime. One soldier wrote: "There were early morning drills, before breakfast, forenoon drills, afternoon drills, evening and night drills, beside guard mounting and dress parade." And the drills were supplemented by more practical soldiering. During July 1862 elements of the brigade participated under Gibbon's command in a hard reconnaissance in force from Fredericksburg toward Orange Court House. On August 5, the entire brigade embarked on the Frederick's Hall Raid. Starting at Fredericksburg, for three days the brigade carried out a complicated and difficult raid on Confederate communications south of that city.

The conduct of soldiers is in many respects a matter of *reflex;* psychologists tell us that when threatened, the human animal will fight or flee. In war, the likelihood of his fighting—making an organized and systematic response—is a matter of training, what is customarily called military discipline. At the crest of the Brawner ridge, the Second Wisconsin

Volunteers and the other regiments did what had become natural—respond to commands, retain a sense of organizational integrity, and effectively use the by then familiar weapons. This was what months of training produced. One may compare it with the fighting at Shiloh in April 1862, where most of the regiments on both sides had been recently raised. The soldiers on both sides fought almost like individuals, advancing and retreating at will.

Regarding *esprit de corps,* the regionalism and distinctive uniform deserve reemphasis. Even today, when it is only a few hours from coast to coast and in spite of homogeneity, we tend to think of ourselves as Hoosiers or Virginians. We also have a regional sense. In his book *The Old Northwest,* R. Carlyle Buley argues that the Middle West historically had a sense of identity, partly because of a cultural paranoia about New England and the East Coast. Surely that regional sense existed in the nineteenth century and was intensified by the sectional nature of the Civil War.

Gibbon shrewdly seized on this as a means of developing an *esprit de corps* in his civilian soldiers. He insisted that his Indiana, Wisconsin, and Michigan men think of themselves as "Westerners" and therefore distinctive. It was not a manufactured point. The brigade *was* the only all-Western one in the East; as a whole, there were relatively few Western regiments in the Eastern armies of the Union. Indiana, for example, raised during the war 150 regiments of infantry, most of them for a three-year enlistment, and only five of these, including the Nineteenth, were in the Army of the Potomac. Because of the success of his identity tactic, in seeking an additional regiment for the brigade in 1862, after the casualties of August and September, Gibbon specified that he wanted the next *Western* regiment assigned to the Army of the Potomac. His efforts resulted in the addition of the Twenty-fourth Michigan. And he uniformed the Westerners distinctively to mark them as unusual and not to allow themselves to overlook their distinctiveness. What better way could there be to act out this identity and sense of regional integrity than by showing the New Yorkers and Pennsylvanians and, of course, the Rebels, how to fight?

The raw material was good, but not uniquely so—it was interchangeable with that of many brigades, both Northern and Southern. But unusual leadership, the coincidental fact of the opportunity to be trained as soldiers, and *esprit de corps* made the Iron Brigade what it was—the best fighting brigade in the Federal armies.

Rufus Dawes' Service with the Sixth Wisconsin Volunteers

S *ervice With The Sixth Wisconsin Volunteers* was originally published in
1890 by E. R. Alderman & Sons of Marietta, Ohio.[1] Long classified
as rare and prized as a collector's item, the book is a combination of the
personal experiences of Rufus R. Dawes and a history of the regiment of
which he was a member. In the vast literature of the American Civil War,
it has long been recognized as exceptional. Its excellence is the product
of three factors: the character and abilities of the author; the historical
techniques and materials which he used; and the events in which he and
his regiment participated. These factors—author, technique and events—
combine to make the book a superb document of its kind. It is appropriate for an editor's foreword briefly to discuss each of these factors.

A lthough principally identified with Wisconsin Civil War history,
Rufus R. Dawes was an Ohioan. One of the six children of Henry
and Sarah Cutler Dawes, he was born at Malta in Morgan County, Ohio,
in 1838. Appropriately enough, his birthday was on Independence Day,
but his relationship to the American story was not only symbolic. His
great-grandfather was William Dawes, Jr., Paul Revere's companion on
the eve of Lexington and Concord, and his mother's family, too, was
rooted in American history. She was the granddaughter of Dr. Manasseh
Cutler, the great Massachusetts clergyman and patriot of the Revolutionary War and the early years of the republic.

Rufus Dawes spent his youth in Constitution, Ohio, near Marietta,
and in Malta. But when the time came for college, he went to Wisconsin

---

[1]In 1937, a limited reprint of the book was issued, containing additional il-
lustrations. The instant edition is a republication of the original 1890 edition.

and entered the University of Wisconsin at Madison. After two years there, he returned to Ohio, to Marietta College, where he graduated in the Class of 1860.

In April 1861, at the time of Sumter, Rufus and his father were on business in Juneau County, Wisconsin, but the onset of the war turned the youth at once to that more urgent matter. Allying himself with Wisconsin instead of Ohio, on April 25 he undertook to raise a company of volunteers in Juneau County. Less than a week later, one hundred men had enrolled. Taking the name of the "Lemonweir Minute Men," the men elected Dawes as their captain. A few weeks later, the company arrived at Madison and was assigned as Company K of the newly-organized Sixth Wisconsin Volunteers. Dispatched to Washington in July, the regiment was shortly thereafter assigned to the brigade which was later to be called the Iron Brigade. Appointed major of the Sixth Wisconsin on June 30, 1862, and to the lieutenant colonelcy of the regiment during the following year, Dawes ultimately became its colonel on July 5, 1864. Even before the colonelcy, he had frequently acted as the regimental commander of the Sixth and was its commander at Gettysburg. On August 10, 1864, his term of enlistment having expired, he was honorably discharged and returned to Marietta, Ohio. In 1866, he was brevetted a brigadier general of volunteers.

Dawes was seldom absent from the field during his term of service. On one occasion, he accompanied the regiment home on veteran furlough in January 1864. While in Marietta, he married Mary Beman Gates of that community. It was a uniquely happy marriage and six children were born of the union. Continuing the family tradition of public service and renown, one of these children was Charles G. Dawes, Vice-President of the United States during the Coolidge Administration.

After the war, Dawes settled in Marietta and turned his attention to his family and to business pursuits. These were interrupted in 1880 when he was elected as a Republican to Congress, a seat which he lost in the election of 1882. Despite the onset of ill health, he remained a prominent figure in Ohio public affairs and was a strong contender for the Republican gubernatorial nomination in 1889. Following this episode, he was appointed by President McKinley as Minister to Persia, a post he declined because of physical incapacity. But he continued his interests in veterans' affairs, and in the temperance movement and education. In the latter respect, he served as a trustee of the Ohio Institute for the Deaf and Dumb and of Marietta College. Finally confined to a wheelchair, he died at Marietta in 1899.[2]

These are the basic biographical facts. They tell us something of Rufus R. Dawes, but his book tells us much more about him. At the outbreak of the war, he called himself an Abolitionist, still a relatively unpopular cause in 1861, especially in the Middle Western states. He wrote of "our destiny, the entire destruction of slavery," and "the eternal overthrow of a monied aristocracy based on slavery." Thus, in addition to a plain and unquestioning loyalty to the "old flag" and to the Union, Dawes also understood the implications of the war in relation to what he called "the great question of liberty." The book also testifies that its author was a secure and well adjusted man. It is wholly free of the pomposity and self-justification which characterize much autobiographical literature. And he was gentle, too, a characteristic which men do not enough admire but which so often marks the truly masculine spirit. Thus, on the eve of battle, he could write to his young fiancée, "You are mustered into service now and must endure your trials and hardships as a soldier, and I doubt not that they will be harder ... than mine, for you see, you are a raw recruit. . . . If I do anything glorious I shall expect you to be proud of me." Between the lines, too, one finds the qualities of idealism and high-mindedness. There was nothing banal or second-rate about Dawes and when one finishes the book he can accept the author's word about his own feeling for the men under his command: "I ... esteem it an honor, worth a better life than mine, to be permitted to lead them in this glorious struggle."

In the light of his idealism about the war, it is fortunate that Dawes had another attribute, courage, a quiet and determined physical courage. This appears not in any self-conscious way. Indeed he wrote to his fiancée that "I do not want to fight" and noted an occasion behind a tree at Second Bull Run when "I must have shrunk to the dimensions of a wafer." But courage is nevertheless there in the swirling ordeal of the

---

[2]Biographical materials about Dawes and his family are from *A Memoir, Rufus R. Dawes* (New York, 1900), pp. 11–31; Alan T. Nolan, *The Iron Brigade* (New York, 1961), pp. 14, 376; *The National Cyclopedia of American Biography* (New York, 1910), Volume XIV, pp. 527–528. Dawes' commission dates appear in *Annual Report of the Adjutant General, State of Wisconsin* (Madison, 1865), p. 1339. The dates given are dates of the commissions, not issue dates or late muster dates.

combat that he told about. A sense of humor was another of his gifts. In addition to the funny episodes which mark the pages, a humorous strain runs through much of his text. Complaining of the early period of the war and the elaborate equipment provided, Dawes remarked that "with us, ponderosity was military science." One of his musicians was described as a man who had "undertaken to crush the Rebellion with a trombone." And as lieutenant colonel commanding, he wrote of his headquarters in a residence, in Virginia, with "three little astonished looking girls with their fingers in their mouths, hanging around the table watching me as I write." It should be especially marked that he was also able to look at *himself* humorously. Thus, when assembling his book in later years, he could characterize as "youthful vapor" some of his own high flown writings from the time of the war.

To all of Dawes' felicitous attributes of character may be added other qualifications of critical importance to a man writing a book. He was wonderfully observant and sensitive to everything around him. And he was a sophisticated and highly literate man, the product of a classical education which equipped him with narrative skills and permitted him to use the English language with uncommon skill and facility. With quiet irony, he mentioned Lee, "using his great power as a military leader, to destroy the Government he had sworn to defend." Turning to a less serious theme, the same satirical insight tells us of his metal scabbard "that tarnishes in half an hour." And he could sum up his feeling about an officer's expensive dress: "fancy uniforms are useless sleeping in the mud." Beyond the satire are the descriptions of the scenes that he saw. As he wrote about them, we, too, can see the "one hundred thousand miserable and discouraged men . . . wading through this terrible mud and rain" after the Federal disaster at Chancellorsville. And we can see the same men again, "tired, sore, sleepy, hungry, dusty and dirty as pigs" on the march to meet Lee at Gettysburg. With these descriptive skills, and with his other traits of character, Rufus Dawes was peculiarly qualified to write the book he chose to write. The fact that such a man was the author is the first element contributing to the value of the book.

The published memoirs of Civil War military personnel are frequently simply the *recollections* of aging men, written down long after the facts and sometimes marked by antagonisms and special pleadings. Most regimental histories are of similar ingredients. Published principally for the veterans themselves, they are usually composed largely of the reminiscences of the soldiers exchanged at regimental reunions and surely enlarged upon and improved by frequent repetition. Such materials have their flavor and interest, but they are of limited historical value. *Service With The Sixth Wisconsin Volunteers* stands apart from all such works of this kind.

Throughout the period of his service, Dawes kept a journal. He was also a prolific correspondent, writing long and articulate letters to his mother, his sister, and to his fiancée, Miss Gates. After he and Miss Gates were married, she became the principal object of the letters, but their quantity increased and the quality did not diminish. To his wife, Dawes credited the keeping of these materials so that they were available to him when he began his book. They provided a contemporaneous chronicle of events, but he was not content to rely on them alone. He also turned to the *Official Records,* verifying and amplifying his own account by references to the reports of both Federal and Confederate participants.

Dawes' journal and his letters were marked by unusual richness of detail. His searching observation and his fluent pen worked to set down not only the obvious and dramatic, but also the ordinary and routine. Thus, his book provides a source of facts about the soldiers' attitudes and the *minutiae* of their daily lives, in and out of combat. The order of camp life was noted, beginning with reveille, proceeding through roll call, breakfast, police duty, guard mounting, inspection, drill, dress parade, retreat, tattoo, and taps. With both whimsy and truth, the soldiers' ordinary diet was recorded, "hard tack plain, hard tack fried, hard tack soaked, hard tack crumbled and stewed, or hard tack otherwise compounded." When his regiment withdrew at night from the front of a much larger enemy, the soldiers "muffled the rattling tin cups" to avoid discovery. In combat there was "the peculiarly mournful wail of the spent bullet," and when Dawes' commander was shot at his side, "I heard a distinct sound of the blow that struck him. He gave a convulsive start and clapped his hand on his leg, but he controlled his voice." After battle, we learn of the "troubled and dreamy sleep . . . that comes to the soldier on a battle field," and of the dolorous task of those assigned to find the dead and wounded: "Several dying men were pleading piteously for water, of which there was not a drop in the regiment, nor was there any liquor. Captain Kellogg and I searched in vain for a swallow for one noble fellow who was dying in great agony from a wound in his bowels. He recognized us and appreciated our efforts, but was unable to speak. The dread reality of war was before us in this frightful death, upon the cold, hard stones. The mortal suffering, the fruitless struggle to send a parting message to the far-off home, and the final release by death, all enacted in the darkness."

These, of course, are only samples of the recorded observations of the author. The fact that he had his own detailed and contemporaneous accounts before him, and his desire to write objective history as well as his own impressions, represent the second element in the excellence of his book.

O riginally called "The Black Hat Brigade" because its men wore the regular army dress black hats instead of the more typical blue cap, the Iron Brigade was the only all-Western brigade which fought in the Eastern armies of the Union. It was perhaps the most distinguished infantry brigade in the Federal armies. Composed initially of the Second, Sixth, and Seventh Wisconsin Volunteers, and the Nineteenth Indiana Volunteers, the brigade also later included the Twenty-fourth Michigan Volunteers. Battery B of the Fourth U.S. Artillery, composed in large part of infantry men detached from the brigade, was not a part of the brigade but was closely associated with it.

Rufus King, a New Yorker who had moved to Milwaukee before the war, was the first commander of the brigade. He led the Western men until the spring of 1862, at which time the remarkable John Gibbon of North Carolina and West Point assumed command. To Gibbon is ordinarily assigned the credit for the peculiar élan and unique effectiveness of the brigade, characteristics which it maintained after Gibbon's promotion to division command and his replacement by General Solomon Meredith, promoted from the colonelcy of the Nineteenth Indiana.

In view of its ultimate casualty record, it is strange that the Iron Brigade waited so long to become a combat unit. It was organized on October 1, 1861, in camp at Arlington, Virginia. Assigned to the Army of the Potomac's First Corps, the brigade was not seriously engaged until almost a year following its organization. But at last on August 28, 1862, on the eve of the Federal defeat at Second Bull Run, its fighting career began at Brawner Farm. Led by General Gibbon, the Westerners showed their mettle in this vicious engagement, standing up to Stonewall Jackson's much larger Confederate force, in spite of the disadvantage of surprise and 33 percent casualties. From that day until Gettysburg, the Iron Brigade was on hand for every significant Eastern battle, frequently at the vortex of the fighting and uniformly fighting with desperate and telling gallantry. On the first day of Gettysburg, numbered as the *First* Brigade of the *First* Division of the *First* Corps, the Western men outdid themselves against overwhelming numbers in the often neglected Federal holding action on McPherson's Ridge and Seminary Ridge, west of the town. At the close of that day, 1,212 of the brigade's 1,883 men were casualties, but not a backward step had been taken except on orders.

Shortly after Gettysburg, a series of Eastern regiments were incorporated into the brigade. In late 1864 and early 1865 three of the five Iron Brigade regiments either left the front or were merged with other regiments and lost their identity. The vaunted name "Iron Brigade" remained in use until the end of the war and some of its original members fought with Grant all the way to Appomattox. But by that time only Dawes' Sixth Wisconsin Volunteers and the Seventh Wisconsin Volunteers existed by name and, heavily infiltrated by late volunteers and drafted men, they were not the same regiments that had originally come from the West. But despite the relatively brief life of the organization, when the statistics were finally assembled, they accorded to the Iron Brigade a sad but proud distinction: a greater proportion of its men had been killed in combat than in any other Federal brigade. To this record, Rufus Dawes' Sixth Wisconsin Volunteers was no small contributor. Indeed, the records also showed that it stood tenth on the list of all Federal regiments in its number of men killed and died of wounds.[3]

This is the outline of the story which Rufus Dawes recorded at the time and later set down in his book. Although he wrote principally of the Sixth Wisconsin, its story could not be separated from those of the Iron Brigade and Battery B. Thus—and this is the third element contributing to the high quality of the book—Dawes chronicled *significant*

---

[3]Nolan, *The Iron Brigade.* Casualty statistics are those of William F. Fox, *Regimental Losses in the American Civil War* (Albany, 1889), pp. 116–17.

military organizations engaged in *significant* events of the war. Although writing about combat is difficult, Dawes was at his best in telling of such activities. When Battery B was summoned at Brawner Farm to respond to the opening artillery fire from the enemy, he saw the battery come driving "down the turnpike on a gallop. Quickly tearing away the fence, they wheeled into position in the open field, and the loud crack of their brass twelve pounders echoed the rebel cannon." Furious was the action at Antietam, in the bloody cornfield north of the famous Dunker Church. Dawes conveyed the ferocity of this most deadly action which befell the Sixth Wisconsin: "Men, I can not say fell; they were knocked out of the ranks by dozens. But we jumped over the fence, and pushed on, loading, firing, and shouting as we advanced.... The soldier who is shooting is furious in his energy. The soldier who is shot looks around for help with an imploring agony of death on his face." And there was also Gettysburg, the climax of the formal career of the Iron Brigade. Leading the Sixth in a celebrated charge on the railroad cut which concluded with the capture of an enemy regiment, perhaps the finest hour of the Sixth Wisconsin, Dawes wrote: "I ordered my men to climb over the turnpike fences and advance ... (into) the heavy fire which they began at once to pour upon us from their cover in the cut ... many were struck on the fences, but the line pushed on ... 'Forward, charge!' was the order I gave.... With the colors at the advance point, the regiment firmly and hurriedly moved forward, while the whole field behind streamed with men who had been shot, and who were struggling to the rear or sinking in death upon the ground. The only commands I gave, as we advanced, were 'Align on the colors! Close up on the colors! Close up on the colors!' The regiment was being so broken up that this order alone could hold the body together. Meanwhile the colors fell upon the ground several times but were raised again by the heroes of the color guard. Four hundred and twenty men started in the regiment from the turnpike fence, of whom about two hundred and forty reached the railroad cut."

With equal skill, Dawes recorded the entire career of his regiment and its companions, until, physically exhausted and broken, he left it at Petersburg to be discharged. Moving in and out of the story are some of the major figures of the war as they were observed by Dawes, including Abraham Lincoln, and Generals Grant, McClellan, Hancock, and Doubleday. The scenes and descriptions of these men are valuable. Visiting the army after Antietam, the homely President "looked serious and careworn. He bowed low in response to the salute of our tattered flags." Referring to McClellan's 1861 order prohibiting the inauguration of army movements on Sunday, Dawes discerningly noted that since "he did not inaugurate them on any other day, it was not of much importance." And U. S. Grant appears at one of his first reviews as General-in-Chief, ignoring those regiments which cheered him, but doffing his hat to the Sixth Wisconsin because it did not. In addition to these materials about leading figures of the war, more detailed and intimate portraits appear of officers identified with the Iron Brigade. Surely Dawes correctly evaluated General John Gibbon: "Thoroughly educated in the military profession, he had also high personal qualifications to exercise command . . . and . . . splendid personal bravery." Iron Brigade commanders King and Meredith also frequently appear. And the book affords perhaps the only published eye-witness observations of a number of other figures of the war. Among these were Brigadier General Lucius Fairchild of the Second Wisconsin, a post-war Governor of Wisconsin; Brigadier General Lysander Cutler of the Sixth Wisconsin, the original colonel of that regiment; Brigadier General Edward S. Bragg, Dawes' immediate predecessor as colonel of the Sixth, a national political figure after the war; Colonel John A. Kellogg, Dawes' successor as colonel of the Sixth, commander of the regiment at Appomattox; and Colonel Frank A. Haskell, originally adjutant of the Sixth, author of a famous Harvard Classics' letter describing Gettysburg, who was killed at Cold Harbor as colonel of the Thirty-sixth Wisconsin.

Like Dawes himself, the brigade and regimental officers and enlisted men of whom he wrote were lesser figures of the war in any comparative sense. As distinguished as the Sixth Wisconsin and the Iron Brigade were, they were but little when considered as a part of the war as a whole. And the experiences of a single officer and his regiment and brigade, however interesting and colorful, are also of limited import in relation to the epic of the Civil War. But *Rufus R. Dawes* and his *regiment* and his *brigade* fought for the Union with signal honor, valor, and devotion. Because of Dawes and his regiment and his brigade, and the efforts of others like them, the Union lived. *Service With The Sixth Wisconsin Volunteers* improves our understanding of the central event of American history. Its availability in this new edition will be welcomed by those who seek such an understanding.

History of the
Sauk County Riflemen

In 1975, the eminent T. Harry Williams wrote that histories of the basic units of the Civil War armies were critical to Civil War scholarship. According to Williams, this "statement was prompted by a recently formed conviction that Civil War writers could not understand the operations of the armies, and hence could not explain them to readers, unless they understood how the smallest units, regiments and brigades, were administered and led."[1] James I. Robertson, Jr. of Virginia Tech, has recently verified this opinion. "Unit histories," he has said, "have long been the most ignored of Civil War studies. This is a keen loss, for in many respects they are the most revealing of military works."[2]

These professional comments suggest a subtle revision that is taking place in the philosophy of historical writing. We are in a transition from concern with the "big picture" to a consideration of the "little pictures," or at least smaller ones and, as Williams and Robertson have suggested, this is an historically valid change. It reflects the elemental proposition that "history," like everything else, is after all, the sum of its parts. It also recognizes that the presentation of the big picture requires such a broad brush that much of significance is unreported, and that history, to that extent, is a distortion. Robertson has expressed this point. Thus, with reference to the specific example of the history of combat, he has written: "Civil War battles did not consist of an army sweeping forward like an unbroken wave against the battlements of an opponent.

---

[1]"Introduction to the 1975 Edition," Alan T. Nolan, *The Iron Brigade* (Madison, 1975).

[2]"Introduction to the 1983 Edition," Alan T. Nolan, *The Iron Brigade* (Ann Arbor and Berrien Springs, 1983).

Rather, armies fought (as well as marched and camped) in increments of brigades."[3] Robertson also knows, of course, that a brigade was composed of regiments and that regiments were composed of the truly basic units, the companies. He would acknowledge therefore that armies also fought, marched, camped—and lived and died—in increments of *companies*. The point is then that unit histories, the "little pictures," must be examined in order for one to construct the "big picture," and to illuminate and correct it.

Unit histories, the "little pictures," are of two general types. On the one hand there are those written in our own generation, using contemporary techniques of scholarship and mining primary sources. There are a few of these. But much the greater number are those written by the veterans themselves and published during the lifetimes of the war's survivors.

Collected and coveted by the dyed-in-the-wool (and sometimes patronized) buff, the volumes produced by the participants are surely of varying quality. Many, perhaps most, are principally after-the-fact recollections of aged men. Published largely for the veterans themselves, unit histories of this genre are frequently composed of reminiscences, probably enlarged upon and improved by repetition. Others, a minority of these older volumes, combine personal experiences with research into the *Official Records* and primary sources and are historical in an academic sense, and are of genuine historical value.

Although the book for which this Introduction is written is of the latter type of unit history written by participants, a book of genuine historical worth, I suggest that both types of veterans' books have a validity. In this respect, I embrace the distinguished Joshua L. Chamberlain's view that "it must be of interest, especially in important transactions, to know how things appeared to those actually engaged in them . . . It has been deemed a useful observance 'to see ourselves as others see us,' but it may sometimes be conducive to a just comprehension of the truth to let others see us as we see ourselves."[4] I believe, in short, that we may learn about the Civil War from the participants' perceptions of what they had done.

Here, then, is the *History of the Sauk County Riflemen,* with the subtitle of: "Known as Company 'A', Sixth Wisconsin Volunteer Infantry

---

[3]Ibid.
[4]Joshua L. Chamberlain, *The Passing of the Armies* (Dayton, 1982), p. xi.

1861 – 1865." Written by Philip Cheek and Mair Pointon of the Company, published in 1909 and long out of print, the book is at once unusual simply because it is a *company* history. Veterans' *regimentals* are commonplace, but there are very few histories that concern a single company.

Like most of the veterans' books, information about the publication and distribution of the *History of the Sauk County Riflemen* is scarce. We do not know about the number of copies originally printed, but the book itself does identify the printer, the Democrat Printing Company of Madison, Wisconsin. According to James L. Hansen, Reference Librarian at the State Historical Society of Wisconsin, *The Madison Democrat* was one of the major Madison newspapers in 1909. The scope of this enterprise is suggested by the fact that it also bound the book.

A s stated in the title of the book, "Sauk County Riflemen" was the *nom de guerre* of Company A of the Sixth Wisconsin Volunteers. The book eloquently tells the story of the Company, but it is appropriate for this Introduction to provide some context for that story.

Raised during the frantic months immediately following Sumter, the ten companies of the Sixth Wisconsin Volunteers rendezvoused in Madison at the State Agricultural Society's Fairgrounds, which had just been re-christened as Camp Randall, in honor of Wisconsin's Governor. Company A was, of course, from Sauk County, slightly north and west of Madison; Baraboo was the county seat town. Following a widespread custom, each of the other companies of the regiment, representing eight other counties,[5] had adopted "fighting names," such as "The Prescott Guards" (Company B–Pierce County), "Bragg's Rifles" (Company E– Fond du Lac County) and "The Lemonweir Minute Men" (Company K– Juneau County). Mustered into Federal service on July 16, 1861, 1084 strong, the Sixth Wisconsin arrived in Washington in August. On October 1, 1861, the regiment was formally brigaded with the Second and Seventh Wisconsin Volunteers and the Nineteenth Indiana Volunteers. Thus began the life of the infantry brigade of which the Sauk County Riflemen were a significant part. That brigade was later to be commanded by General John Gibbon and identified as the Iron Brigade. The history

---

[5]As has been said, there were ten companies but two of them, Companies D and F, were from Milwaukee County. The names of the companies appear in the *Annual Report of the Adjutant General, State of Wisconsin,* 1861 (Madison, 1861).

of the Sauk County Riflemen is inextricably a part of the Iron Brigade's story.[6]

Initially called the "Black Hat Brigade" because its men wore the regular army's dress black hat instead of the more typical kepi, the Iron Brigade was the only all-Western brigade in the Eastern armies of the Union. Reinforced late in 1862 by the newly-raised Twenty-fourth Michigan Volunteers, the Iron Brigade was the most famous and distinguished of all Federal brigades, "the best fighting brigade in the army," according to T. Harry Williams.[7] Because of this quality, the records show that the Iron Brigade led all Federal brigades in percentage of deaths in battle.[8] The Sixth Wisconsin contributed heavily to this doleful distinction. Its losses place it *tenth* on the list of Federal regiments with the highest total losses in the war.[9]

Focusing on their own beloved Company A, Cheek and Pointon recount the events that resulted in the foregoing statistics. The narrative starts in 1861 in Sauk County and wonderfully describes the quaint and picturesque beginnings of the Company. The story ends with the Grand Review in Washington and the regiment's return to Madison on July 16, 1865, precisely four years after the muster into Federal service. Along the way, the authors describe the day-to-day happenings of the soldiers' lives as well as the storied stations and events, including Gainesville (Brawner Farm), Second Bull Run, South Mountain, Antietam, Fredericksburg, Chancellorsville, and Gettysburg, where the brigade was virtually destroyed. They then follow the Sixth Wisconsin and the remnants of the Iron Brigade into the Wilderness in 1864, through the constant warfare of Grant's final Virginia campaign and on to Appomattox. The book concludes with casualty statistics; brief sketches of the post-war

[6]Information regarding the Iron Brigade hereinafter is from Alan T. Nolan, *The Iron Brigade,* published by the Macmillan Company (New York, 1961), the State Historical Society of Wisconsin (Madison, 1975) and the Historical Society of Michigan and Hardscrabble Books (Ann Arbor and Berrien Springs, 1983).

[7]The Southern historian, James I. Robertson, Jr., is the source of the "most famous" characterization in the "Introduction to the 1983 Edition," Alan T. Nolan, *The Iron Brigade* (Ann Arbor and Berrien Springs, 1983). Williams is quoted from the "Introduction to the 1975 Edition" of the same work.

[8]William F. Fox, *Regimental Losses in the American Civil War* (Albany, 1889), p. 117.

[9]Ibid., p. 3

careers of some of the members of the Company; a roster of the Company that identifies each soldier's home town, date of enlistment, and military record; and an anecdotal section.

Based on the authors' observations and recollections, and on diaries, letters and at least some consulting of the *Official Records* and such authorities as Fox's *Regimental Losses in the American Civil War,* the book presents an interesting mix in terms of substantive content. It also provides a similar mix in terms of style—marked by sentimental Victorian flourishes, laconic and understated facts, and the soldier's ultimate weapon, humor. Cheek was, by any standard, a funny man, and he also had the typical enlisted man's impudence where officers were concerned. At an Iron Brigade reunion campfire held in Detroit in 1890, Cheek chided the Military Order of the Loyal Legion, whose membership was limited to officers. Addressing the gathering in a speech not reported in the *History of the Sauk County Riflemen,* he said, "We are all 'loyal legioneers'—that is, I am not; I was a private. There are so many officers now, though, that I enjoy the distinction of being the only surviving private of the war."[10]

Cheek and Pointon put their book together with appropriate humility. They are referred to only when necessary to the narrative or statistical data. This is to their credit, but readers today will presumably want to know more about the authors. Fortunately collateral sources tell us about them.

Philip Cheek, one of six children,[11] was born in Somersetshire, England, in 1841. The family immigrated to Newark, New Jersey in 1852. Shortly thereafter, they moved to Rhode Island, but in 1856, the Cheeks went west, settling in Excelsior Township in Sauk County. A carpenter by trade, Cheek's father devoted most of his time in Sauk County to farming. Philip had attended school in England and continued his edu-

---

[10]O. B. Curtis, *History of the 24th Michigan of the Iron Brigade* (Detroit, 1891), p. 469.

[11]Information about Cheek is taken from Harry Ellsworth Cole, *A Standard History of Sauk County, Wisconsin* (Chicago and New York, 1918), Vol. II, pp. 666–668, and the *Soldiers' and Citizens' Album of Biographical Record Containing Personal Sketches of Army Men and Citizens Prominent in Loyalty to the Union* (Chicago, 1890), pp. 710–712.

cation in New Jersey, Rhode Island, and Wisconsin. In his young manhood he helped his father on the Excelsior farm.

Just prior to his twentieth birthday, Cheek enlisted as a private in Company A. As evidence of the youth of the nation, and the great tide of mid-nineteenth century immigration, Wisconsin's Adjutant General was carefully classifying Wisconsin's volunteers by his perception of their "nationality," listing "Americans," "Germans," "Irish," etc.[12] Since Cheek did not bother to become a citizen until 1869, he was presumably not counted in the "American" column. Had he been aware of the Adjutant General's classifications Cheek might have been resentful, but he had something else on his mind at the time. On the eve of the regiment's departure from Madison he married his Sauk County sweetheart. Only then was he ready to go to war.

Philip Cheek shared the life of the Company through the Iron Brigade's early career in 1861 and 1862, a period marked by a peculiar absence of combat. Thereafter he passed unscathed through the brigade's hard fighting at Brawner Farm, Second Bull Run, and South Mountain, where the Iron Brigade acquired its proud name. But in the First Corps' furious action on the Federal right at Antietam on September 17, 1862, Cheek went down with a serious wound in the right ankle. Temporarily hospitalized in a nearby house, he was later transported to a Washington hospital. For Philip Cheek, the war ended along the Hagerstown Turnpike, near the storied and bloody cornfield, the West Woods, and the Dunker Church. On December 18, 1862, he was discharged. Returning to Sauk County, he convalesced until the summer of 1863, when he was finally able to resume working on the family farm.

Cheek's post-war career was busy and distinguished. In the fall of 1863, he was appointed Deputy Provost Marshall for the Third Congressional District of Wisconsin and served in this capacity until the close of the war. During this period his brother Robert of the 19th Wisconsin Volunteers was killed at Petersburg on August 7, 1864.

In 1870, Cheek was elected Clerk of the Circuit Court of Sauk County and moved from Excelsior to Baraboo. While occupying this position he read law and on January 1, 1876, was admitted to the Wisconsin bar and opened an office in Baraboo. His professional career included

[12]*Annual Report of the Adjutant General, State of Wisconsin,* 1861 (Madison, 1861), p. 56.

election and service as District Attorney of Sauk County, which was followed by election and re-election to the state-wide office of Insurance Commissioner. In 1891, during the last year of his term as Insurance Commissioner, Cheek resigned that office to become the special agent for Wisconsin of the Hartford Fire Insurance Company. In this position, which he held for the rest of his life, Cheek traveled the state from his residence in Baraboo.

Like so many veterans, Cheek blended veterans affairs with politics. His success in the latter respect has already been described. A vigorous Republican and an accomplished speaker, he was a charter member and first Commander of his local post of the Grand Army of the Republic (G.A.R.), and was Assistant Adjutant General, Senior Aide-de-Camp and twice elected Department Commander for Wisconsin of the G.A.R. He also served for four years on the Executive Board of the National Commander of that organization. He was a frequent speaker at its National Encampments. As will be noted hereinafter, he was also busy in the Iron Brigade Association, an organization described at the conclusion of this Introduction.

In his political-veteran activities, Cheek practiced the prevailing "bloody shirt" politics. He was an ally of fellow Republican Lucius Fairchild, wartime Colonel of the Second Wisconsin of the Iron Brigade, postwar Governor of Wisconsin and a National Commander of the G.A.R.[13] Ironically, this placed Cheek in opposition to Edward S. Bragg, Colonel of Cheek's own regiment but a prominent Wisconsin Democrat, Congressman and veteran activist.[14] Unhappily, this political conflict extended to the Iron Brigade Association. In 1887, in a move related to Republican plans to prevent President Grover Cleveland's re-election in 1888, the Iron Brigade Association's reunion in Milwaukee was marked by strident political conflict, centering around the election of officers. Cheek was one of the leaders of the Republican forces and these forces succeeded in unseating Congressman Bragg as Senior Vice President of the Association.[15] Cheek was also a trustee of the Waupaca Home for

[13] *Dictionary of American Biography* (New York, 1931), Vol. III, pp. 253–254.
[14] Ibid., Vol. II, pp. 587–588. In 1896, Bragg was a "Gold Democrat" and he refused to support Bryan. He supported McKinley in 1900 and thereafter was identified as a Republican.
[15] Milwaukee *Sentinel,* September 14, 1887; September 15, 1887. Fond du Lac *Commonwealth,* September 16, 1887.

Veterans, an active Mason and a member of the Baraboo Methodist Church. He died in 1911 at the age of seventy.

According to the 1900 Census of the United States, Mair Pointon, like his co-author, was born in England. The Census states that his birthdate was May, 1845, and that he had immigrated to the United States in 1854. In May of 1861, he was living in Baraboo and on May 10 of that year, at the age of sixteen, he enlisted as a private in the Sauk County Riflemen.[16] Unlike Cheek, Pointon served throughout the war. In May of 1864, at Laurel Hill, Virginia, en route with Grant from the Wilderness to Spottsylvania, he and his long-time tent mate, William Palmer of the Company, were wounded, but Pointon was only briefly out of action. The details of Pointon's wounding are worth noting because they show the value of history that concentrates on the "little pictures" and thereby corroborate James I. Robertson, Jr.'s above quoted comment about the revealing character of unit histories:

> Bill Palmer and Mair Pointon were the last to leave the field, remaining and firing after the rest of the company had gone. Before long, the enemy hit Bill on the jaw and cut off the lobe of his ear, which caused him to bleed profusely. He went to Pointon and asked him how badly he was hurt. Pointon told him and advised him to go to the rear ... Bill took off from his knapsack, their frying pan and a two quart tin pail and gave them to Pointon, who took out his pocket book and divided its contents with Bill and he went to the rear. During all this time, the enemy was plugging away at both of them. Pointon remained until struck by two bullets, one entering his knapsack, the other cutting him on the upper left arm, making a painful but not serious wound. He went to the rear soon after he was hit, but did not go to the hospital.[17]

[16]Biographical data about Pointon are from the census, Arthur P. Rose, *An Illustrated History of Yellow Medicine County, Minnesota* (Marshall, 1914), pp. 101 – 102, Carl and Amy Narvestad, *A History of Yellow Medicine County, Minnesota* (Granite Falls, 1971), p. 702, and the Canby *News*, January 14, 1921. There is conflict in these sources concerning whether he was born in 1843 or 1845. The latter date is adopted here.

[17]Philip Cheek and Mair Pointon, *History of the Sauk County Riflemen* (Madison, 1909), p. 96.

May of 1864 was a horrible time in Virginia, the beginning of the constant blood-letting that would ultimately end the war, and this vignette, in the midst of the awfulness, tells us a number of things about what it was to be a Civil War soldier: tent mates were each other's Guardian Angels, even to the point of advice about the nature of a wound; there was a division of labor between tent mates, with one acting as quartermaster, responsible for cooking utensils and the other serving as treasurer; even when bleeding profusely the quartermaster dared not leave the field with the frying pan or tin pail that served the two men; and the treasurer was required to account if the other was leaving the field, because they did not know the future but did know that money might come in handy.

As a result of his relative invulnerability in a company and regiment with unusually high casualties, Pointon was regularly advanced in rank—to Corporal, Sergeant, First Sergeant and then to Sergeant Major. On October 19, 1864, during the siege of Petersburg, he was appointed First Lieutenant of Company A, apparently without even a stop-off as Second Lieutenant.[18] The book graphically illustrates this rise, initially picturing Pointon without stripes or straps and showing him finally as an officer in Richmond in 1865, with the war finally over.[19]

Like Philip Cheek, Pointon returned to Sauk County from Appomattox. Married in 1868, he also pursued a political career. He was Deputy Postmaster and Town Clerk of Baraboo, before becoming Register of Deeds for Sauk County, a position he occupied for eight years. In June of 1870, he was commissioned Captain of the Sauk County Light Guard, a Wisconsin National Guard Company. But in 1877, together with his wife and two children, Pointon moved to Yellow Medicine County in western Minnesota. There he homesteaded in Oshkosh Township, eventually owning 480 acres. He called his farm "Elmwood." From 1889 to 1901 he served as Auditor of Yellow Medicine County. In about 1910, the year after the publication of *The Sauk County Riflemen*, Pointon sold Elmwood and moved into Canby, a small town in Yellow Medicine County, close to the South Dakota line. As a result of his poor health, at an undetermined time Pointon and his family went south to Bedford,

[18]Ibid., p. 191.
[19]Ibid., pp. 27, 127.

Virginia, where they operated an eighty-acre fruit farm. From Virginia, for health reasons, they sought the climate of Southern California, moving to Alhambra, where the old soldier died in 1921 after "a long and painful illness." He was seventy-six years old.

In June of 1880, the Wisconsin Soldiers and Sailors Reunion Association staged the "Great Reunion" in Milwaukee. It is estimated that as many as 25,000 Wisconsin veterans attended. Ex-President Grant and General Philip H. Sheridan were also on hand.[20] In the course of this gathering, and with the participation of visiting veterans of the Nineteenth Indiana and Twenty-fourth Michigan Volunteers, the Iron Brigade Association was formed.[21] A five-pointed badge, a modification of a Maltese cross, with each point engraved with the name of one of the five regiments of the brigade, was adopted as the Association's emblem in 1885.[22]

The badge of the Iron Brigade Association was imprinted on the front cover of *The Sauk County Riflemen.* On the back was stamped a circle, insignia of the Army of the Potomac's First Corps, and the Maltese cross, badge of the Fifth Corps, into which the First Corps was merged on March 23, 1864.[23] These were surely appropriate decorations. Speaking at the Association's meeting in Detroit in 1890, Cheek said, "I wouldn't give for these little badges of the Iron Brigade any possession I have or could have outside of my wife and children."[24] *The Sauk County Riflemen* betrays the feeling that the soldiers of the Iron Brigade also had for the corps in which they had fought so desperately.

Joshua L. Chamberlain once wrote that the Civil War was "a war to test and finally determine the character of the interior constitution and real organic life of this great people." The Northern volunteers of 1861 and 1862, he added, "would settle the fact that they had a country and

[20]Racine *Journal,* June 2, 1880; Milwaukee *Sentinel,* June 7, June 11, June 12, 1880.

[21]Milwaukee *Sentinel,* June 9, June 11, June 12, 1880; *National Tribune,* June 15, 1922; J. A. Watrous, *Richard Epps and Other Stories* (Milwaukee, 1906); Milwaukee *Sentinel,* July 23, 1882; Fond du Lac *Reporter,* September 11, 1916.

[22]Milwaukee *Sentinel,* September 16 and September 17, 1885.

[23]*War of the Rebellion, Official Records of the Union and Confederate Armies,* (Washington, 1882–1900), Serial Number 60, pp. 717, 722–723.

[24]Curtis, *History of the 24th Michigan of the Iron Brigade,* p. 469.

then consider the reasons and rights of it."[25] Here, then, is the story of 100 or so of these men and their involvement in the nation's ordeal. T. Harry Williams stated that unit histories "tell the story of a democracy at war."[26] This intimate account does exactly that.

[25]Chamberlain, *The Passing of the Armies*, pp. 12–13.
[26]"Introduction to the 1975 Edition," Alan T. Nolan, *The Iron Brigade* (Madison, 1975).

The Twenty-Fourth Michigan of the Iron Brigade

The eminent Southern historian, James I. Robertson, Jr., has recently written that among Northern brigades "by far the most famous of them all was the Iron Brigade, the only pure Western brigade in the North's premier Army of the Potomac."[1] Originally called the "Black Hat Brigade," because the soldiers wore the Army's dress black hat instead of the more typical blue cap, the Iron Brigade was initially made up of the Second, Sixth, and Seventh Wisconsin and the Nineteenth Indiana Volunteers. In 1862, it was reinforced by the newly-raised Twenty-fourth Michigan Volunteers.

Because of its exceptional valor and élan, the Iron Brigade led all Federal brigades in the percentage of its men killed and mortally wounded. The Twenty-fourth Michigan was a significant contributor to this record. Among Federal regiments at Gettysburg, the Michigan regiment, with losses of 80 percent, ranked first in percentage of casualties. For the war as a whole, William F. Fox ranked the Twenty-fourth as nineteenth on his honor roll of regiments suffering the highest percentage losses in battle.[2]

---

[1]"Introduction to the 1983 Edition," Alan T. Nolan, *The Iron Brigade* (Ann Arbor and Berrien Springs, 1983). Materials regarding the Iron Brigade hereinafter are from this book, published by the Macmillan Company (1961), the State Historical Society of Wisconsin (1975), and the Historical Society of Michigan and Hardscrabble Books (1983).

[2]William F. Fox, *Regimental Losses in the American Civil War* (Albany, 1889), pp. 116–17. *War of the Rebellion, Official Records of the Union and Confederate Armies* (Washington, 1882–1900), Serial Number 43, p. 173. This work is hereinafter cited as *O.R.*, followed by the serial number of the volume and the page number in that volume.

Regimental histories exist for two of the five Iron Brigade regiments. In 1890, E. R. Alderman & Sons of Marietta, Ohio, published Rufus R. Dawes' *Service With The Sixth Wisconsin Volunteers*.[3] In 1891, Winn & Hammond of Detroit published the *History of the Twenty-Fourth Michigan of the Iron Brigade,* by O. B. Curtis. The title of the book also recited that the Twenty-fourth was "known as the Detroit and Wayne County Regiment." According to the Detroit City Directory for 1892, Winn & Hammond was located at 152–156 Wayne, in Detroit. The firm was described as "(Henry R. Winn, George S. Hammond), Printers, Binders and Engravers, Zinc Etchings and Half-Tones." No information is available about the number of copies of Curtis' book that were originally printed, but it is now quite rare.

On this occasion of the republication of the Twenty-fourth Michigan regimental, it is appropriate for an Introduction to tell readers about author Curtis and to comment on his book.

O rson Blair Curtis[4] was born in 1840, in Wayne, a small town in Wayne County, Michigan, just west of Detroit.[5] Nothing is known of his antecedents or background. From 1856 to 1858, he attended the Michigan Normal School (now Eastern Michigan University) at Ypsilanti. He then enrolled in Ypsilanti Union Seminary. In the fall of 1859, he entered the University of Michigan at Ann Arbor. He left the university in the summer of 1862 and enlisted in the Twenty-fourth Michigan, which was at that time being raised in Detroit.

Curtis' attitude toward slavery and the black race is plain from his book. He was apparently not an Abolitionist before the war, but he does not deprecate abolitionism, remarking that "the barbarism of slavery begot abolitionism." Like Lincoln, he recognized the great American

---

[3]This exceptional work was reprinted in 1962 by the State Historical Society of Wisconsin.

[4]Curtis' book contains some information about him, but the principal sources of data about him are the admirable records of the Alumni Records Office of the University of Michigan at Ann Arbor. These contain several responses, written in his own hand, to university inquiries. Except as specifically noted hereinafter, biographical information about Curtis comes from these records.

[5]There is an unexplained conflict about Curtis' birthplace. In his book (p. 329) he states that he was born in Nankin, in northwest Wayne County, identified in contemporaneous Michigan gazetters as a post hamlet. But he consistently advised the Alumni Records Office that he was born in the town of Wayne.

contradiction. Speaking of the War for Independence, he states that "the colonists were seeking sympathy from the civilized world in their efforts for liberty, and yet, were holding in slavery their own fellow human beings!" He is also articulate in his descriptions of the "barbarism" of slavery and recites that "the edicts of heaven were against it."[6]

Having been grievously wounded at Fredericksburg in December of 1862, Curtis was mustered out and returned to the University of Michigan. In June of 1865, he received the degree of Bachelor of Arts. In 1868, after further work at the university, he was awarded the degree of Master of Arts. In view of his later employment in public education, it is likely that he concentrated on this field of study.

As has been said, Curtis volunteered for the Twenty-fourth during the raising of that regiment in July and August, 1862, enlisting as a private in Company D. His book notes with some pride that he did not "join in the scramble for position,"[7] but he was nevertheless promoted to Corporal shortly after his enlistment. Mustered into Federal service at Camp Barns, Detroit, on August 13 and August 15, under the command of Colonel Henry A. Morrow, the regiment reached the Army of the Potomac at Sharpsburg, Maryland, on October 8. A fateful order was issued on that day, assigning the Michigan men to the Iron Brigade, then commanded by General John Gibbon:

> HEADQUARTERS FIRST ARMY CORPS,
> Camp near Sharpsburg, October 8, 1862
> Special Orders,)
> No. 24   )
> . . .
>
> II. The following new regiments now en route for this corps are assigned as follows: First Division (Gibbons' brigade), Twenty-fourth Michigan Volunteers . . .[8]

Curtis' military career was cut short at Fredericksburg. Since the circumstances of that event are unusual, and illuminating of Curtis' character and personality, they deserve to be described in detail.

---

[6]O. B. Curtis, *History of the Twenty-fourth Michigan of the Iron Brigade* (Detroit, 1891), pp. 9, 12, 19. Cited hereinafter as *Curtis*. A postwar photograph of Curtis appears on page 414 of his book.

[7]*Curtis*, p. 264.

[8]*O.R.*, 107, p. 877.

On the eve of the Fredericksburg Campaign, the Army of the Potomac was encamped at Warrenton, Virginia. General George B. McClellan was removed from command and was replaced by Ambrose Burnside. General Burnside did not change the existing corps structure, but he superimposed on the Army three "grand divisions," the right, the left and the center, each made up of two corps. The Left Grand Division, commanded by General William B. Franklin, was composed of the Sixth Corps and Reynold's First Corps. The Iron Brigade, enlarged by the addition of the Twenty-fourth Michigan and commanded by General Soloman Meredith, was identified as the Fourth Brigade of Doubleday's First Division of the First Corps. General Edwin V. Sumner was placed in command of the Right Grand Division. It included the Ninth Corps and Couch's Second Corps. The Third Brigade of the Second Division of the Second Corps was composed of six regiments, one of which was the Seventh Michigan Volunteers.[9]

During the Federal movements prior to Fredericksburg, the First Corps, including the Iron Brigade, marched to Brooks Station on the railroad between Aquia Creek and Fredericksburg. Arriving there on November 25, the brigade was to remain until December 9, 1862. The weather during this interval was unusually bad, marked by freezing rains, and the soldiers were poorly housed. Casualties from disease were widespread and Corporal Curtis was one of those who fell ill. He was hospitalized and describes himself as "sick with pneumonia at Brooks Station, sixteen miles from the field of Fredericksburg."[10]

The Iron Brigade moved out from Brooks Station on December 9, bound for Fredericksburg. Corporal Curtis remained behind in the hospital. His book contains three references to what then happened to him. Sometime between the 9th and 11th of December, Curtis "heard firing on the Rappahannock," from the direction of Fredericksburg. According to his own account, "knowing that absence from the ranks in the engagement might be misconstrued and result in being outranked by others on the promotion list," with the consent of Assistant Surgeon Charles C. Smith, Curtis left the hospital in search of the regiment. Having proceeded fourteen miles on foot, he was unable to find the Twenty-fourth,

[9]For composition, strength, and losses of the Army of the Potomac at Fredericksburg see *Battles and Leaders* (New York, 1884, 1888), Vol. III, p. 143–146.
[10]*Curtis,* p. 265. See also p. 386.

but he did find some Michigan men, soldiers of the Seventh Michigan Volunteers, in the Second Corps of Sumner's Right Grand Division. According to Curtis, he "fell in with the Seventh Michigan Infantry."[11]

Burnside's plan for the Battle of Fredericksburg required the Army's crossing the Rappahannock in front of Fredericksburg and southeast of that town. Two pontoon bridges were to be laid directly in front of the town, another, the "middle bridge," three quarters of a mile down the river, and two more, placed side by side, were to be located a mile southeast of the middle bridge. These last bridges, known historically as Franklin's Crossing, were the destination of the Iron Brigade and their comrades of the First Corps and Franklin's Left Grand Division. On December 12, without the services of Corporal Curtis, the Iron Brigade crossed the river southeast of the town and was engaged until the night of the 15th, when it withdrew as Burnside, badly defeated, abandoned the fight. In this action, the Twenty-fourth Michigan distinguished itself.

Sumner's Right Grand Division was to cross the river on December 11 in front of the town, above which loomed Marye's Heights. This crossing did not go well. By early morning on December 11, the Fiftieth New York Engineers had made considerable progress in laying down the three pontoon bridges opposite the town, but the bridges were not complete. Behind the engineers, Sumner's troops, and Hooker's Center Grand Division, waited for the engineers' work to be accomplished. At about 6:00 A.M., Barkdale's Brigade of Mississippians opened fire on the bridge builders from houses on the south river bank, and from behind walls and fences. Unarmed, suffering casualties, the engineers were driven away. The Federals then turned to artillery to dislodge the Mississippians. A heavy fire did great damage to the town, but when the engineers were sent forward they were again driven off by Barksdale's men. At last, General Burnside ordered that infantry were to be crossed in the pontoon boats. Volunteers were called for from the nearby regiments.

There is some conflict in the accounts of which regiments were involved in storming across the river, with several regiments being credited, but all accounts agree that the Seventh Michigan contributed a share of the volunteers. Among these volunteers was Corporal O. B. Curtis.

[11] *Curtis*, pp. 386, 265, 88, 99.

The Federal artillery resumed a heavy covering fire as the volunteers clambered into the boats. Four hundred feet ahead of them was the south bank of the Rappahannock. The artillery ceased firing, the engineers gave each boat a hearty shove, and the race was on. Under a heavy musketry fire, the soldiers furiously poled the boats across. Striking the bank first, the Seventh Michigan leaped ashore and proceeded up Farquhar Street, becoming immediately engaged. Behind them other regiments crossed and ultimately, after hard fighting, a firm bridgehead was established. At last at 4:30 P.M., the engineers could complete their work.[12] There were, of course, casualties in this kind of work, and one of them was Curtis. In his own words, he "crossed the Rappahannock with (the Seventh Michigan) in boats, and helped clear the enemy from the rifle pits; wounded in subsequent engagement; left arm amputated on the field."[13] A Detroit newspaper obituary states that Curtis' wound was caused by an enemy artillery shell. In his handwritten account in the university Alumni Records Office, having described the plight of the engineers, Curtis put it this way:

> Then the 7th Michigan volunteered to cross in pontoon boats and drive the rebels from the opposite banks, which they gallantly did in the face of a shower of bullets. Corporal Curtis jumped into a boat with his new found comrades, fought his way across the river in this historical 'Forlorn Hope' charge . . .

Curtis was sent to Washington's Harewood Hospital.[14] In March of 1863, he was mustered out.[15] As has been said, he promptly returned to Ann Arbor and resumed his schooling.

Curtis' post-war activities and employment were many and varied. Quick to involve himself in veterans' affairs, in 1866, he was elected Vice President of an organization called Michigan Boys-in-Blue. In the same year he traveled to Pittsburgh and was elected Secretary of the Soldiers and Sailors National Convention. In 1868, he was elected Senior Vice

---

[12] *O.R.*, 31, pp. 169–171, 167–168, 174, 175–176, 180–189, 183, 262, 265, 310. *Battles and Leaders* (New York, 1884, 1888), Vol. III, pp. 108, 121, and 127, contains good descriptions of this action and also discloses the conflict about the participants.

[13] *Curtis*, p. 386.

[14] *Curtis*, p. 81.

[15] *Curtis*, p. 386.

Grand Commander for Michigan of the Grand Army of the Republic. He was also President and Orator of the Twenty-fourth Michigan Association, a post-war regimental organization.

Curtis' employment record embraced the fields of public education, newspaper publishing, and government service. During the three years that he was working on his master's degree, he was employed as the Principal of the Sturgis Union Schools in southwestern Michigan, an indication that the master's program involved correspondence work and what is today called independent study. In 1868, he became the editor and publisher of the Sturgis *Star,* but he also sold the newspaper in that year to become Superintendent of the Bay City Public Schools. In the following year, he moved to Tecumseh, Michigan, and became its school superintendent. Apparently in demand, in 1870, he was elected Superintendent of the Muskegon City Schools, to which position he was three times re-elected. During the period of the Muskegon employment, he also served as Vice President of the Michigan State Teachers' Association. In 1871, he was married to a woman from Hillsdale, Michigan.

The year 1874 marked the end of Curtis' career in education. In that year he returned to newspaper work, becoming the editor and publisher of the Muskegon *Chronicle*. But four years later, in 1878, he sold the *Chronicle* and moved again, this time to Wayne, Michigan, where he was an unsuccessful candidate for State Senator in that year. At about this time, he was appointed Deputy Collector of Customs for Detroit. Although remaining with the customs service, he subsequently was classified as Statistical Clerk, the occupation in which he served for the rest of his life. During at least part of this time, he was also Secretary of the Detroit Civil Service Board and an examiner to select cadets for the United States Military Academy.

Curtis' book was not his first experience with the publication of military history. Reacting to an article for *Battles and Leaders* by a Second Wisconsin soldier that referred to the Twenty-fourth Michigan as "bounty men," Curtis contributed a response to that publication. In his article, Curtis discussed the bounty question and otherwise set forth the record of his regiment.[16]

In March of 1889, at which time he advised the University of Michigan that his address was 290 25th Street in Detroit, Curtis was appointed

[16]*Battles and Leaders* (New York, 1884, 1888), Vol. III, p. 142.

by Michigan's Governor to one of the committees planning Michigan Day at Gettysburg. On this day, July 12, 1889, the Michigan monuments were to be dedicated at Gettysburg, the fated field for the Twenty-fourth Michigan. Curtis describes these activities in detail in his book.

A modest obituary in the *Detroit Free Press* tells of the death of O. B. Curtis, aged 60, at his 25th Street residence on January 11, 1901.[17] The cause of death was given as diabetes, a disease that he had recently developed. He was survived by his wife and two sons. One of the sons, Heber D. Curtis, was employed at the Leander McCormack Observatory, in Charlottesville, Virginia, not many miles from the place of his father's wounding. The other, Walter, was said to be working for the Northwestern Railway in Chicago.

Dedicated with Victorian flourish "To Our Heroic Dead . . . ," Curtis' Introduction to his book acknowledges the assistance of several members of the regiment, including "Sergeant Robert Gibbons of the Publication Committee." The reference to a committee suggests that although Curtis was the author of the book—and he refers to his labors as gratuitous—it was a group enterprise. The Introduction also refers to Curtis' many months of research through wartime letters, diaries and official records.[18]

Structurally, the book begins with a historical discussion of "The Slaveholders Rebellion" and a survey of the war down to the stalemate on the Penninsula in the summer of 1862. The book proceeds to a description of the raising of the Twenty-fourth in July and August of 1862, its transportation to the Army of the Potomac, and its assignment to the Iron Brigade. This is followed by an account of the Michigan soldiers' career, beginning with Fredericksburg and ending with the regiment's withdrawal from the front and assignment to Springfield, Illinois, in February, 1865. After a brief description of the Springfield duty, the book returns to Virginia and Appomattox. It then resumes the story of the regiment to June of 1865, when the Michigan men were mustered out in Detroit.

Curtis did not cease his account with the mustering out of the regiment. He proceeded with eight more chapters. Chapter XVI lists the original members of the regiment by name, rank, place of birth, age, occupa-

[17]The edition of January 11, 1901.
[18]*Curtis,* p. 3.

tion, residence, and date of enlistment. Earlier, in Chapter II describing the raising of the regiment, Curtis included tables showing the composition of the regiment by place of birth, age, occupation, and residence. Taken together, these data tell a good deal about the depth of Curtis' interest and research. He was, by any standard, a fact man. Curtis continues this detail in Chapter XVII, in which he identifies the regiments' recruits; Chapter XVIII, the "Roster of Officers"; Chapter XIX, "The Dead of the Twenty-fourth Michigan"; and Chapter XX, "Records of the Survivors." Each of these chapters contains a painstaking accounting.

Having completed Chapter XX, Curtis had told the story of the regiment, essentially a chronological account with statistical data, but he added four more chapters, "Michigan Day at Gettysburg" (XXI); "Confederate Prisons" (XXII); "The Iron Brigade" (XXIII); and "Our Last March" (XXIV). Although these chapters, especially the one about the Iron Brigade, contain interesting information, they are not up to the standard of the rest of the book and tend to disrupt its structural integrity. The chapter on Confederate prisons surely exaggerates the comforts of Federal prisons and is angrily indiscriminate in its condemnation of their Southern counterparts.

What, then, may be said about the *History of the Twenty-fourth Michigan of the Iron Brigade?* Regimental histories invariably have an interest to the aficionado, whether or not they are accurate or well written. But Curtis' book has a value beyond that of the ordinary regimental, a value that results from several factors. His claim to having consulted letters and diaries and official records is supported by the text. He went far beyond the campfire and reunion yarns of the old soldiers. In addition, his statistical data about the members of the regiment give valuable insights into the sociology of that organization. He also includes letters and speeches, otherwise unavailable, of members of the regiment and these provide useful information. Colonel Morrow's letter of May 19, 1865, stands out in this respect. And there are indelible flashes that remind us of the awfulness of the much-romanticized Civil War. Thus Mason Palmer was wounded at Gettysburg on July 1, 1863: "Arm amputated. Death hastened by his jumping out of a window in delirium." A few lines later, the fate of Seymour Burns is described. Wounded in the Wilderness on May 5, 1864, his body was "burned up in the woods" when the Wilderness caught fire during that battle.[19]

[19] *Curtis,* p. 375.

With final regard to the contents of the book, it contains an articulate statement of what Curtis thought about the celebrated question of the cause of the war. Unconsciously influenced, one suspects, by early twentieth century racist attitudes, academicians have sought until recently to find the cause of the war in something other than slavery. For years many Northern and Southern historians virtually exorcised slavery as a cause, or trivialized it as incidental to the conflict. This has always seemed an anomaly because both before, during, and after the war the *participants* in the struggle found slavery at the root of their disagreements. In the last several years, in a different context in terms of racial attitudes, the professional historians have begun to concede that perhaps the participants were right. The most persuasive of the more recent professional analyses is Kenneth M. Stampp's *And the War Came*.[20] Let is be said that Corporal Curtis understood the problem. At the outset of his book he states what is surely true: "The cause of this terrible and unjustifiable war was an unsuccessful *effort to expand and perpetuate slavery of the African race in the United States*."[21]

S erious historians of the war tell us that histories of regiments and brigades are the missing link in Civil War studies. James I. Robertson, Jr., has recently said this: "Unit histories have long been the most ignored of Civil War studies. This is a keen loss, for in many respects they are the most revealing of military works."[22] In 1975, T. Harry Williams described his "recently formed conviction that Civil War writers could not understand the operations of the armies, and hence could not explain them to readers, unless they understood how the smallest units, regiments and brigades, were administered and led."[23] In 1961, Bell I. Wiley wrote that "good unit histories are one of the most urgent needs of Civil War history."[24]

Here, then, is a good unit history of a distinguished regiment that belonged to a distinguished brigade, "probably the best fighting

[20]Kenneth M. Stampp, *And the War Came* (Baton Rouge, 1950).

[21]*Curtis*, p. 9.

[22]"Introduction to the 1983 Edition," Alan T. Nolan, *The Iron Brigade* (Ann Arbor and Berrien Springs, 1983).

[23]"Introduction to the 1975 Edition," Alan T. Nolan, *The Iron Brigade* (Madison, 1975). This is also the source of Professor Williams' quotation, set forth later herein, about the fighting qualities of the Iron Brigade.

[24]*Atlanta Constitution and Journal*, July 9, 1961.

brigade in the Army," according to T. Harry Williams. In 1884, Oliver Wendell Holmes, Jr., made his famous remark about the generation of soldiers who fought in the Civil War: "Through our great good fortune, in our youth our hearts were touched with fire." Late in life, O. B. Curtis struck a similar note. Writing to the University of Michigan, he said that his participation in the forced crossing of the river at Fredericksburg, in which he was maimed for life, was "the choicest gem in my history."

Corporal Curtis' book reflects this spirit. Its availability in this new edition will be welcomed by all students of the Civil War.

Giants in Tall Black Hats

On October 1, 1861, a new infantry brigade was organized at Arlington, Virginia. It was composed of four regiments—the Nineteenth Indiana and the Second, Sixth, and Seventh Wisconsin Volunteers. Command of the brigade was assigned to Brigadier General Rufus King of Milwaukee. General King's grandfather, a Massachusetts delegate to the Continental Congress, had originally drafted that portion of the Northwest Ordinance which forever forbade "slavery and involuntary servitude" in the Northwest Territory. Thus General King was an unusually appropriate commander of the only all-*Western* brigade assigned to the Eastern armies of the Union.

Although the Second Wisconsin had fought at First Bull Run, King's other regiments were untried. The regimental field officers were equally green. Some famous American names were among the officers, like Major Charles A. Hamilton of the Seventh Wisconsin, Alexander Hamilton's grandson, and Captain Rufus Dawes of the Sixth Wisconsin, great-grandson of William G. Dawes, Paul Revere's companion on the eve of Lexington and Concord. Rufus Dawes was now to distinguish himself, and was also to sire a vice president of the United States, (Charles Gates Dawes, vice president under Calvin Coolidge, 1925–29). In addition to these well-descended men, another name was later to be famous. This was Frank A. Haskell, a captain in the Sixth Wisconsin, who was to write a famous letter about Gettysburg. These officers provided the brigade with some promise of distinction, as did the association with a crack regular army outfit, the honorable and historic Battery B of the Fourth U. S. Artillery. Commanded by Captain John Gibbon of West Point and North Carolina, a *Union* man whose three brothers were in Confederate service, the battery was assigned to the Western soldiers' division. The battery was understrength and it was soon filled up by the detachment of men from the Western infantry regiments. This process, which was to be repeated over the next two years, and the fact that the brigade and the battery were to fight together, created an intimate relationship between the two organizations.

L ike most of the Army of the Potomac, the Western Brigade was inactive throughout the winter of 1861–1862. And when the army moved to the Peninsula in the spring, the Westerners, part of the First Corps, marched instead to Falmouth and Fredericksburg. There, on May 7, 1862, John Gibbon was commissioned a brigadier of volunteers and promoted to command the brigade. Gibbon was a thoroughly professional soldier and a natural leader. Ultimately he was to command a corps in the Army of the James. But in May of 1862, he set about to make first-rate soldiers of his Western men. Reflecting a fine sense of *esprit de corps*, he first ordered a special uniform for them. The uniform was largely that of the United States army regulars—the frock coat and the stiff, black Hardee hat. He also obtained white leggings and white gloves for the Western men. Of these items, only the Hardee hat was to survive and be reissued to the soldiers, and the head gear was to become their trademark. Having thus distinguished the *appearance* of his volunteers, Gibbon embarked upon a rigorous training program designed to distinguish their conduct.

Gibbon's regime was afforded more than three months to make soldiers of his volunteers. But, at last, on August 28, the brigade was suddenly and furiously engaged at the Brawner Farm between Gainesville and Groveton, Virginia, as Pope and Lee maneuvered for their struggle at Second Bull Run. The Westerners were surprised that day by two divisions of Jackson's Corps. But despite the surprise and the fact that they were heavily outnumbered, Gibbon's men stood their ground out in the open and blazed away at Jackson's men at a range of a hundred yards. In doing so, they suffered casualties in excess of 33 percent. But they inflicted a similar percentage on the outnumbering foe. The eminent Douglas Southall Freeman was later to find the battle one of Stonewall Jackson's costliest for the numbers engaged. And Jackson's great British biographer, G. F. R. Henderson, has said this about the day: "The Federals, surprised and unsupported, bore away the honours. The Western Brigade . . . displayed a coolness and a steadfastness worthy of the soldiers of Albuera."

After their first fight at Brawner Farm, the Western Brigade, then known as the "Black Hat Brigade," went on to similar exploits at Second Bull Run, always joined in their efforts by their kinsmen of Battery B. At South Mountain they earned their proud title of "Iron Brigade," and they lived up to this promise at Antietam, giving up 42 percent of their numbers in the First Corps' hideous fight in the cornfield and near the Dunker Church. After this bloodletting, the reduced Westerners were reinforced by another Western regiment, the newly-raised Twenty-Fourth Michigan, commanded by a Detroit judge, Colonel Henry A. Morrow, a native of Virginia. John Gibbon reviewed the Michigan men before advancing to division command. His iron soldiers condescendingly received the newcomers. But this condescension disappeared after Fredericksburg where the Michigan men earned a place in the brigade. After Burnside's "Mud March," Chancellorsville was also added to the battle honors of the brigade, before the fateful first of July, 1863, at Gettysburg.

As was true of the rest of the Army of the Potomac, everything else was but prelude to Gettysburg. The Iron Brigade, commanded now by another North Carolinian, Solomon Meredith, originally colonel of the Nineteenth Indiana, was by this time the *First* Brigade of the *First* Division of the *First* Corps.

Arriving during the morning fight between Heth's Division and the Federal cavalry on July 1, the Westerners' division was the first Federal infantry on the field. Unaware the Federal army was on hand in force, the Confederates anticipated that militia would join the blue cavalry west of the town. But at the order of General John F. Reynolds, the Iron Brigade was sent at once into the fray. Up and down the Confederate battle line went a cry of recognition: "Thar comes them black hats! It ain't the militia, it's the Army of the Potomac!"

At the outset the Westerners routed Archer's Confederates in McPherson's Woods. Then the Sixth Wisconsin led the Federals in bottling up Davis' Brigade in the railroad cut north of the Cashtown Road. In the afternoon, joined by the rest of the First Corps and Howard's Eleventh Corps, the Iron Brigade participated in the First Corps' brilliant defense against overwhelming numbers, before withdrawing to Cemetery Hill. There on the night of Gettysburg's first day, as the rest of Meade's army moved into position on the ridges and hills which became the Federal position, the regiments of the Iron Brigade counted their losses: Twenty-fourth Michigan—80 percent; Second Wisconsin—77 percent; Nineteenth Indiana—72 percent; Seventh Wisconsin—51 percent; Sixth Wisconsin—48 percent. All of this meant that the Iron Brigade was to lead the entire army in its percentage of losses at Gettysburg, *but the Western men had not taken a single backward step except on orders.*

R educed to 600 men, the Iron Brigade was reinforced just after Gettysburg by a series of Eastern regiments. Gradually the brigade lost its identity. It was also gradually divorced from Battery B, which was to lead all Federal field batteries in killed and wounded for the entire period of the war. Battery B remained in the field until Appomattox, as did some of the veterans of the brigade. The vaunted name "Iron Brigade" also remained on the roster, but after Gettysburg it was not the same organization which Rufus King had organized, John Gibbon had perfected, and Solomon Meredith had led on its greatest day. Even before this greatest day, one of Berdan's Sharpshooters had seen the Iron Brigade and he was later to write an appropriate epitaph for the Westerners. Referring to the army's march away from the Chancellorsville defeat, Berdan's man recorded:

> Loud cheers were frequently given when some particular regiment or brigade passed by. Especially when, while resting on the roadside . . . the great Western or Iron Brigade passed, looking like giants with their tall black hats . . . and giants they were, in action. . . .

"Looking like giants . . . and giants they were" to their companions. And this was not simply rhetoric, because the records show that the Iron Brigade suffered a higher percentage of battle deaths than any other Federal brigade. This is the real testament of the men in the black hats, the only exclusively Western brigade of the Eastern war.

Brave Men's Tears: The Iron Brigade at Brawner Farm

We are again in the midst of a renaissance of interest in the Civil War. Since it is generally regarded by historians as one of the principal events in American history, the renaissance is surely appropriate. The question is what kind of scholarship the new surge of interest will produce. It is my view that we do not need additional attention to the "big picture." Retelling the story of the big picture is not only redundant, it also typically requires such a broad brush that much of significance is unreported and the history to that extent is a distortion. "History" is, after all, the sum of its parts. What is needed, I believe, is more concern for the parts, for the "little pictures," or at least smaller ones. The little pictures must be examined in order for one to construct the big picture. The little pictures permit the kind of detail that illuminates, enriches, and corrects the big pictures. In short, what is needed are such things as unit histories and histories of individual battles and engagements.

This book by Alan D. Gaff precisely fits my sense of the needs of Civil War scholarship. It is a book about a single battle. It is, moreover, an excellent book. It owes its excellence to three factors: the character of the soldiers who fought at Brawner Farm; the nature of the battle itself; and the manner in which the author has described the event. These factors—the *participants,* the *battle* and the *authorship*—combine to make the book uniquely worthwhile. It is appropriate for this Introduction briefly to discuss these factors.

For the Confederates, although Stonewall Jackson's entire corps was at hand, the fighting was largely done by four brigades: Baylor's Stonewall Brigade and A. G. Taliaferro's Brigade from William B. Taliaferro's Division, and Trimble's and Lawton's Brigades from Ewell's Division. Several Confederate batteries were also in action.

The principal Federal participants were the soldiers of Gibbon's Brigade and their artillery companions of Battery B of the Fourth U. S. Artillery, made up largely of infantry soldiers who had transferred from Gibbon's infantry regiments. Gibbon's men were vigorously assisted by two regiments from Doubleday's Brigade, the Fifty-sixth Pennsylvania and the Seventy-sixth New York, and by Battery D of the First Rhode Island Light Artillery. Gibbon's Brigade and Doubleday's Brigade were of the First Division (Rufus King's) in McDowell's Corps of Pope's Army of Virginia.

For Gibbon's Brigade, the battle was the prophetic beginning of a storied career. Composed initially of the Nineteenth Indiana and the Second, Sixth, and Seventh Wisconsin Volunteers, the brigade was organized on October 1, 1861. It was the only all-Western Brigade in the Eastern armies of the Union. Because they wore the regular army's dress uniform, the Western men were known for a time as the "Black Hat Brigade." Shortly after Brawner Farm, at South Mountain, this sobriquet was changed to "Iron Brigade." Reinforced after Antietam by the Twenty-fourth Michigan, the Iron Brigade was, in T. Harry Williams' words, "the best fighting brigade in the army." In the final accounting, it suffered a higher proportion of battle deaths than any brigade in the Federal armies. A similar doleful distinction marked the career of Battery B: the greatest aggregate losses of any field artillery battery in the Federal service.

These, then, are the soldiers at Brawner Farm. They establish the first reason for the significance of this study.

S ometimes confusingly identified as Groveton or Gainesville, Brawner Farm took place on August 28, 1862, on the eve of Second Bull Run, in the midst of the complicated maneuvering of the armies that led to that battle. Brawner Farm was thus a part of the Second Bull Run Campaign, but it had an existence and integrity of its own, an existence and integrity that have been overshadowed by the tumult of the immediately following days. It is not an "unknown" battle, but it has never before been studied in the detail that its dramatic character deserves.

The drama of Brawner Farm arises from several circumstances. In the first place, although Gibbon's Western regiments had been brigaded on October 1, 1861, Brawner Farm was the baptism of fire for the brigade. One of his regiments, the Second Wisconsin, had fought at Bull Run in 1861, but the other Wisconsin regiments and the Hoosiers of the

Nineteenth Indiana had not been seriously engaged. Having in mind the ultimate distinction of these soldiers—the Iron Brigade—it is important to know how their combat career began.

The battle was, in addition, in every sense a surprise to the Federals. Caught in the Federal army's command confusion associated with the Second Bull Run Campaign, and without effective direction at the *army, corps* or *division* level, the brigades of Gibbon and Doubleday appeared on the Warrenton Turnpike at the farm of John C. Brawner, unaware that Jackson's Corps was encamped and in hiding nearby. They appeared in front of Jackson just as that general learned that Longstreet's Corps, from which Jackson's had been separated, was nearby, so that Jackson was free to attack. Jackson did attack the unknowing Federals who, according to Rufus Dawes of the Sixth Wisconsin, were passing along the turnpike "as unsuspectingly as if changing camp."

There is also a David and Goliath aspect to the battle. The Federals were not only surprised and inexperienced in combat. They were also heavily outnumbered. Of his superior numbers available, Jackson committed approximately 5900 infantry to the battle. Even after reinforcement by Doubleday's two regiments, Gibbon was able to field only 2500 infantry. Unlike David, the Federals did not fell the giant, but in the words of Jackson's report, they "maintained their ground with obstinate determination," and the disengagement in the final darkness was a mutual act.

Finally, it is plain that the battle was unusually intense, a stand-up fight, with little maneuver and little available cover. The participants, including Generals William B. Taliaferro, Isaac Trimble, and John Gibbon, remarked on the extraordinary ferocity of the conflict. Gaff records the fateful consequences of this aspect of the battle: the casualties were very high. Stonewall Jackson's admiring biographer, G. F. R. Henderson, said this about Brawner Farm: "The men who faced each other that August evening fought with a gallantry that has seldom been surpassed." Henderson also went further: "The Federals, surprised and unsupported, bore away the honours. The Western Brigade, commanded by General Gibbon, displayed a coolness and steadfastness worthy of the soldiers of Albuera."

A lan D. Gaff is, in my view, unequaled as a historical researcher. Literally no one else that I know who is writing today goes as far and as deep as he does. Having researched and written about Brawner Farm myself, I know something of the research possibilities. I genuinely believe that this is the final, definitive account of the battle. It corrects some of my own interpretations of the sources and goes far beyond my search.

Another secret of the book is structural. The author deftly places the battle in context, so that it is meaningful in the campaign as a whole, but he does not lose the focus on Brawner Farm and its integrity and meaning.

Gaff also uses his exceptional sources in a very good way. The participants are frequently allowed to speak for themselves about what they had done at Brawner Farm. When not directly quoting, the author concentrates on telling the story in large measure as the soldiers saw it. There is thus a three-dimensional character to the account.

Finally, although Gaff feels and writes of the high drama of combat, he is not a sentimentalist. The plain awfulness of this battle is here, as is its ultimate irony. Having found Jackson's Corps, and thereby provided the Federal army with the logistical opportunity to prevent the joinder of Jackson and Longstreet, the soldiers of King's Division were ordered to march away to Manassas. Behind them Jackson and Longstreet joined, which signaled the decisive Federal defeat on the succeeding days.

Because of the detail of this account and Gaff's unusual insights, this book tells us a lot about what it was like to be a Civil War soldier and what the Civil War was like. His book is a major contribution to Civil War scholarship.

As I write this Introduction, I see on my desk a faded silk ribbon dated 1871 and worn at the "First Annual Reunion" of the Nineteenth Indiana Volunteers. The reunion took place in Cambridge City, Indiana, home of General Solomon Meredith, the colonel of the regiment at Brawner Farm. It is, of course, not a coincidence that the ribbon identifies the date on which the reunion took place: *August 28*, the anniversary of Brawner Farm. It occurs to me that the Hoosier soldiers and the others who fought there would especially appreciate Alan Gaff's book. They would like the realism. They would say, I believe, "Yes, that's the way it was."

John Brawner's Damage Claim

The Battle on the Farm

People interested in the Iron Brigade are generally aware of its first full-blown combat on the Brawner Farm on August 28, 1862, the eve of Second Bull Run.[1] It was a stunning engagement in which the brigade and Battery B, surprised and outnumbered, fought to a standstill men of Stonewall Jackson's wing of Lee's army. Jackson's wing had separated from Lee and Longstreet's wing on August 25 at the Rappahannock River. Flanking Major General John Pope's Army of Virginia, Jackson had fallen on Manassas in Pope's rear on August 26. Aware that his wing was vulnerable by itself in northern Virginia, Jackson had moved his 25,000 men to wooded Stony Ridge immediately north of the Brawner Farm. There he waited for Lee and Longstreet to follow him into northern Virginia.

The farm of John C. Brawner, a tenant farmer, was located along the north side of the Warrenton Turnpike between the crossroads villages of Gainesville and Groveton, Virginia. The countryside was rolling with occasional ridges and in 1862 was marked by patches of woods and marginal farms.[2] Brawner's farm was composed of approximately 300 acres.

---

[1]There are three detailed accounts of the battle at Brawner Farm: Alan D. Gaff, *Brave Men's Tears: The Iron Brigade at Brawner Farm* (Dayton: Morningside House, Inc., 1988); John J. Hennessy, *Return to Bull Run* (New York: Simon & Schuster, 1993), 153–93; Alan T. Nolan, *The Iron Brigade*, third edition (Bloomington: Indiana University Press, 1994), 80–98.

[2]The physical descriptions of the farm area are based on close personal examination of the ground, maps, and participants' descriptions. *Maps:* (1) "Map of

It was owned by the widow Augusta Douglas of Gainesville, and since 1858 had been leased to Brawner. Brawner was sixty-four years old in 1862. Prior to the war, his household included his wife, two sons, and three daughters. In August of 1862, the sons were away in the army. The whereabouts of his wife in 1862 are unknown.[3]

Brawner's farm was not imposing. The farmhouse and barn were located a quarter of a mile north of the Warrenton Turnpike on the crest of a gentle ridge. A farm lane led from the turnpike to the farmhouse. In the yard, extending to the east, was an orchard. Except for the orchard and a small grove of trees at the house and barn, the ground near the buildings was cleared so that the fields in front and behind the buildings were open. Brawner's fields were bordered on the east by a rectangular wood that lay south and east of the farm buildings. The wood was approximately a fifth of a mile long. Its north edge, enclosed by a zigzag rail fence, began seventy-five yards south of the crest of the farm building ridge and extended down to and south of the turnpike. Inside the wood, the ground was rugged and irregular and dipped down to the

---

the Battle-Grounds of August 28–29–30, In the Vicinity of Groveton, Prince William County, Va., Made by Authority of the Hon. G. W. McCrary, Sec. of War, Surveyed in June 1878 by Bvt. Maj. Gen. G. K. Warren, Major of Engineers, 1878, U.S.A." National Archives, Washington, D.C.; (2) U.S. War Department, *The War of the Rebellion: A Compilation of the Official Records of the Union and Confederate Armies*, ser. I, Volume 12, Part 2 Supplement, facing page 1052; (3) Esposito, Col. Vincent J., ed., *Atlas to Accompany Steele's American Campaigns* (West Point: United States Military Academy), map 60; (4) U.S. Army Corps of Engineers, United States Department of the Interior Geological Survey, *Gainesville Quadrangle* (Washington, 1953); (5) Rufus R. Dawes, *Service with the Sixth Wisconsin Volunteers* (Marietta: E. R. Alderman and Sons, 1890), 66; and (6) Gibbon, *Personal Recollections*, 53. *Participants' descriptions:* Theron Haight, *Gainesville, Groveton and Bull Run*, War Papers, Wisconsin Commandery, Military Order of the Loyal Legion, Volume 2 (Milwaukee: 1896), 345–56. Personal examination of the ground, now a part of Manassas National Battlefield Park, establishes that it is unchanged since 1862 with the exception of an additional barn, miscellaneous trees and bushes, and the wood which is larger now, north and south, with an extension in the northeast corner. The farmhouse and barn are postwar but located where the 1862 buildings were. The remnants of an orchard are visible.

[3] *Petition of John C. Brawner, Prince William County, Southern Claims Commission*, Commission No. 1335, Office No. 13, Report No. 1, U.S. National Archives (Washington, D.C.), hereinafter identified as "Brawner Claim File."

level of the turnpike at the eastern edge of the wood, where another open field extended to the north from the turnpike.

A Confederate general officer later characterized the Brawner Farm as simply "a farm-house, an orchard, a few stacks of hay, and a rotten 'worm' fence,"[4] but Virginia was a border state and the farm was perilously close to Washington, thirty miles to the east. When the Virginia Convention voted on April 17, 1861, to secede,[5] northern Virginia became a marchland. Confederate troops had advanced toward the Potomac and the Union moved divisions across the river onto Virginia soil.

Brawner's first brush with the war, a near miss for his property, had taken place in July of 1861. The Federals had undertaken their first major offensive in northern Virginia and had been defeated in the First Battle of Bull Run. Sixty thousand soldiers, Northern and Southern, had engaged in a confused and bloody struggle around the Henry House Hill and Bull Run, five miles east of the farm. The Federals had then retreated to the Washington defenses, leaving the Confederates in Brawner's neighborhood until March of 1862. Anticipating another Union advance, the Confederates had then withdrawn southward toward the Rappahannock River and the Federals had moved before marching farther south. For almost four months during the late spring and early summer of 1862, things were quiet around the Brawner Farm.[6] Then in August of 1862, the armies had again marched into northern Virginia and the fighting had moved toward the farm.

Brigadier General Rufus King's Division, including Brigadier General John Gibbon's Brigade of Western men, mustered approximately 10,000 officers and men of all arms[7] and was assigned to Major General Irvin McDowell's Third Corps of Pope's army. On August 28, 1862, the division was marching east on the turnpike en route to Centreville as a part of Pope's inept and ill-informed effort to find Jackson before Lee and Longstreet's wing of the Army of Northern Virginia joined Jackson. The route of march was past the Brawner Farm. Immediately behind

---

[4]Robert Underwood Johnson and Clarence Clough Buel, eds., *Battles and Leaders of the Civil War,* Volume 2 (New York: Century, 1884–87), 510.

[5]*Official Records,* Volume 2, 1.

[6]These early months of the war are well described in James M. McPherson, *Battle Cry of Freedom* (New York: Oxford University Press, 1988).

[7]*Official Records,* Volume 12, Part 3, 580, 584.

Gibbon's Brigade in King's column was the brigade of Brigadier General Abner Doubleday.

From his post on Stony Ridge, Stonewall Jackson saw King's apparently isolated division marching across his front, past the Brawner Farm.[8] It was approximately 5:00 P.M. and the sun was beginning to set. At about the same time, Jackson heard from Lee. Longstreet had reached nearby Thoroughfare Gap, was expected to force it, and was within supporting distance. Jackson immediately disposed his troops to attack. As the head of Gibbon's column emerged from the cover of the wood at the eastern edge of the Brawner property, a Confederate battery fired on it from a position north and east of the farm. Another battery, firing from the north and west of the farm, promptly opened on other brigades of King's Division that were marching to the rear of Gibbon's men. Believing that the enemy guns were unsupported horse artillery, Gibbon ordered Battery B to the head of his column to respond to the battery firing from the east and directed the Second Wisconsin Volunteers, his only combat veterans, to silence the battery firing in his rear.

Battery B drove rapidly up the turnpike, unlimbered, and went into position on a knoll east of the Brawner woods and just north of the turnpike. As the Federal artillery commenced firing, the Second Wisconsin moved through the woods. Having formed line of battle in the open field south of the Brawner farmhouse and barn, it started forward. Approaching the crest of the ridge on which the farm buildings were located, the unsuspecting Federals were suddenly fired on from their right flank by skirmishers from Starke's Brigade of Brigadier General William B. Taliaferro's Stonewall Division. In spite of their surprise, the Wisconsin men did not falter. They wheeled to their right and returned Starke's fire. The flank companies of the Wisconsin regiment were sent forward as skirmishers and Starke's Confederates withdrew over the crest of the ridge followed by the Wisconsin skirmishers. Within a few yards, the Federal skirmishers confronted a larger group of Confederates posted in a small grove of trees. Shots were exchanged as the other Second Wisconsin companies, moving with the skirmish line, reached the crest of the ridge. Looking north from the crest, the Western men at last knew the truth: Long columns of Confederate infantry were filing out of wooded Stony Ridge and advancing on the Brawner property. At once

[8]See note 1, above

Baylor's Stonewall Brigade, also of Taliaferro's Division, opened fire on the Second Wisconsin. Rejoined by its skirmishers, the embattled Second Wisconsin returned this fire and held its ground.

At last comprehending the force of the Confederate assault, having dispatched calls for help to division commander King and the other brigades of the division, Gibbon sent the Nineteenth Indiana to form on the left of the Second Wisconsin, extending his line toward the Brawner farm buildings. The Seventh Wisconsin went in to the right of the Second. Gibbon committed the Sixth Wisconsin to the right of the Seventh, to a position in the lower ground in the field east of the Brawner woods. Behind the Sixth, the guns of Battery B were at work.

The battle was now joined. Gibbon's line was just south of the crest of the Brawner farmhouse ridge. From left to right it followed the ridge line, passed along the northern edge of the wood and extended into the field east of the wood. There was a large gap in the line between the positions of the Seventh and Sixth Wisconsin. Having driven off the Confederate battery that had begun the affair, Battery B now moved to a new position so that it could fire into this gap. Both of Gibbon's flanks were in the air and were overlapped by the larger Confederate forces, even before Confederate reserves entered the battle.

In addition to Starke's Brigade, the Confederate skirmishers that had surprised the Second Wisconsin, and Baylor's Stonewall Brigade, Jackson now committed the brigade of Colonel A. G. Taliaferro from the same Division. He also sent in the brigades of Brigadier Generals Isaac R. Trimble and Alexander R. Lawton from Major General Richard S. Ewell's division, and additional artillery. Although not ordered to do so, Doubleday sent the Seventy-sixth New York and Fifty-sixth Pennsylvania from his Brigade into the gap between the Seventh and Sixth Wisconsin. His remaining regiment, the Ninety-fifth New York, moved to the support of Battery B. Battery D of the First Rhode Island Light Artillery of Doubleday's brigade also joined the battle. It appears that Jackson committed between 5,900 and 6,400 infantry. Gibbon was able to field between 2,500 and 2,900 infantry, including the regiments from Doubleday's Brigade. The two sides were relatively even in artillery engaged.[9]

---

[9]The difficult question of numbers is discussed in Nolan, *The Iron Brigade,* 78, 84, 88, 89. See also Gaff, *Brave Men's Tears,* 156–60.

Darkness and the tacit consent of the generals terminated the engagement. From the first Confederate artillery fire to the last desultory infantry fire, it lasted for approximately three hours, perhaps two of which were intense. The participants have adequately characterized the nature of the fight. According to Brigadier General Taliaferro, "It was a stand-up combat, dogged and unflinching, in a field almost bare. There were no wounds from spent balls, the confronting lines looked into each other's faces at deadly range, less than a hundred yards apart, and they stood as immovable as the painted heroes in a battle-piece."[10] The Confederates held the farmhouse and the northern edge of the orchard and their line then extended in front of the Brawner wood and into the low ground in the field east of the wood. The Federals clung to the farmyard, the southern edge of the orchard, and the northern face of the wood, extending their line eastward into the same low ground. Gibbon, who was to be in many battles, later said that it was "the most terrific musketry fire I . . . ever listened to."[11] Brigadier General Taliaferro reported it was "one of the most terrific conflicts that can be conceived of." Brigadier General Trimble stated that "I have never known so terrible a fire as raged . . . on both sides." And Doubleday wrote that "there have been few more unequal contests or better contested fields during the war."[12] Perhaps Brigadier General Taliaferro provided the best summary description of the engagement. After the war, and referring to the Federal as well as Confederate participants, he wrote: "out in the sunlight, in the dying daylight, and under the stars, they stood, and although they could not advance, they would not retire. There was some discipline in this, but there was much more of true valor."[13]

And, of course, this kind of fighting exacted a fearful toll. Thirty-seven percent of Gibbon's Western men were casualties, including three of four regimental commanders, the lieutenant colonel of the Seventh Wisconsin, and the majors of three of the four Western regiments. Doubleday's regiments also lost heavily. On the Confederate side, the total

[10] Johnson and Buel, *Battles and Leaders,* 510.

[11] Gibbon, *Personal Recollections,* 54.

[12] *Official Records,* Volume 12, Part 2, 657; Isaac R. Trimble, "Trimble's Report of Operations of His Brigade from 14th to 29th of August, 1862," *Southern Historical Society Papers,* 8 (1880), 306–309; Abner Doubleday Journal, Harpers Ferry Center Library, Harpers Ferry, West Virginia.

[13] Johnson and Buel, *Battles and Leaders,* 510.

losses exceeded those of the Federals, and the Federal rifles accounted for division commanders William B. Taliaferro and Richard S. Ewell. Nine regimental commanders, including three in the Stonewall Brigade, were killed or wounded. Douglas Southall Freeman has written that the battle was one of Jackson's costliest, for the numbers engaged.[14]

Leaving their dead and wounded on the farm, the surviving Federals returned to the turnpike and ultimately made a painful night march to Manassas. Jackson's men returned to Stony Ridge. Confederate physicians tended the Federal wounded as well as their own and Confederate burial parties buried the dead of both sides in shallow graves on Brawner's property. On the next two days, August 29 and 30, Second Bull Run, a major battle and a spectacular Confederate victory, took place just east of the farm. The Confederates remained on the farm and Southern artillery batteries placed there participated in the Confederate victory.

Stonewall Jackson's admiring biographer, the Englishman G. F. R. Henderson, was later to write of Brawner Farm: "The men who faced each other that August evening fought with a gallantry that has seldom been surpassed. . . . The Federals, surprised and unsupported, bore away the honors. The Western Brigade, commanded by Gen. Gibbon, displayed a coolness and steadfastness worthy of the soldiers of Albuera."[15] Brawner Farm was in fact the prophetic beginning of a storied career for the soldiers from the Old Northwest and for Battery B. Later reinforced by the newly raised Twenty-fourth Michigan Volunteers, the Western brigade went on to earn the sobriquet "Iron Brigade."

The Claim

In 1871, the Forty-first Congress of the United States enacted a war claims statute. The legislation authorized the payment of claims "of those citizens who remained loyal adherents to the cause of the government . . . during the war, for stores or supplies taken or furnished during the rebellion for the use of the army of the United States in States proclaimed as in insurrection against the United States." A three-member

[14]Nolan, *The Iron Brigade*, 95–96; Gaff, *Brave Men's Tears*, 156–60.
[15]Henderson, G. F. R., *Stonewall Jackson and the American Civil War* (New York: Grosset, 1936), 451.

commission was created, to sit in Washington, to adjudicate the claims on the basis of "testimony of witnesses under oath, or from other sufficient evidence." The commissioners were required to keep a journal of their proceedings and a register of claims.[16] These papers are now in the National Archives.[17]

John C. Brawner was quick to file his claim. The statute was approved March 3, 1871. Brawner hired Uriah B. Mitchell, a Washington attorney, and filed his claim on April 27, 1871. Identified in the claim form as a resident of Prince William County with a Gainesville Station post office address, Brawner apparently still lived on the wartime farm or close by. Taken down in longhand by someone acting for the Commission, the testimony of Brawner, his daughter Mary, and two witnesses in his behalf, Richard Graham, and John Crop, are in the claim file. Also included in the file is the statement of one Jackson Tippins.

Sworn before Justice of the Peace G. A. Simpson, Brawner asserted that he had supplied corn, hay, wheat, bacon, oats, salt, and flour to the soldiers of General King's Division. These men, he said, had also killed and eaten a cow and twenty-two hogs and taken $23.00 worth of fowls. His horse was shot and died from wounds. Some of his household and kitchen furniture was taken for use by wounded men. His vegetable garden was destroyed. Finally, axes, hoes, spades, and other farm tools were appropriated. The total claim was for $1,153.75. The claim concluded with Brawner's certification that he did not "voluntarily serve in the Confederate army or navy . . . that he never voluntarily furnished any stores, supplies or other material aid to said Confederate army or navy, or to the Confederate government . . . or yielded voluntary support to the said Confederate government."

In support of his claim, Brawner testified that he was a native of Maryland and had moved to Virginia at seven years of age. He had witnessed the First Battle of Bull Run in July of 1861. When the Confeder-

---

[16]Chapter 116, Forty-First Congress, Session III, "An Act Making Appropriations For The Support Of The Army For The Year Ending June Thirty, Eighteen Hundred And Seventy-Two, And For Other Purposes," Sections 2–6, 524–25.

[17]See note 3 above. The facts concerning the claim appear in the Brawner Claim File.

ate army had fallen back toward the Rappahannock in March of 1862, Brawner had remained on the farm although his neighbors in the area had left. When the Federals moved in during the spring of 1862, officers had visited Brawner and had asked him why he had remained. According to his testimony, he had explained that he was crippled and could not leave and that he did not believe that the Union soldiers were "barbarians." The officers, he said, had then given him "protection papers."

Brawner also stated that he had stayed inside during the August 28 battle on his farm, although bullets had crashed through the house. His home and farm were "broken up" by the battle of August 28 and he and his family were "driven away." They left the morning after the battle and went to a neighbor's house to the north of the combat area.

To perfect his claim, Brawner needed to establish three things: the identification and value of the goods furnished by him, that *Federal* troops had taken those goods, and that he had been loyal to the United States. Having listed the goods, Brawner's statements were principally directed to two issues, presumably reflecting the questions with which the claims commissioners were concerned: whether the Federals or Confederates were responsible for his losses and whether or not he met the statute's loyalty requirement.

On the issue of which army was responsible, Brawner asserted that "General King sent to my house and officers came for supplies." Regarding the loss of the hogs included in his claim, these, he said, were butchered by the soldiers and then carried off. When he left the farm on August 29, the day after the Iron Brigade's fight, Union soldiers were in his house. When he returned, they were still there, but the furniture was gone or "used up." Among the soldiers were Union wounded. Brawner and his daughter waited on them, he said. The farm tools, presumably the spades, were used by the soldiers to dig graves.

Regarding his allegiance to the Union, despite his certification Brawner admitted a number of incriminating facts. He was uncertain whether he had voted in the election of delegates to the Virginia Convention that had ultimately voted to secede. He did not think he had voted "on the adoption of the Constitution," presumably a reference to the balloting of May 23, 1861, when Virginia voters had approved the earlier secession ordinance.[18] But Brawner's sons were a major problem.

[18] *Official Records,* Volume 2, 911–12.

He said they had left the farm in March of 1862, when the Confederate army had fallen back toward the Rappahannock, and had then entered the rebel army. Brawner said that they had been drafted and he was questioned about them at length. He had, he said, advised them against enlisting. Although they had reached their majority and he had no control over them, they had listened to him and had not volunteered. He and his sons "agreed about the war and did not want the government broken up." He had not heard from them and did nothing for them while they were in the army. The younger son had been captured and imprisoned for approximately two years. Having been exchanged, the son "came home from prison," returned to the army, and was again captured by the Federals.

Pursuing the loyalty issue, the examiners questioned Brawner about his neighbors. Although he identified Philip Smith, with whom he had taken refuge after the battle on the farm, as "with the South," others whom he named were "all Union men," including his witness, Richard Graham. Returning to questions about his own views, Brawner said that his "sentiments were peace," "let the Union stand as it was and have no war." Apparently pressed about his feelings, he made this answer:

> I had no sympathy for either side when the battle was going on.
> I suppose my feelings naturally were with my sons when in bat-
> tle and I suppose I wanted them to whip. But I had no sympa-
> thy with either side, for they brought it on themselves.

Mary B. Brawner, John C. Brawner's daughter, had moved away from the farm sometime prior to the hearing. Her statement essentially conformed with her father's but she also added some interesting details. Part of the time the farm was within the Confederate lines and part of the time within the Union lines, "the Union army was passing backward and forward all the time after the Southern army left" in March of 1862. At times when the rebel army was nearby, Confederate officers came to the farm and either purchased or took such things as milk and butter. Her brothers had indeed been drafted into the Confederate army. One was a cavalryman and the other an infantry soldier. Her father had not furnished either of them a horse or anything else. They had come home occasionally during the war.

With reference to which army had supplied itself on the farm at the time of "the battle . . . all around my father's house," the daughter testified that a quartermaster and soldiers who came for supplies said that they were from General Rufus King, the Federal, and that they would bring receipts for what was taken. "But then," she said, referring to August 28, "the battle came on, and we did not get any receipt." She generally verified her father's statements as to what goods had been taken and said that she had seen the soldiers who took some of the goods.

Brawner's remaining witnesses were two men who purported to testify as to his loyalty. Neither was particularly helpful to him. Richard Graham's nearby store was the prewar post office, presumably the Gainesville Station site. He testified that Brawner was often in the store and in the discussion there "he always took a stand against it," an apparent reference to secession. Graham and Brawner were in agreement on this point. Graham further testified that he himself had "hesitantly" voted for secession in the Virginia referendum and "went with the state" after it seceded. He did not know Brawner's feelings after Virginia seceded. When the Confederate army withdrew from northern Virginia in March of 1862, Graham left the area and moved to Richmond. John Crop, an acquaintance of Brawner for twenty years, corroborated Graham regarding Brawner's prewar opposition to secession. "He said he was in favor of U.S. Govt.," before the war. Concluding his statement, Crop added what one suspects was a touch of realism. "Nobody could talk in favor of the Union after the state seceded."

The most interesting testimony in the Brawner file is that of Jackson Tippins, identified in the record as a "colored employee of the Commission." He had lived, he said, in Stafford County, the county immediately south of Brawner's Prince William County. Nothing in the record tells whether Tippins had been a free black or a slave before the war, or whether he was called to the hearing or simply happened to be on hand in Washington at the time. His testimony, however, was plainly damaging to Brawner: "I know Brawner. . . . I know he was no Union man. I heard him talk. . . . His reputation was that of a rebel." And Tippins testified to an overt act. At some unstated time, he said, a man named Underwood had "put up a Union flag in Occaquan," a Virginia village that has since disappeared from the map. According to Tippins, "Brawner was with the men who cut it down."

The claim file ends with the Commission's brief decision. The issue of which army had taken or destroyed Brawner's property was not addressed or resolved by the Commission. Although the record of the proceedings does not say so, in view of the logistics of the battle on the farm, there is reason to doubt that Federal troops were responsible for the losses. When attacked, the Iron Brigade was marching on the turnpike that ran past the farm. It fought on the part of the farm around the house and east of it, and retreated then toward Manassas Junction. At no time had it been encamped on the farm. It is much more likely that Confederate troops, who had encamped nearby before and occupied the farm after the battle, were the takers.

Concerned entirely with the loyalty issue, the decision noted the two sons in the Confederate army, recited Brawner's statement that they were of age and beyond his control, acknowledged that he had opposed their entering the army, but quoted his admission that he wanted them to "whip" in battle. The decision then set forth the substance of Tippins's testimony and concluded: "This claimant fails to establish his loyalty. . . . We reject the claim." A reading of the decision suggests that the word of the lowly and disenfranchised black man was a material factor in the deliberations.

Brawner's file contains two later entries that were not before the Commission that denied his claim. Dated November 30, 1875, and March 31, 1879, respectively, these facts were apparently turned up during the War Department's early work in assembling for publication the 127 volumes of *The War of the Rebellion: Official Records of the Union and Confederate Armies*. The first entry closely paraphrased a First Bull Run battle report of General P. C. T. Beauregard, the victorious Confederate commander, which stated: "Messrs. McLean, Wilcoxen, Kinchelo, and Brawner, citizens of the immediate vicinity . . . have placed me and the country under great obligations for the information relative to this region, which has enabled me to avail myself of its defensive features and resources. They were found ever ready to give me their time without stint or reward." The second reported that "Mr. Brawner sold to the Confederate States 3000 lbs Hay at 75 Cts, amt $22 50/100. Paid at Centreville, Va. Dec. 9th, 1861." The document recording this transaction, presumably a receipt, was signed by Captain John Page, a quartermaster of the Confederate States of America.

Whether these documents referred to John C. Brawner or one of his sons will now never be known. Brawner is in fact a relatively common name in northern Virginia. But the incidents took place very close to the Brawner Farm and would surely have interested the claims Commission.

The Significance of the Claim

The claim file provides dramatic insight into what happened when Civil War armies met on one's property. It also suggests the complicated circumstances of life and loyalty in a Civil War marchland. The crediting of the black man's word is a specific example of the social revolution wrought by the war.

And the file does more. The evidence verifies the precise location of the battle of August 28, 1862. It did take place on John C. Brawner's farm. This, in turn, validates the naming of the battle as the Battle of Brawner Farm, the unique name I gave it in 1961 when my military history, *The Iron Brigade*,[19] was first published. Prior to 1961, there was widespread confusion about the name of the Brawner Farm fight. Federal writers at the time of the war, like Rufus R. Dawes of the Sixth Wisconsin Volunteers, called it the "Battle of Gainesville," as did the *Official Records*.[20] This was not apt because the battle did not in fact take place at Gainesville. Modern authorities like Kenneth P. Williams called it "Groveton,"[21] which was also inappropriate from a location standpoint and tended to confuse it with the larger and foreshadowing engagements of the next two days. Other modern authorities, including Douglas Southall Freeman, avoided the name problem entirely by leaving the battle unnamed. I believe that in a history of the Iron Brigade, the event on August 28, 1862, simply has to have a meaningful name.

I selected the Brawner name because it was distinctive, and thus confusion with other days' events was avoided, and because it was geographically accurate. For identification of the Brawner ownership prior to the finding of the National Archives claims file, there were two widely different authorities. The first of these was Stonewall Jackson, whose report of the affair, written April 23, 1863, accurately set forth the name of Brawner.[22] The second was Joseph Mills Hanson, former superintendent of the Manassas National Battlefield Park. An unpublished manuscript in the park's files contained an excerpt from a letter written under date of

[19]Nolan, *The Iron Brigade* (New York: The Macmillan Company, 1961).

[20]Dawes, *Service with the Sixth Wisconsin*, 60; *Official Records*, Volume 12, Part 2, 845.

[21]K. P. Williams, *Lincoln Finds a General*, Volume 1 (New York: The Macmillan Company, 1950), 318–20.

[22]*Official Records*, Volume 12, Part 2, 645.

December 21, 1946, by Hanson to the author of the manuscript, Fred W. Cross. Hanson said: "I believe . . . investigation would show the name of the place should be Brawner's. . . . Brawner is a common name around Manassas; there are many here today."[23] The only published Federal source that attempted to identify the property called it by the name of the owner rather than the tenant of the farm. In his *Personal Recollections of the Civil War*, John Gibbon included a rough map at page 53 which set forth the farmhouse, and called it "Douglass House." On the following page, this name is spelled "Douglas."[24] But the name applied by Stonewall Jackson at the time, and approved by Mr. Hanson, seemed to me to be preferable. The only other Confederate participant who tried to name the farm was not so successful. Captain J. B. Evans's report for the Fourth Virginia in the Stonewall Brigade refers to the name as "Brown," incorrect but not unlikely.[25] Since my application of the name Brawner Farm to the battle, other historians have adopted the Brawner Farm name. Among these other historians are Alan D. Gaff, Lance Herdegen, William J. K. Beaudot, and John J. Hennessy. The battle is now aptly identified with the Iron Brigade.

[23]Joseph Mills Hanson to Fred W. Cross, 21 December 1846, Manuscript File, Manassas National Battlefield Park, Manassas, Virginia.

[24]Gibbon, *Personal Recollections*, 53–54.

[25]*Official Records*, Volume 12, Part 3, 661.

IV

Selected
Reviews

Selected Reviews

Introduction to Book Reviews

People who write books sometimes find themselves asked to review others' books. This is a great boon for the reviewer. He or she gets a free book and, because the reviewer learns from the books and has his own thoughts sharpened in the process, it is a valuable activity. Mindful as a matter of personal experience of George Orwell's saying that "writing a book is like a bout with a serious illness," I am usually friendly to others' books because I appreciate what they have been through and why. Thus I resist the frequent tendency of many reviewers to approach a book so as to fault it. Occasionally, as will be seen hereinafter, a book arrives that seems to me inexcusably biased or uniformed, in which event I say so. I also try in my reviews to set forth my own substantive historical opinions related to the subject matter of the book I am reviewing. These characteristics of some of my reviews encourage me to include them in this volume.

Generals McClellan and Hancock

George B. McClellan: The Young Napoleon. By Stephen W. Sears. Ticknor & Fields, 1988. Pp. xii, 482.
Winfield Scott Hancock: A Soldier's Life. By David M. Jordan. Indiana University Press, 1988. Pp. xii, 393.

Robert Penn Warren has written that "The Civil War is, for the American imagination, the great single event of our history. Without too much wrenching, it may, in fact, be said to *be* American history." Whether or not this is an exaggeration, we are now embarked on another renaissance of Civil War writing. As in the past, both popular writers and the academic historians are at work. Much of the new scholarship is promising. If one may venture a cautious generalization, it may be said that the new writing, unlike that of prior generations, is marked by two principal characteristics. It is unromantic. Instead of glorifying or celebrating the war, the new scholarship treats it as the harsh tragedy that it surely was. In addition, today's writers are unapologetic to the South. The "Lost Cause" tradition, created in the South after the war and embraced by the North, has contained an implicit acceptance of the justification or logic of the Southern course of conduct. This is no longer the case among today's thoughtful writers. Stephen W. Sears' biography of General George B. McClellan and David M. Jordan's biography of General Winfield Scott Hancock, concerned with two of the war's leading military figures, are representative of the new genre.

In 1983, Sears authored an excellent book, *Landscape Turned Red,* a history of Robert E. Lee's 1862 Maryland Campaign and the Battle of Antietam. That book was marked by the writer's growing feeling of distaste for General McClellan, focused on McClellan's failure to support Pope's Army of Virginia at Second Bull Run on the eve of the Maryland Campaign, his slowness to realize the opportunity that Lee's movement into Maryland afforded, and his inept conduct of the Battle of Antietam. Indeed, the inadequacies of McClellan became the thesis of that book. A reader of Sears's McClellan biography senses that the study of the Maryland Campaign provoked in Sears a need to examine in detail the life and character of McClellan. *The Young Napoleon* is the result. It is a well researched and well written factual account of McClellan's life together with reasoned interpretations of his conduct. The general represents a classic case of self-incrimination, betrayed by his own letters, especially the numerous letters to his wife. Although Sears has mined a wide range of manuscript sources, he draws his sharpest insights into McClellan's motives and character from these letters. He emerges as a seriously flawed human being.

Born in 1826 into a Philadelphia family of intellectual and social distinction, McClellan graduated from West Point in 1846 and entered the Corps of Engineers. Distinguished in the Mexican War, he was also identified as a military theoretician. He resigned from the Army in 1857 to become a railroad executive, but shortly after Sumter was appointed Major General of Ohio Volunteers by the Governor of that state and placed in command of Ohio's forces. This was quickly followed by Lincoln's commission as Major General in the United States Army. In Ohio he was responsible for organizing and drilling the early regiments raised in that state. In June he took the field and conducted the Federals' successful Rich Mountain Campaign in western Virginia, before being called to Washington in August of 1861 to take command of the Army of the Potomac. It was the combination of his success in the early fighting in western Virginia and the Union's defeat at Bull Run in July of 1861 that propelled McClellan into this command. On November 1, 1861, he became the General-in-Chief of the Armies of the United States. He was thirty-four years old.

During the relatively brief period between his Ohio commission and the call to Washington, McClellan manifested several attributes. In the first place, his administrative and organizational skills were of the highest order. In the chaotic early days in Ohio he was effective in mustering, organizing, equipping, and training the early volunteers. He also had a gift for rhetoric in the Napoleonic style. He sounded like a great soldier. Related to this posing was the capacity to inspire the confidence and affection of his soldiers, developing what would today be called "personality cult" leadership. In the western Virginia campaign, he overestimated the enemy's numbers and exhibited a mindless caution, which he carried to the point of leaving a portion of his army in peril. He also showed that he perceived army command as something more than simply obeying orders and dealing in purely military matters. Antagonistic to the anti-slavery cause, he had a pronounced sense of the grand strategy of the war from the standpoint of the Union. It was to be a limited war in which Southern civilians and their property, including slaves, would be protected.

In Washington McClellan exhibited two additional tendencies. One was contempt for his superiors. As early as August 16, 1861, he was referring to the President as an "idiot," "baboon," and "gorilla." In addition, he involved himself directly with political questions and with politicians, and identified himself as a conservative Democrat. He was, he wrote, "fighting for my Country & the Union, not for abolition and the Republican Party." Bitterly racist, McClellan was hostile to abolition as a war aim; yet he was not sympathetic to slavery.

Sears ably recounts McClellan's organizational and administrative activities as he trained and equipped the Army of the Potomac during the winter of 1861–62. During this period he was also heavily involved as General-in-Chief in the Administration's consideration of the appropriate use of that army. The outcome of these deliberations was the well known Peninsula Campaign, undertaken on March 17, 1862, at which time McClellan was stripped of his status as General-in-Chief.

On the Peninsula McClellan's advance toward Richmond was slow and cautious. Insisting that he was outnumbered by the much smaller forces of Confederate defenders, he sent forth repeated, impassioned demands to Washington for reinforcements, including the request for the assignment of divisions that Lincoln believed to be required for the safety of the capital. On May 31, 1862, at Seven Pines, the Confederates attacked. Although unsuccessful, this show of offensive spirit further daunted McClellan. Ultimately, the Confederates initiated a series of battles known as the Seven Days, which caused McClellan to change his base of operations to Harrison's Landing on the James River, which point his army reached on July 2nd. From Harrison's Landing McClellan continued to proclaim that he was outnumbered and reiterated his demands for reinforcement. He also indulged his penchant for criticism of his superiors. This criticism was especially directed at Secretary of War Edwin M. Stanton. His correspondence from Harrison's Landing accused the Secretary of incompetence, treachery, and the intentional sacrifice of Federal soldiers. When visited by Lincoln on July 8, the general presented the President with a letter setting forth his views concerning the conduct of the war. This letter rejected the idea of confiscation of rebel property and also rejected the "forcible abolition of slavery."

After much debate and controversy, on August 3, 1862, the newly appointed General-in-Chief, Henry W. Halleck, ordered the Federal army withdrawn from the Peninsula. On August 13 Lee's Army of Northern Virginia moved north in Virginia toward the newly-organized Federal Army of Virginia commanded by General John Pope. General Halleck's order to McClellan promptly to reinforce Pope introduced another sad chapter in the McClellan story.

Preoccupied with the question of his own command status, McClellan procrastinated in moving his divisions to the scene of action in northern Virginia. His correspondence suggests that he sought to extract from the Administration commitments as to his command status as the price of cooperating with Pope. On its face, the inference of this correspondence is also that McClellan wanted Pope to be defeated. Other writers have believed this, but Sears finds this "too much to say" and concludes instead that "captive of his delusions, he put his own interests and his messianic vision ahead of doing everything possible to push reinforcements to the battlefield" (p. 254). Pope was, of course, defeated at Second Bull Run. His divisions and those of McClellan were drawn into the defenses of Washington as Lee crossed the Potomac into Maryland.

In Washington, the armies of Pope and McClellan were merged with the Army of the Potomac as the survivor and with McClellan in command, to the great pleasure of the soldiers. With the vigor and skill that he customarily displayed away from the battlefield, McClellan reorganized the badly disorganized Federal army. On September 6, he undertook the pursuit of Lee into Maryland. At Frederick, he came into possession of Lee's Special Order No. 191 which disclosed that the Confederate leader had split his outnumbered army into four separated parts. McClellan waited sixteen hours from this discovery before acting on this unique opportunity to attack Lee in detail. He then advanced, forced a crossing of South Mountain on September 14 and proceeded toward Sharpsburg.

By early morning of September 16, 1862, McClellan had seventy-five thousand troops assembled along Antietam Creek. Opposing them were eighteen thousand Confederates, Lee's detached commands having not yet rejoined his army. McClellan did not attack and Lee's force rapidly increased as the day progressed. There was sharp fighting late in the afternoon of September 16 as McClellan positioned a portion of his army to attack Lee's left flank. The following day, September 17, witnessed the bloodiest single day of the war as the Federals assaulted Lee's line.

Badly outnumbered, his back to the Potomac and with inadequate fords for retreating, Lee gambled the life of his army at Antietam. Sears is correct that McClellan "squandered the unique opportunity of winning a battle of annihilation" (p. 322). He "lost his inner composure and with it the courage to command under the press of combat" (p. 323). Withholding a third of his army, he forfeited his numerical advantage by bloody piecemeal assaults on September 17. He then did not attack the crippled and decimated enemy on the following day, in spite of the fresh troops available to him. He let Lee retreat into Virginia.

After another period of delay, McClellan followed Lee, but at last, on November 7, Lincoln had had enough. McClellan was removed. Although he did not actually resign from the army until election day 1864,

McClellan never again had an active military command. Residing variously in New Jersey and New York after his removal, McClellan occupied his time with a defensive report of his service, efforts to obtain an active command, and conservative Democratic politics. In 1864, he was nominated on the Democratic ticket to run against Lincoln, but suffered a decisive defeat.

Sears is more interested in McClellan the soldier than McClellan the civilian. His account of the presidential campaign is succinct and conventional. In detailing McClellan's well-known disavowal of the so-called peace plank of the Democrats' platform, Sears suggests that his doing so was motivated as much by political as by patriotic considerations. The general's later years were marked by long sojourns in Europe, occasional writing, occasional employment in corporate management or engineering, and, from 1878 to 1881, a term as Governor of New Jersey. He died in 1885 at the age of 59.

David M. Jordan carefully recounts the story of Winfield Scott Hancock. Born in Pennsylvania in 1824, the son of a small town teacher who was to become a lawyer, Hancock was graduated from West Point in 1844. His pre-war service included the Mexican War, Western Indian fighting, and the Utah expedition against the Mormons. He was a birthright Democrat and wholly unsympathetic to the free soil movement, as evidenced by his having voted for Kentucky Democrat John Breckinridge for President in 1860. Fortunately for the Union, Hancock was a staunch nationalist. Although disapproving of the North's course there was never any doubt of his allegiance.

A captain when Sumter was fired on, Hancock was stationed in Los Angeles as chief quartermaster for the Southern District of California. He arrived in Washington after McClellan's appointment to command the Army of the Potomac and was at once appointed a brigadier general of volunteers in that army. He and his brigade rendered excellent service in the Peninsula Campaign. During the Battle of Antietam he succeeded the mortally wounded General Israel B. Richardson as commander of the First Division of the Second Corps, which led to his major generalship. Further distinguished at Fredericksburg and Chancellorsville, he took command of the Second Corps after the latter battle.

On July 1, 1863, the first day of Gettysburg, Hancock was with General George Gordon Meade, commander of the Army of the Potomac, at the latter's headquarters in Taneytown, Maryland. Serious fighting had begun at Gettysburg. Two Federal corps and General John Buford's cavalry were there. Another corps was nearby. It had been reported that First Corps commander John F. Reynolds was either seriously wounded or dead. On this assumption regarding Reynolds, who had in fact been killed, Hancock was ordered by Meade to assume command and decide whether or not to give further battle at Gettysburg. This assignment evidences the high esteem in which Hancock was held by Meade.

Hancock arrived at Gettysburg to find the Federals defeated. With a sure hand, he took charge, established the Federals effectively on the high ground, and made the critical decision to defend that ground. General Meade and the balance of the Federal army arrived at Gettysburg that night and on the following morning. Hancock continued to serve with distinction until seriously wounded on July 3. Jordan accurately observes that "Gettysburg was Hancock's field" (p. 100).

Recuperating from his wound, Hancock stayed on leave until late in 1863. Although the wound was to cause a lifetime of suffering and occasional disability, he resumed command of his corps in December. In Grant's Overland Campaign of 1864, Hancock and his corps continued to perform well. His service included the storied battles of the Wilderness, Spotsylvania, and Cold Harbor. Because of the Gettysburg wound, Hancock was sent from the field in November of 1864 to various commands behind the lines.

A lifetime soldier, Hancock after the war was assigned as commander of the Middle Military District which included Washington, D.C. In this role he was responsible for carrying out the warrant for the execution of the Lincoln assassination conspirators. Because of the questionable processes of the military commission that tried the conspirators and the hanging of Mary Surratt, the general was criticized, it would seem unjustly, for his involvement in these events. In 1866, a major general in the regular army on the recommendation of U. S. Grant, he was assigned as the commander of the Military Department of the Missouri, the focal point of warfare with the Indians of the plains.

At General William T. Sherman's direction, in 1867 Hancock led an army expedition into Kansas, a show of force intended to intimidate and pacify the Indians. His conduct of this campaign was obtuse, insensitive, and provocative, a prime example of the government's Indian policy. This service was followed by assignment to command the Fifth Military District with headquarters in New Orleans. Apparently believing that, regardless of the war, the historic leadership of the region was to resume its authority, in this post Hancock uniformly favored the white, Democratic faction. Although Jordan's bibliography includes recent revisionist analyses of Reconstruction, he writes of Hancock during Reconstruction from the traditional premises and does not question his acts which were anti-black and anti-reform. Hancock's activities during the Louisiana command identified him with President Andrew Johnson as anti-black and an enemy of the developing Republican position. This brought him into conflict with U. S. Grant. Relieved in New Orleans at his own request, Hancock left that post thoroughly identified as a conservative Democratic general.

Estranged from Grant, Hancock was assigned to command obscure military departments beneath the level of his seniority and experience. In 1868 he was a serious candidate for the Democratic presidential nomination against Grant but was defeated in the convention by Governor Horatio Seymour of New York. In 1870 Hancock was assigned to the Department of Dakota where his mission was to carry out the government's effort to prevent white encroachment on the Black Hills, which had been ceded to the Sioux by the 1868 Treaty of Laramie. He was again interested in the Democratic presidential nomination in 1872 but withdrew from consideration by the convention.

As the senior major general in the army, Hancock was appointed in 1872 to command of the Division of the Atlantic with headquarters in New York City. He was to occupy this post for the rest of his life. His name was placed in nomination in the Democratic Convention that nominated Tilden in 1876. During the railroad strikes of the late 1870s, which were accompanied by violence and riots, he commanded the army's efforts at suppression, although he objected on philosophical grounds to the use of the army as a police force. Although not an intellectual man or military theoretician, he conducted himself with respect for military justice and the appropriate role of the army.

At the age of 56, Hancock was nominated for President by the Democrats in 1880. He ran on the proposition that the states should be free from interference by the Federal government and accepted the Democratic platform position that tariff was to be for revenue only. The Democratic Campaign of 1880 was unusually inept. Hancock made his own contribution by remarking that the issue of tariff was "a local question." Ohio Republican James A. Garfield defeated him by slightly more than

7,000 popular votes, but by a broader margin in the electoral college. Jordan suggests that Hancock had limited understanding of the political processes, but concludes that the general would have been "an adequate if undistinguished president" (p. 308). Hancock died in New York City in 1886 of diabetes.

Jordan's book is at its best in its descriptions of the general's Civil War career. The post-war years are less carefully treated. In summarizing Hancock's life, his comment regarding his attitude toward the Indians seems both to beg the question and not to follow from his earlier description of the general's activities: "He developed feelings of benevolence toward the Indian, so long as interference with the westward spread of the white settler did not result" (p. 318). The context in which Jordan views Hancock's Reconstruction role also appears in his summary. He states that "the course of the Radicals in Reconstruction kept the wounds of conflict fresh and raw" (p. 318). He does not acknowledge that the Southerners' political and racial goals contributed to this conflict.

These then are the two generals who became politicians. As is obvious from these books, they had many things in common: background, political point of view, education, the military profession, and political activity. They were also faithful husbands and family men of exemplary personal habits. But their biographies make plain that despite these similarities they were vastly different men. Hancock was a "good soldier," fully grasping the constitutional role of the military. A lack of this understanding was the source of some of McClellan's problems. But their differences were at a more profound level. Although neither book purports to be a psychohistory, it is plain that the men are to be distinguished in terms of basic character and personality.

McClellan had what would today be called charisma. In an era in which people were more vulnerable to sentimentality and romance, his Napoleonic ideas of esprit de corps were useful to his military leadership. It is also apparent that he was highly competent at military administration, for which Sears gives him full credit. One may even attribute to McClellan good faith. But he failed because of the cast of his mind and heart, his psychological makeup. The evidence of Sears's book makes it difficult to exaggerate McClellan's weaknesses. He was erratic and unstable. His moods and attitudes, like those of a manic depressive, swung in wide arcs between extreme confidence and self-congratulation on the one hand, and hysterical despair and self-pity on the other. Paranoid and conspiratorial by disposition, he had difficulty with reality and with truth and frequently dissembled when the facts were not to his liking. He sought positions of great responsibility but shrank from taking that responsibility in a practical sense. Someone else was always to blame. McClellan lacked moral courage and, Sears suggests, his occasional absences from the scene of action may have been caused by a lack of physical courage. He had intemperate contempt for those whom he believed, often wrongly, did not support him without question. Although Sears does not refer to it, his account of McClellan's military career fits the characterization made by the military historian Kenneth P. Williams: "McClellan was not a real general. McClellan was not even a disciplined, truthful soldier. McClellan was merely an attractive but vain and unstable man, with considerable military knowledge, who sat a horse well and wanted to be President."

In essential character and personality, Hancock was none of the things that McClellan was. Genuinely confident, he took and also accepted responsibility. At each level of military command, he was appropriately aggressive. Possessing physical and moral courage, he and his soldiers were frequently at the center of the action. He was candid and realistic. Finally, although possessing his share of vanity and ambition, he was not self-indulgent on the battlefield.

Since both McClellan and Hancock were presidential nominees, their biographies provide convenient vehicles for exploring the political history of that era. The books complement each other. Because of their common experiences each protagonist moves in and out of the other's life. Read separately or together, those books illuminate the Civil War and post-war periods. Their authors have made a substantial contribution to scholarship.

Generals Lee and Jackson

Lee and Jackson: Confederate Chieftains. By Paul D. Casdorph. Paragon House, 1992. Pp. xii, 498.

Beginning with prewar biographies of Robert E. Lee and T. J. "Stonewall" Jackson, Paul D. Casdorph proceeds to their Civil War careers and concludes with a brief epilogue sketching the war in the East after Jackson's death and Lee's postwar career. The result is a brisk, well-written account.

Casdorph states a traditional thesis with no questions asked. What was Lee's strategic view of how the war was to be won? Was his aggressive warfare, with his disproportionate casualties, wise or unwise? No consideration is given to such larger questions. Lee's campaigns are considered simply from a tactical standpoint. The usual justifications for Lee's acts are provided. When he entered Maryland in 1862 he had "no option" (p. 312), a Lost Cause assertion that has never been convincingly explained. The standard villains are here. James Longstreet is, as usual, the principal *bête noire*. He, not Lee, was "bullheaded" (p. 396) at Gettysburg. The implication is that George Pickett's charge would have succeeded had Longstreet handled it correctly. Richard Ewell's "defeatism" (p. 396) late on the first day of Gettysburg is also criticized, without analysis. The author is mistaken that Lee had ordered Ewell to take the high ground "if possible" (p. 396). Lee's words were "if practicable," a quantum difference from "if possible," and Lee's instruction added the further caveat that Ewell was to "avoid a general engagement."

Casdorph adopts John Esten Cooke's statement that Lee's army in Maryland conducted itself "with perfect regard for the rights of property and the feelings of inhabitants" (p. 316) although Lee officially reported that "a great deal of damage to citizens is done by stragglers . . . wantonly destroying stock and other property." Lee was the principal military leader of a government expressly based on slavery. He owned slaves, did not voluntarily emancipate them, saw to the capture of his fugitive slaves, trafficked in slaves, characterized slavery as "necessary," and late in the war wrote that he considered "the relation of master and slave . . . as the best that can exist between the white and black races." Nevertheless, Casdorph identifies Lee as "the man who had opposed slavery" (p. 404).

Since the book concentrates on the Lee-Jackson relationship, Jackson's death at Chancellorsville is seen as a decisive event. Casdorph is clearly of the view that Jackson's effectiveness was the key to Lee's tactical successes. For example, although George McClellan's failure of will was surely his undoing before Richmond in 1862, the author writes that "with Abraham Lincoln's help, [Jackson] had ruined McClellan's peninsula campaign" by keeping Federals in the valley (p. 248).

The book's problems result from the author's unquestioning reliance on numerous questionable writers, then and now, advocates of or
apologists for the Lost Cause, among these being Cooke, J. W. Jones,
A. L. Long, Robert L. Dabney, and the later neo-Confederate, Clifford
Dowdy. Casdorph's use of quotations from such writers to characterize
critical events provides an apologetic gloss to the book.

Concluding with the obligatory panegyric to Lee, this time a Biblical quotation that describes Lee as "the perfect man" (p. 408), the book
is a conventional restatement of the Southern tradition.

Atlanta, Pea Ridge, and Chickamauga

Decision in the West: The Atlanta Campaign of 1864. By Albert Castel. Uni-
versity Press of Kansas, 1992. Pp. xvi, 665.
Pea Ridge: Civil War Campaign in the West. By William L. Shea and Earl J.
Hess. University of North Carolina Press, 1992. Pp. xiii, 417.
This Terrible Sound: The Battle of Chickamauga. By Peter Cozzens. Uni-
versity of Illinois Press, 1992. Pp. xii, 675.

These three new tactical studies of major Civil War campaigns are representative of the burgeoning rush of Civil War literature. Civil War
readers are reasonably apprehensive about this rush. There are already
hints that a dominating economic motive may be driving this process
and may cause a decline in the quality of the genre. Fortunately, the
three books under review are not involved in that indictment.

The distinguished Albert Castel's Atlanta book is nothing short of
excellent. Begun in May, 1864, under Sherman's command, the campaign was one of the several prongs of newly-appointed General-in-
Chief Grant's effort to subdue the Confederacy. The author has a sound
grasp of the importance of the war in the West and the logistical, military, political, and morale significance of the Atlanta campaign. Conventional accounts have suggested that the Federal progress from Dalton to
Atlanta was essentially a matter of maneuver. The book reminds the
reader that in fact there was much fighting along the way, at Pickett's
Mill and Dallas and other previously ignored battlefields. Among several
persuasive revisionist themes, the most striking concerns Sherman,
whom the author faults for candor, strategic capacity, and tactics and
compares unfavorably to General George H. Thomas. Castel notes that
Sherman unilaterally modified Grant's intent for the campaign. Grant

wanted Sherman to destroy the Army of Tennessee. Sherman concentrated instead on the more modest objective of capturing Atlanta.

On the Confederate side, the major figures of the campaign were Generals Joseph E. Johnston and John Bell Hood and President Jefferson Davis. General Braxton Bragg was also active as Davis's military advisor. Castel appropriately labels Johnston "overrated" and Hood "over-aggressive." These leaders did not cooperate among themselves, and the controversy among them was a factor in the Confederate defeat. Johnston simply ignored the instructions of his government. Having disloyally undermined Johnston, Hood replaced Johnston late in the campaign and failed in the ultimate battles at Atlanta. As the author makes clear, the fall of Atlanta on September 1 and 2, 1864, was a major factor in Lincoln's reelection. The campaign was therefore literally a "decision in the West."

Implicit, and sometimes explicit, in Castel's evaluation of the military leaders in the campaign is his admiration of General Robert E. Lee's leadership in the East. This reviewer rejects Lee as *the* criterion of generalship. Frequently a brilliant tactician, Lee's grand strategic sense of the war was premised on the military defeat of the North, an unlikely goal, rather than on wearing out the North's will to fight, a realizable objective. This led him to aggressiveness that produced disproportionate, irreplaceable, and unaffordable casualties destructive to the Confederacy's chances of victory. Regardless of the Lee issue, which is not central to the Atlanta campaign, Castel's book is wonderfully researched and written, has refreshing original insights, and is plainly a definitive work on the campaign.

The 1862 Pea Ridge campaign, pitting the Federal Army of the Southwest against the Confederate Army of the West, has never been adequately reported. Indeed, William L. Shea and Earl J. Hess have provided the first detailed account of this campaign in southwestern Missouri and northwestern Arkansas. It is an exceptional work. One suspects that the campaign has been overlooked in part because of historians' undue emphasis on the war in the Virginia theater and preoccupation with the romanticized eastern battles involving the Army of the Potomac and the Army of Northern Virginia. As the authors accurately state, the "victory at Pea Ridge was the turning point of Federal efforts to dominate the Trans-Mississippi" (p. 308). Fought in the depths of winter and fraught with almost unbelievable logistical difficulties, the campaign featured remarkably valiant soldiers and an interesting array of general officers. Principal among the latter was the underrated General Samuel R. Curtis, the Federal commander, and the erratic Federal General Franz Sigel. General Earl Van Dorn incompetently led the Southern participants.

The research base of the book is impressive, and the book is marked by the authors' fine strategic grasp and capacity to present a complex campaign with great clarity. The reader discovers that the resolute Curtis anticipated Sherman's strategy of foraging and living off the country. Curtis also emancipated slaves without hesitation, and his actions were not reversed or criticized by the Washington administration. The significance of the campaign is accurately characterized: "By the time Curtis led his dusty blue column into Helena in the summer of 1862, Missouri was safe for the Union, half of Arkansas was lost to the Confederacy, and the strategic balance in the Mississippi Valley was altered permanently" (p. 306). In presenting this decisive campaign the authors have made a significant contribution to the scholarship of the war.

Chickamauga, the only marked Confederate victory in the West, was a bloody melee in which neither army commander had control of his army. For the Federal Army of the Cumberland the commander was the mercurial Major General William S. Rosecrans. His command opponent was the ill-fated General Braxton Bragg, commander of the Army of Tennessee. The battle also featured Rosecrans's lieutenant, Major General George H. Thomas, who was to replace Rosecrans in command of the army after the battle, and Lieutenant General James Longstreet who brought several brigades of his corps from the Army of Northern Virginia to the event. It was Thomas's dogged defense at Snodgrass Hill on the second day of the battle, after Rosecrans and much of the Federal army had retreated to Chattanooga, that saved the Federals from a total defeat and the loss of Chattanooga.

Peter Cozzens has written of the battle in the way it happened, in segments, detailing the unsystematic fighting even at the regimental level. As a consequence, the larger context of events and of the battle as a whole is sometimes obscured by detail. At the command level, Cozzens has fine insights into the problematic Rosecrans, and he details the controversy in the Confederate army that continuously surrounded Braxton Bragg, including President Jefferson Davis's post-battle inept efforts to quiet the controversy between Bragg and his commanders. These accounts underline two major Confederate tragedies. As Bell I. Wiley once wrote, "strife was the Confederacy's evil genius and no major organization or activity escaped its crippling influence."[1] And the valiant and gutsy Army of Tennessee never had the kind of leadership that it was entitled to and which could have reversed its doleful history of defeat and losses. An immediate consequence of this lack was the failure of the Confederates to realize on the promise of the Chickamauga victory. The Union held on to Chattanooga and in November decisively defeated Bragg's army at Missionary Ridge.

Tennessee's War

Tennessee's War, 1861–1865, Described by Participants. Compiled and edited by Stanley F. Horn. Tennessee Civil War Centennial Commission, 1965. Pp. 364.

Stanley F. Horn's *Tennessee's War* does not have the general appeal of Milligan's book. Published by the Tennessee Civil War Centennial Commission, it appropriately focuses attention on the war as it directly affected that state. In view of the trite but true saying that the war was fought in Virginia and Tennessee, a book about Tennessee's war is concerned with large aspects of the conflict. Because the author is Stanley F. Horn, the book is well done. Before the emergence of K. P. Williams, Bruce Catton, Bell Wiley, T. Harry Williams, and others of the great Civil War writers, Horn was already writing distinguished Civil War books. His *The Army of Tennessee,* initially published in 1941, is still the definitive book about that Southern army and is still the best single book about the war in the West.

Tennessee's War is organized chronologically and begins with the fateful decision on the part of the state to leave the Union and join the Confederacy. It proceeds to a description of the state's preparations for the war and then to the fighting. Forts Henry and Donelson, Shiloh, the fall of Memphis, Stones River, Chickamauga, Missionary Ridge, and Hood's campaign, culminating in the defeats at Franklin and Nashville, are included. The method of the book is what may be called documentary; that is, the statements of the participants are used to tell of the events and these statements are brought together by means of brief narratives by Horn. Although there is little new, the story is well told; and the method is effective.

---

[1] Bell I. Wiley, *The Road to Appomattox* (Memphis, 1956), 98–99.

An episodic characteristic marks the book, a characteristic forced on the author by the nature of the contents. Regrettably, the work is not indexed and the sources are not well identified, both of which would have contributed much to its value. It is, nevertheless, a valuable book and is another item of evidence in behalf of the Centennial.

Old Abe the War Eagle

Old Abe the War Eagle: A True Story of the Civil War and Reconstruction. By Richard H. Zeitlin. State Historical Society of Wisconsin, 1986. Pp. vi, 113.

In this unusual book Richard H. Zeitlin presents the history of "Old Abe," the eagle mascot of the Eighth Wisconsin Volunteers of the Civil War. Old Abe's career is in itself remarkable and worth recounting in the midst of the current renaissance of interest in the Civil War, but Zeitlin also uses the bird's story as a vehicle for a number of other stories. The book is, therefore, a veritable potpourri of mid– and late–nineteenth century history with the eagle as the unifying force.

A Disney Studio writer could not improve on the true story of Old Abe. Born in rural Wisconsin, the eagle was originally captured by Chippewa Indians in 1861 and traded to a farm family for a bushel of corn. Adopted by the newly raised Company C of the Eighth Wisconsin Volunteers, the eagle went to war and participated in the long and hard service of that regiment. Returning to Wisconsin after the war, he became a pet of the state and a genuine national celebrity and traveled widely as a feature of patriotic meetings and conventions until his death in 1881.

The eagle's story is, of course, inextricably connected with the story of the Eighth Wisconsin. The book, therefore, contains a regimental history of that organization. Its marches and battles are included, as are the details of the common soldiers' lives and the incredible hardships of their service. Also recorded are biographical sketches of a number of the officers and enlisted men of the regiment.

Old Abe's postwar career is then recounted, and this story leads to an account of the activities of the veterans in that era, activities with which the eagle was intimately associated. Because the postwar veterans' organizations were in the forefront of Republican "bloody-shirt" politics, these, too, are described. Adopted by the veterans' groups for this purpose, in the author's words, "Old Abe became a perfect symbol of nationalistic Republicanism, a living version of the Bloody Shirt" (p. 80). The eagle's involvement in the centennial celebration of 1876 permits the author to describe that episode of Americana. And because all of the postwar events touched by the eagle took place during the heyday of American Victorianism, the reader grasps the flavor of that sentimental and colorful time.

The book contains a number of fine photographs of the eagle and the events and people with which the book is concerned. These enliven the text significantly. Zeitlin is a professional historian and a careful and deep researcher, as his copious citations attest. He is also a graceful writer, thoroughly at home in Civil War history and the period and events about which he writes. Replete with information and insights, this book is an excellent exposition of its several themes.

Why the Confederacy Lost

Why the Confederacy Lost. Edited by Gabor S. Boritt. Oxford University Press, 1992. Pp. xii, 209.

In 1958 distinguished Civil War historians David Donald, Richard N. Current, T. Harry Williams, Norman A. Graebner, and David M. Potter participated in a conference at Gettysburg College and addressed the issue of "Why the North Won the Civil War." In 1960 their papers, each containing useful insights, were published by Louisiana State University Press. In 1991 James M. McPherson, Archer Jones, Gary W. Gallagher, Reid Mitchell, and Joseph T. Glatthaar—among today's leading Civil War historians—met at Gettysburg College and revisited the issue, albeit slightly rephrased. This book, surely a significant contribution to the history of the war, collects the papers presented on that occasion.

The issue is, of course, a perennial one, valid in and of itself and also as a convenient vehicle for larger consideration of the military, political, economic, and social history of the war. Following a graceful introduction by Gabor S. Boritt, each of the essays has a different focus. The initial essay is McPherson's, an excellent analysis of the prominent theories propounded over the years in answer to the book title's question. His conclusion suggests that the answer lies in an understanding, not yet achieved, of turning points in the war, what he calls "points of contingency." Jones's thesis concentrates on the relationship between military events and the politics of each section, surely a crucial factor. Gallagher's contention has Napoleonic premises: superior Federal generalship, especially in the persons of Grant and Sherman and in spite of Lee, was decisive. Mitchell revises the Lost Cause romance of the superior Confederate soldier, arguing that "the ideology and the morale of the Union soldier made a key contribution to a Union victory; one reason the Union could triumph was the perseverance of its soldiers" (p. 111). Glatthaar's concluding essay asserts that the role of African-Americans was decisive. Their soldiering and laboring for the Union contributed largely to the Federal effort. Further, their rejection of the Confederate cause and flight into the Union lines destabilized the Confederate home front, another advantage to the Union cause.

The book contains a significant implicit premise. Each of the essayists assumes that the Confederacy could have won the war. The loss of the war was not inevitable. Although it surely predates this book, this revisionist premise has profound implications for the historiography of the war, implications of which we may not yet be fully aware. The "history" of the war continues to be marked by the romantic traditions of the Lost Cause that arose in part from a vague and unstated Northern apology to the South. The apology was based on the view that winning the war was impossible for the Confederacy. The abandoning of that belief significantly compromises the apology and opens the door to reconsideration of important questions about the war.

Lee and Grant: A Dual Biography

Lee and Grant: A Dual Biography. By Gene Smith. McGraw-Hill Book Company, 1984. Pp. xiv, 412.

A dual biography of Robert E. Lee and Ulysses S. Grant is an exceptionally good idea. Very different in background, style, and personality, they became the principal military antagonists of the Civil War. As the author of this book suggests, in many ways each was typical of his cause: the aristocratic and anachronistic Old South, a strange mixture of gentility and brutality, versus the industrializing, rough-and-ready, egalitarian North. Admirably organized around the counterpoint suggested by its protagonists, the book traces their origins and careers. The author plays no favorites; an effort is made to characterize both men fully. A prolific and successful trade writer, Gene Smith writes very well. Granting all of these positive points, the book is significantly flawed.

In the first place, Smith relies entirely on secondary sources. Regardless of the general acceptability of this method, it appears that Smith has consulted them indiscriminately. (His imprecise method of footnoting adds to readers' doubts.) Thus, he has overlooked well-known authoritative historians (Bruce Catton and K. P. Williams, for example) and turned instead to such doubtful sources as W. E. Woodward and Sylvanus Cadwallader. The truth is that Smith is far from home in dealing with the military history of the Civil War. He has grabbed whatever was handy to advance his manuscript and apparently had neither the knowledge nor the time to evaluate his sources.

The author's poor research base shows up in a number of ways. For example, he accepts Cadwallader's account of Grant's binge during the Vicksburg campaign. Smith is presumably unaware of K. P. Williams's persuasive destruction of this story. He characterizes other Civil War personalities with dubious stereotypes. His treatment of General Henry Halleck, for example, shows that he has made no inquiry into the very complicated role of that very complex man.

Numerous outright errors about the war also appear, of which the following are simply examples: it is not accurate to say that Fort Donelson is "11 miles downstream from Fort Henry" (p. 113); Grant had not "committed his last reserves" on the first day at Shiloh (p. 121); it is not true that "almost as one man the right wing of Hooker's army turned and ran" at Stonewall Jackson's attack on the Eleventh Corps on May 2, 1863, at Chancellorsville (p. 160); Hooker did not "turn and run for it" on the morning after Jackson's stroke at Chancellorsville (p. 161)—there was fighting on May 3, 4, and 5, and the retreat took place on May 6; James Longstreet was not "Jackson's replacement" in any meaningful sense (p. 164); to state that Grant expected no great results from Benjamin F. Butler's 1864 campaign below Richmond (p. 188) is simply wrong; the "entire course of the war" did not devolve on the two forces opposed in the final Virginia campaign (p. 211), and the statement reflects and promotes a misunderstanding of the war; Lee did not "have to" invade Pennsylvania in 1863 (p. 163) and to say that he did moots a question that a biographer should address.

Each of the men was an enigma, and each is ultimately a tragic figure. Lee, the aristocratic soldier, initially opposed secession; he was one of the few who foresaw the horrors of the war and its ultimate outcome. Somehow he converted his position of not *opposing* Virginia into the role of the slaving Confederacy's aggressive and bloody point man. He could write during the war that "the warmest instincts of every man's soul declare the glory of the soldier's death." In the name of his own honor, he clung to the war long beyond his own awareness of any practical possibility of success, although every day intensified the agony of his beloved Virginia and all the people, North and South. These undisputed facts make Lee a tragic hero. They also suggest his unique and anomalous place in American history. Other historical figures are evaluated with reference to the ultimate morality of their acts, but history is curiously neutral where Lee is concerned. Universally credited with purity of motive, he is somehow therefore absolved of the destructive and inhumane consequences of that motive. Grant has surely not enjoyed Lee's immunity from history's inquiries and judgments, but his tragedy appears in the aftermath of Appomattox when he exhibited his moral obtuseness in regard to postwar gifts from wealthy friends; his perception of the presidency as a "sinecure," a gift from the people because of his wartime service; and his role in "Grantism," the awful corruption of American politics during the Gilded Age.

In short, there is much to say about Grant and Lee, but, in view of its defects, this book poses the classic question: is there validity to this kind of popular history? On the one hand, such works may be the general reader's only source of history. On the other hand, the commercial imperatives seem to require broad brush oversimplification, exaggerated and categorical characterization when the truth is highly uncertain, and the publishing of outright error—so that what the general reader gets is erroneous or distorted information.

The best-seller lists notwithstanding, people who take their history seriously have cause to be disappointed with this book.

Commanders of the Army of the Potomac

Commanders of the Army of the Potomac. By Warren W. Hassler, Jr. Louisiana State University Press, 1962. Pp. xxi, 281.

In this book, Professor Hassler presents an exposition of the command careers of the generals who headed the Army of the Potomac. Taken chronologically, these men were McDowell, McClellan, Burnside, Hooker, and Meade. Chapters are also devoted to Pope, whose shortlived Army of Virginia was merged into the Army of the Potomac after Second Bull Run, and Grant, who was Meade's overshadowing superior during the final Virginia campaign.

The scheme and organization of the book are good. A well-written account of the conduct of each officer appears. This is followed by a Conclusion in which the men are compared and measured against such criteria as strategy, tactics, administrative skill, and use of naval power.

In his statements of objective *fact,* Professor Hassler is a sure teacher. The book is marked by careful basic scholarship. With one notable exception, the author's judgments of the men are the traditional ones, although—subject to the same exception—it sometimes seems that he is extravagant in his condemnations. Thus, in the case of the usual villains—Pope, Burnside, and Hooker—there is hardly a good word said, although at least Pope and Hooker had certain gifts despite their ultimate failings.

McDowell, Grant, and Meade are accorded "balanced" treatment. This reviewer had the impression that Professor Hassler has no predilections about these men and therefore presents their stories thoughtfully. It is when McClellan is under discussion that the author seems to labor. He is a staunch defender of McClellan and his brief for him is the point of departure for the book as a whole. The impression is given that Professor Hassler tends to view the other leaders from the vantage point of one championing McClellan. The analysis of these men seems colored by efforts to bolster McClellan.

Reasonable men may—or, in any event, *do*—differ about George B. McClellan. A reviewer has no right to reject an author's thesis simply because it defends McClellan. At the same time, certain things appear in this book which one would seem to have the right to question. Thus, the McClellan view of all of his celebrated controversies is invariably adopted and couched in "good guy–bad guy" terms inconsistent with scholarship. For example, the Radicals appear as unmitigated "bad guys," moving always to harm McClellan; the government was always "meddling" in McClellan's affairs; McClellan was right—or almost right—and Lincoln was wrong about the defenses of Washington in 1862; McClellan was cautious, but he was not really slow; and his subordinates were at fault when he failed. Antietam, the one failure that McClellan's defenders have never been able to explain, is largely blamed on Burnside. McClellan's conduct—*before, during,* and *after* this unmatched lost opportunity—is explained on the ground that McClellan had been "informed" that Lee had 120,000 men and McClellan was, after all, "a circumspect man" (p. 85). Nothing at all appears to rationalize the corps-by-corps manner in which McClellan wasted his vastly superior manpower.

Beyond these basic issues, a number of other defenses of McClellan are offered. Thus, we are told that McClellan's custom of pressing on Lincoln his *political* views was "customary" among the generals of the period (pp. 28–29). But was it? It was not done by McDowell, Pope, or Burnside. More significant, it was not done by Grant, Meade, Sheridan, or Thomas. Professor Hassler also states that McClellan was "generally deferential and proper in his intercourse with his superiors [unless] he believed an error or injustice was being committed" (p. 39). This qualification successfully begs the question. McClellan was insolent and insubordinate to Lincoln, Stanton, and Halleck on a number of occasions simply because *he* believed that they were in error. Professor Hassler is also quick to downgrade even incidental figures who were at odds with McClellan. General Wadsworth—one of the men who believed that McClellan had left Washington insecure when he moved to the Peninsula—is called an "elderly political general" in 1862 (p. 41). It might also have been said that this "elderly" man ably led the First Division of the First Corps at Gettysburg, and was killed in action in the Wilderness in 1864. General Halleck is referred to as a "moral coward" (p. 54), surely an oversimplification of this complicated man. An inference is left to cloud the reputation of Stanton simply because he did not defend himself against McClellan's well-known hysterical letter which accused the Secretary of War of *intentionally* trying to sacrifice the army on the Peninsula (p. 50). In his affirmative case, Professor Hassler cites the chestnut that Lee said after the war that McClellan had been his ablest opponent (p. 249)—a "fact" based on multiple hearsay and not generally accepted by scholars. Finally, and most illuminating of Professor Hassler's comprehension of the military character of the war, is his statement that there was "too much 'nursing' of the Union infantry . . . too much lying down and firing at short range, and too little use of the bayonet charge, pressed home" (p. 245). It may be candidly said that no serious student of military tactics of the period—a period of *rifled* arms, earthworks, and effective anti-personnel artillery—shares this view. On the contrary, their criticism of Civil War tactics argues precisely the contrary. But this is the kind of thing that McClellan himself would have *said,* or, more likely, written in a letter to his wife.

It is generally conceded that McClellan had certain high qualifications. Even Professor Hassler grants that he also was not perfect. The interesting question is what made the difference between a great commander and those who were not great. There is much to suggest that basic elements of character—*integrity* of personality in the classic sense—were decisive, especially in those days when military organization was not institutionalized and the *person* of the leader was so meaningful. It is in this respect that writers may appropriately consider McClellan. He had technical skills and understandings, to be sure, but he was also the man who, when defeated, could write to the Secretary of War: "I have seen too many dead and wounded comrades to feel otherwise than that the government has not sustained this army. . . . If I save this army now, I tell you plainly I owe no thanks to you or to any other persons in Washington. You have done your best to sacrifice this army" (p. 50). Even three weeks later, McClellan would say that this was all "quite true" (p. 50). And when finally removed from command, he could write, "Alas, for my poor country! I know in my inmost heart she never had a truer servant" (p. 93). A final glance at Burnside is worthwhile here. Regarding his own removal, that general wrote, "in view of the glorious results which have since attended the movements of this gallant army [the Army of the Potomac], I am quite willing to believe that my removal was for the best" (p. 125). The pity of it all was that such a man as Burnside lacked the technical skills of McClellan.

Stonewall Jackson: The Man, the Soldier, the Legend

Stonewall Jackson: The Man, the Soldier, the Legend. By James I. Robertson, Jr. Macmillan, 1997. Pp. xxiii, 940.

This book sets forth in unusual detail the now-familiar life and legend of Confederate Gen. Thomas J. Jackson, one of the major figures of that American tragedy, the Civil War. Stonewall Jackson was a complex and interesting man. His quirky personality was marked by contrasts. Thus, on the one hand, he could be playfully affectionate with his wife and, on the other, like Cromwell among the Irish, manifest a steely zest for killing people for the glory of God.

We are reminded here of the general's birth into an undistinguished Scot-Irish family in 1824 in the part of Virginia that became West Virginia. He was an orphan, and his hardships in that respect are described. He went on to West Point, class of 1846, and the Mexican War, in which he earned brevets as a captain and major.

Resigning from the army in 1852, Jackson became a member of the faculty of the Virginia Military Institute. A slaveholder who believed that God had sanctioned slavery, he went without question with Virginia into the Confederacy. Initially a colonel in Virginia's militia, he rose to lieutenant general in the Confederate army and corps command of the Second Corps in Gen. Robert E. Lee's Army of Northern Virginia.

Distinguished at First Bull Run, where the sobriquet "Stonewall" was acquired, he earned fame with his highly effective Shenandoah Valley campaign in 1862. His performance thereafter in the Peninsula campaign was strangely inadequate, but he redeemed himself at Second Bull Run, Antietam, and Fredericksburg and achieved the apogee of his career in his famous flank march against the federal troops at Chancellorsville in May 1863. There he was mistakenly wounded by Confederate troops and did not survive the amputation of his left arm, succumbing to pneumonia on May 10, 1863.

Widely mourned in the South, Jackson was a thoroughly compelling person—his military reputation having extended well beyond American borders.

James I. Robertson Jr., Distinguished Alumni Professor in History at Virginia Tech, is very strong on historical facts and writes gracefully.

For this reviewer, the book is nevertheless marred significantly. Mr. Robertson is a romantic Confederate in his point of view; his interpretation of men and events places him squarely in the "lost cause" tradition. His implicit and sometimes explicit premise is that there was a nobility about secession and the Southern cause, that the leaders of the Confederacy were heroic and superior men and that the war itself was a glorious martial competition.

Confederate leader biographies of the lost-cause tradition are invariably, like this one, of the "Lives of the Saints" variety. Mr. Robertson's foreword frankly declares this. There, he states that Jackson's "devotion to God, duty and country remain treasured legacies of the American people, just as they are inspirations to people everywhere."

Classified as a "martyr," Jackson was a "spiritual prince," who "began each task by offering a blessing and he completed every duty by returning thanks to God."

Jackson also rigidly kept the Lord's day—if forced to write a letter on Sunday, something he sought to avoid, he mailed it Monday. An "extraordinary man," he "stands alone on a high pedestal" and, in the description of his death, he is referred to as a "saint."

This is all very well in the context of the lost cause myth. In the context of history, it is plain that the secessionist movement was not noble. Quite the contrary. It was historically a grievous mistake. With respect to glory, the mistake led to a powerful tragedy for the American people, North and South.

More than 600,000 men were killed, including one of every four Southern men between the ages of 20 and 40, and many more were wounded and disabled. Further, Southern wealth was decreased by 60 percent. The sole reason for secession was protection of slavery against a disapproving national constituency, a cause in the interest of a distinct minority of Southern men, the slaving planter aristocracy.

Dismantling the American union was not in the interests of the American people, North or South, for any reason, let alone to preserve slavery. It would have led to constant conflict between the two nations about such things as access to the Mississippi River and the division of the territories. It also would have meant that the losing side in a democratic election could successfully resort to warfare, which was what Lincoln hoped would not happen, as stated in the Gettysburg Address.

The leaders of this great erroneous crusade were hardly superior men. They were unwise and shortsighted and acted against the public interest.

Jackson, although plainly an accomplished military leader, was intolerant and unusually contentious, carrying on destructive conflict with fellow Confederate officers such as A. P. Hill, Richard Garnett, and William Starke.

Demonizing the Northerners, he advocated early in the war that the Confederates take no prisoners. Indeed, he urged on Virginia's governor the policy of the black flag and proposed himself to set the example. This he believed would have provoked a similar policy on the part of the federal forces, which would have had the added benefit of making Southern soldiers fight more desperately, knowing that capture meant death.

This is Mr. Robertson's sainted hero.

As indicated above, the author, like other lost cause biographers, insists that Jackson was a great Christian. A book review is hardly the place for a theological discussion. However, with respect to religiosity, Jackson was a convert of the Old Light Presbyterian sect, well known for blood-and-thunder intolerance and rigidity. Mr. Robertson, again like other lost cause biographers, makes no distinction between religious pietism and rhetoric on the one hand and humane and Christian conduct on the other.

Now that the wounds of the nation have been sewed up, surely it is time for historians to write about Confederate leadership free of the Margaret Mitchell Confederate mystique.

War in Kentucky

War in Kentucky: From Shiloh to Perryville. By James Lee McDonough. University of Tennessee Press, 1994. Pp. xvii, 386.

Civil War scholars have long debated the relative decisiveness of the war in the East and the war in the West. It is surely true that the consistent, almost invariable Federal successes in the West were a significant offset to the Confederate victories in the Virginia theater during the first two years of the war. It is also true that the western war receives less public attention than do the eastern activities of the armies. James Lee McDonough is a western war writer. He has a keen grasp of western strategy and pays needed attention to the involvement of railroads in that strategy. Having previously published books about Shiloh, Stones River, Chattanooga, and the Battle of Franklin, he now turns his attention to the Kentucky war that took place between the time of Shiloh and Perryville. The events there and then were significant and deserving of close attention.

The Confederacy was initially thrust on the defensive in the West by Grant's successes at Henry and Donelson in February, 1862, "the first turning point of the war" (p. 15). Attempting to regain the initiative, the Confederates were then defeated at Shiloh in April, 1862. Following Shiloh, Buell's Army of the Ohio was dispatched to march against Chattanooga. Belabored by guerrillas and cavalry under Generals Forrest and Morgan, Buell did not reach Chattanooga. Instead, Braxton Bragg arrived there and compelled Buell's withdrawal to the north. Bragg and

Kirby Smith then led separate and ineffectively cooperating armies through Tennessee and into Kentucky. The Kentucky campaign, like Lee's move into Maryland, was in part motivated by a Confederate belief that Kentucky would rise for the Confederacy. The campaign represented another Confederate attempt to restore itself in the West.

Crossing the Cumberland River, Bragg moved into Kentucky toward Glasgow, and Kirby Smith's army entered the state about one hundred miles east of Glasgow. The book contains good discussions of the Battle of Richmond, Kentucky, where Smith soundly defeated a smaller Federal force. McDonough also describes the interesting encounter between Bragg and a Federal force under Indiana's Colonel John Thomas Wilder at Munfordville. The book climaxes with a fine description of the Battle of Perryville on October 8, 1862. Perryville was a bloody and confused drawn battle from which Bragg and Smith retreated into Tennessee, thus ending this Confederate effort to recover from the result of Forts Henry and Donelson. The campaign was a failure for the Confederacy for several reasons, including the absence of unified command between Smith and Bragg, their inept cooperation, and the fact that Kentuckians did not rally to the Confederate banner in any significant way.

Concentrating on a relatively brief period of the war in a circumscribed area, the book informs the reader significantly about the war in the West. It contains careful evaluations of the protagonists' leadership, Halleck and Buell for the Union and Bragg and Kirby Smith for the South.

Indiana in the War of the Rebellion

Indiana in the War of the Rebellion, Report of the Adjutant General: A Reprint of Volume 1 of the Eight-Volume Report Prepared by W. H. H. Terrell and Published in 1869. Indiana Historical Collections, Volume XLI. Indiana Historical Bureau, 1960. Pp. xii, 603.

In 1869, W. H. H. Terrell, adjutant general for the state of Indiana during the latter part of the Civil War, issued the *Report of the Adjutant General of the State of Indiana.* The work included eight volumes and covered the entire period of the Civil War. The first of the eight volumes was the most significant one as a historical source. It was composed of 466 pages of text supplemented by 372 pages of statistics and documents describing Indiana's participation in the great war. The remaining seven volumes were largely composed of rosters of Indiana officers and soldiers.

The volume under review is a reprint of the major portions of Terrell's Volume I. It corrects certain typographical errors and changes punctuation in a manner consistent with better usage. It has also been organized into chapters. Minor text material and most of the statistical and documentary supplements have been omitted. These omissions have been noted in the new edition, and reference is made by means of footnotes citing the original Volume I. The remaining statistical and documentary supplements which are reprinted include the summary of troops furnished by the state of Indiana, the chronological list of engagements in which Indiana troops participated, and the campaigns in which Indiana troops participated. An index for the volume has also been supplied. In addition, there is a thoughtful Foreword by the eminent Bell I. Wiley, of Emory University, chairman of the Committee on Historical Activities of the National Civil War Centennial Commission, and an anonymous editorial note with biographical data concerning Terrell.

In considering the value of this reprint, it should first be said that any study of Indiana's participation in the Civil War begins with the Adjutant General's report. Because it is in many respects a direct transcript of original documents, it is a primary source for a wide range of *facts*. For these facts, there is no usable substitute for this volume. These facts include such things as the number of Indiana regiments raised and their terms of service; the operations of the draft in Indiana; facts about the Indiana Legion, the "home guard" of the period; military financing; relief of soldiers and their families, including the activities of the Indiana Sanitary Commission; and the manufacture of ammunition in Indiana. The reprint also contains a caveat pointing up the limitations of the work when it departs from factual data and pursues interpretations of Indiana politics of the Civil War period.

The caveat attached to the reprint is in the form of Wiley's Foreword. Although he was not asked and did not set forth details, he does refer to the widely accepted traditional view of Indiana politics during the period of the Civil War and immediately thereafter. According to this tradition, Oliver P. Morton and his faction of the Republican party appear as the exclusive champions of the Union in Indiana. The Democrats are cast as Southern sympathizers, men actively seeking to destroy the Union. Also featured are the Knights of the Golden Circle and the Sons of Liberty, secret organizations with loyalties to the Confederacy. According to the tradition, the line between these latter organizations and the Democratic party is very indistinctly drawn.

As is true of so many historical traditions, that concerning Indiana Civil War politics is elusive. Within each of the traditional characterizations of the warring political elements there lies sufficient truth and apparent truth to make rebuttal difficult. Only in relatively recent years have studies appeared raising any questions about the tradition. In 1949 Kenneth M. Stampp issued *Indiana Politics during the Civil War* (Indianapolis, Ind.), an able book which mutes the high colors of the tradition. Frank L. Klement has recently carried the revision further with an exposition which is also well done (*The Copperheads in the Middle West* [Chicago, Ill., 1960]). In addition to questioning the stereotypes of the tradition, these studies show that Governor Morton and his colleagues actively and consciously assisted in the creation of the tradition by accusations of disloyalty against their opponents and by elaborate charades designed to create the impression of imminent peril to the state. W. H. H. Terrell was a Morton man. Not surprisingly, his report accepted the premises of the Morton administration and therefore assisted in carrying along the myth. This is the point which Wiley makes in his Foreword, so that the reprint, unlike the original, may be evaluated with a view to its limitations.

A republication and wider dissemination of the *facts* contained in this volume make this reprint worthwhile. This value is increased because of the better organization and indexing of the reprint as compared to the original work. And because of the caveat, the benefits of the reprint are not mitigated by the inclusion of the traditional partisan view of internal politics. The Indiana Historical Society and its editors have therefore done extremely well in bringing forth this book.

The North Fights the Civil War

The North Fights the Civil War: The Home Front. By J. Matthew Gallman. Ivan R. Dee, 1994. Pp. xi, 211.

J. Matthew Gallman has written an intensive account of the Northern home front during the Civil War. It is the author's thesis that "to understand the Civil War home front we must consider both how individual

Northerners experienced the war years and how the North collectively reacted to the conflict's challenges in its communities, organizations, and businesses" (p. x). Although the book is concerned primarily with the North's activities, Confederate counterparts are occasionally identified because "such comparisons are useful in that they suggest both the significance of the North's superior economic capacity and the critical importance of the regions' different cultural traditions" (p. xi).

The book is admirable in scope. Some of the topics discussed are those one would expect, such as the role of women, race, medicine and nursing, and politics. Others are unusual, including the impact of the war on entertainment, sports, the arts, trade unions, and commemorations and celebrations. The book gives illuminating details of the Northern methods for financing the war and information concerning the U.S. Sanitary Commission and the U.S. Christian Commission.

The book persuasively contradicts certain conventional observations about the war. It is commonly said that the war stimulated and advanced the growth of the Northern economy and imposed permanent harm on the Southern economy. The author notes that "available evidence suggests that although Northerners enjoyed prosperity during the war years, the pace of growth probably slowed in most sectors" (p. 184). The war neither sparked the North into a dramatic industrial takeoff nor permanently crippled the Southern economy. In most respects, according to the author, there was a continuity in the North's wartime experience, which underwent adjustments but involved very few dramatic changes. "The Union never adopted the wholesale mobilization of resources under federal control that we associate with total war" (p. 194). Southerners were forced to accept far more dislocation. In the North, in spite of Emancipation and the growth of Federal power, attitudes of Northerners did not change significantly as a result of the war; "they persisted in their faith in tradition and localism while clinging to a world governed by race, gender, and class hierarchies" (p. 195).

Packed with information, this book is tightly written and well organized and responds to significant historical questions. It contains neither footnotes nor endnotes and the note on sources is fairly brief. Nevertheless, the index means that the book will be convenient as a resource.

A. Lincoln, Prairie Lawyer

A. Lincoln, Prairie Lawyer. By John J. Duff. Rinehart & Co. 1960. Pp. vii, 433.

In 1906, Frederick Trevor Hill wrote *Lincoln The Lawyer*,[1] a study of Lincoln's period at the bar and the legal aspects of his later career. In 1936, on the eve of the centennial of Lincoln's admission to the bar, Albert A. Woldman published a second fullscale analysis.[2] Numerous reminiscences, articles, and pamphlets have also appeared, concerned with one or another aspect of Lincoln's legal career. Now John J. Duff, a practicing New York lawyer, has issued his book, a study of Lincoln's legal education and the period of his practice, which only incidentally makes reference to the presidential years.

Although Mr. Duff's book overlaps with the older works, the new study is justified by three factors. In the first place, there has been a gradual but sure development of new historical techniques in the field of American history. These techniques emphasize documents and are skeptical of the latter-day reminiscences of contemporaries of the subject, men with hindsight who spoke after the legends had begun. The Hill and Woldman books, as well as Herndon's biography[3] and others, are limited in value because of their reliance on the latter type of materials; Duff is committed to the newer technique. The second factor which merits new attention to lawyer Lincoln is the discovery of many new documents. In addition to the Lincoln Papers, which themselves were generally disappointing to scholars, Lincoln legal documents, some of them in his own hand, continue to turn up in the courthouses of the old Eighth Judicial Circuit of Illinois. Finally, Duff's book is appropriate because it rejects what he calls the "stained glass" approach which has marked Lincoln literature and especially those books which have dealt with his career as a lawyer. This is not to say that Duff is simply a debunker. Indeed, he understands the exquisiteness of Abraham Lincoln, but he insists on analyzing him as a man and not as a demigod, with the result that a truer picture emerges.

[1]Hill, *Lincoln the Lawyer* (1906).
[2]Woldman, *Lawyer Lincoln* (1936).
[3]Herndon & Weik, *The Life of Lincoln*, 3 vols. (1890).

An interesting aspect of the "stained glass" approach is that it has surely been unconscious on the part of previous writers. Woldman began his work with the express intention of avoiding the halos and what he called the "silly twaddle" which saw Lincoln "as a Don Quixote of the judicial circuit: ... an oafish country lawyer ... naive almost to the point of simplicity. ..."[4] But Woldman, like the others, became enraptured as he went along. The story—the true story—of the journey of this unpromising backwoodsman, from Kentucky to Ford's Theatre, was too much for Woldman, as it has been for so many conscientious writers. Duff, of course, knows this story. It is a tribute to his skill that it has not obscured his analysis of the prairie lawyer. It is the refusal to fabricate or rationalize events which do not fit the myth which affords the principal difference between Duff's book and the prior art.

A comparison of the treatments of the so-called *Matson Slave Case*[5] is perhaps the best example of the value of Duff's book. The record shows that one Robert Matson of Kentucky was the owner of a farm in Coles County, Illinois. Matson farmed the land with slaves which he brought from Kentucky each spring and returned to Kentucky after the harvest. This technique prevented the Negroes from acquiring a situs in Illinois, which would have jeopardized their status as chattels. There was one exception in Matson's arrangement. This was Anthony Bryant, a former slave, who remained continuously in Coles County, acting as an overseer for Matson and thus becoming a freeman. In 1847, Matson brought his slaves from Kentucky to Coles County. Among them were Anthony Bryant's wife and their four children. During the course of the sojourn, Matson's white housekeeper became annoyed with Mrs. Bryant and threatened to have her and the children sent to Kentucky and sold to a plantation in the deep South. When Bryant learned of this, he contacted local abolitionists and with his family went into hiding under their protection in Illinois. Matson invoked the law, employing Usher F. Linder, a skillful lawyer and contemporary of Lincoln's, and eventually Lincoln himself became associated with Linder in behalf of Matson. Opposing them were other well-known lawyers of the area, Orlando B. Ficklin and Charles H. Constable. Ultimately, the issue was presented in a *habeas corpus* proceeding, on petition filed on behalf of the Negroes,

[4] *Preface* to Woldman, op. cit. supra note 2, at vi.
[5] Discussed at pp. 130–49.

who by this time were in jail in response to the slave owner's writ for possession.

On the merits, Matson's case depended on whether the Negroes had acquired a situs in Illinois or were simply seasonal workers, chattels carried into the state and intended to be returned to Kentucky in accordance with their owner's practice. Lincoln and his co-counsel divided their presentation into two parts. Lincoln argued that the slaves were in fact *in transitu* and thus that Matson's ownership was entitled to protection. He also challenged the form of the petition on technical grounds, contending that in any event the action was defective. At length the court decided against Matson and the slaves were freed.

Many of Duff's predecessors have simply overlooked the *Matson* case. Those who have concerned themselves with it have uniformly resorted to elaborate apologies in an effort to exorcise this episode which collides so sharply with the Lincoln image. The apologies have taken two principal forms. Some, like Woldman, have found in the *Matson* case evidence of Lincoln's paramount devotion to due process and his ability to overcome his general principles because of a deeper and more significant commitment to a system of law.[6] Others, including Beveridge[7] and Benjamin P. Thomas,[8] have rationalized on the ground that Lincoln was ineffective in his presentation, and have either hinted or stated that Lincoln intentionally "threw" the case. Those writers who have taken this view have said that Lincoln's devotion to freedom either overpowered his professional commitment to Matson and his oath as a lawyer or deprived him of his skill as an advocate.

Duff meets the *Matson* question head-on. As a lawyer, he has studied the case and evaluated the strengths and weaknesses of each side of the issue, enabling him to make a judgment about Lincoln's presentation. He convinces us that Lincoln presented the case with both vigor and skill, effectively demolishing the theory that Lincoln either compromised his client or was paralyzed in his effort. Duff also concerns himself with the more significant question of *why* Lincoln accepted the employment. Although his tone here is slightly defensive, he concludes

[6]See Woldman, op. cit. supra note 2, at 66.

[7]Beveridge, *Abraham Lincoln 1809–1858*, 396–97 (1928). Beveridge also suggested that Lincoln desired to represent the other side, but by a combination of circumstances was not able to do so. Id. at 395.

[8]Thomas, *Abraham Lincoln* (1952).

from the evidence that there is no basis for the theory that Lincoln was asserting some absolute moral in taking the case. Granting that Lincoln may have had misgivings about the position of his client (and what lawyer has not?), Duff concludes that Lincoln accepted Matson's cause because he was a lawyer, a member of that "cruel calling" which requires practitioners "to repress their own sometimes deep-seated convictions and become, at times, articulate advocates of ideas and clients abhorrent to their own inner feelings."[9] Thus, Duff points out the elemental proposition that the lawyer's essential role in our legal system assumes that he will accept employment in an honest cause regardless of "an inherent or emotional bias which predisposes . . . [him] in favor of one side or the other."[10] Duff concedes that the economic self-interest of the lawyer is consistent with this role. But he also knows that a system of laws requires this status for lawyers. Surely it is apparent that laymen, even sophisticated ones, do not understand this, and it becomes increasingly apparent that many lawyers themselves either do not understand it or cannot take the consequences. This has led to an always increasing tendency of the citizen to merge the identities of lawyers and their clients and an always diminishing number of lawyers willing to maintain an independence from the views and interests of their clients. A system of due process assumes the availability of the technicians who know how to operate it. But the growth of the dependent bar tends to wither due process, and the unpopular cause or unpopular client, including those of an unorthodox political flavor, have more and more difficulty in invoking the system of law. Duff's book does not set out to make these points, but they nevertheless emerge because we see that they were generally accepted a hundred years ago in the unsophisticated Eighth Judicial Circuit of Illinois, by Abe Lincoln and by his contemporaries.

The *Matson* case is only a part of Duff's correction of the record of Lincoln's legal career. He also disposes of Hill's error in asserting that Lincoln had little relationship with capital cases and that he "was not well qualified for work of this character, and . . . avoided the practice of criminal law as far as possible."[11] Duff shows us that Lincoln was in fact frequently employed in the criminal practice and unhesitatingly repre-

[9]P. 144.
[10]Ibid.
[11]Hill, op. cit. supra note 1, at 235.

sented the defense in homicide matters. We also lose other illusions. Thus, the recurring theme that Lincoln "thoroughly believed in the justice of his cause"[12] before acting professionally is shown to be an error. Lawyers, at least, will be pleased to learn that Lincoln accepted employment in a number of cases in which the law and the facts were stacked against him. Also satisfying is the knowledge denied us by Duff's predecessors that Lincoln was never reluctant to resort to highly legalistic and technical arguments when these seemed to be the likely course.

Some readers may quarrel with Duff's writing style. He is not above the slang expression and the use of the homespun idiom. Others may find this appropriate to the subject matter; in any event style is a matter of taste about which reasonable men may differ. Most important is the fact that the book as a whole is a comprehensive and detailed analysis of the subject. All of the cases are there, beginning with the little ones and gradually proceeding to the big ones, including the then landmark utility and water rights cases which demonstrate Lincoln's professional growth. Thus, we see the unpromising young man beginning at the bottom and rising to leadership and comparative wealth at the Illinois bar. One of the most charming aspects of the book is the picture it gives of the practice of law more than a hundred years ago. Office procedure, fee practices, and the personal habits and experiences of a lawyer of the time all appear. In treating them, as in treating Abraham Lincoln, John J. Duff has combined thorough research, a writer's gift, and a concern for the facts into a first-rate contribution to Lincoln literature.

Lincoln as a Lawyer

Lincoln as a Lawyer. By John P. Frank. University of Illinois Press, 1961. Pp. xiv, 144.

In the vast body of Lincoln literature, A. Lincoln the lawyer has not been neglected. In addition to a number of reminiscences, articles, and pamphlets, three major works have been concerned with his professional career. In 1906, Frederick Trevor Hill wrote *Lincoln The Lawyer,* a study of Lincoln's period at the bar and the legal aspects of his later

---

[12]Hill, op. cit. supra note 1, at 237–38.

career. In 1936, on the eve of the centennial of Lincoln's admission to the bar, Albert A. Woldman published a second full-scale analysis.[1] In 1961, John J. Duff, a New York practicing lawyer, issued a new book.[2] Lawyer Lincoln has also been described in the major biographies by Beveridge, Sandburg, Thomas, and others.

With the exception of the Duff book published in 1961, most of the writing about lawyer Lincoln has been of limited worth. It has been marked by a number of unhistoric characteristics, including implicit apologies for the fact that he was a lawyer at all. (Popular mythology would have preferred that he had been a soldier, an Indian scout, or, God forbid, a physician.) The imperfections of the prior art justified Duff's excellent book. John P. Frank's book is also justified by the imperfections of the previous works. In addition, Frank approaches the subject from a wholly new standpoint. The previous books have been principally expositions of the *facts* of Lincoln's career as an attorney. Having examined all of the materials available, Frank writes about what kind of a lawyer Lincoln was with reference to the traditional criteria by which lawyers evaluate one another professionally. Lincoln practiced law for twenty-five of the thirty-five years of his adult life. As stated by Frank, practicing law "in terms of time and energy and preoccupation . . . was in bulk the largest single factor of his life."[3] Accordingly, a close analysis of Lincoln as a lawyer is a means of learning a great deal about Lincoln as a human being. Frank's unique vehicle is therefore a good one for seeking out new insights into the character and personality of the man.

Frank's book begins with an excellent short description of what the practice of law was like in Illinois during the period of Lincoln's career. He describes the physical circumstances of the lawyer's life—the types of cases presented, the clerical and financial characteristics of the practice, the circuit riding, and all the rest. Since Lincoln was principally a trial and appellate lawyer, these aspects of the practice are highlighted. Lawyers today will be amused—and perhaps reassured—by the fact that the circuit riding practice often afforded almost no opportunity for preparation for trial. Also comforting is the knowledge that Lincoln's practice always included a number of small and unremunerative cases,

---

[1]Woldman, *Lawyer Lincoln* (1936).
[2]Duff, *A. Lincoln, Prairie Lawyer* (1961).
[3]P. 5.

even after he had become an outstanding and prosperous member of the bar in Illinois.

Having briefly set the scene in the old Eighth Judicial Circuit of Illinois, Frank uses the Lincoln legal materials to explore "The Mind Behind The Practice." This mind, he convinces us, was orderly, despite the oft-told tales of Lincoln's disordered office procedures. The mind was also sensitive, both to the technicalities and the equities of the legal conflicts to which it was applied. It was combative—Lincoln had "an unbridled enthusiasm for combat"[4]—but it was also realistic, so that Lincoln saw the imperfections of his own cases and fairly anticipated the contentions of his adversaries. Finally, the mind had the capacity for diligence. Lincoln was an extremely hard working practitioner and when the occasion presented itself he was capable of careful and thoughtful workmanship over a sustained period of time. All of these intellectual attributes lay behind the better known Lincoln qualities—his uncommon facility as a writer and speaker, his ability to marshal facts, and his exceptional skill in making the right decision when confronted with alternatives and required to decide between them. Running through the analysis of Lincoln's mind one sees a capacity for maturing. Growth in all of the qualities essential to his profession was a marked characteristic of the man.

From the practice of law, Frank follows Lincoln into public life. Here he searches for those professional characteristics which were transferred to the Presidency. Lincoln's administration was unusually beset with desperate and fundamental issues which were also essentially legal issues: the nature of the Union, Emancipation, the power of the Executive, and the status of civil liberties in the midst of massive rebellion. Frank shows us that Lincoln approached these and all of the problems of his administration in terms of legal concepts and as a lawyer works. More specifically, from the practice of law Lincoln carried with him his incredible industriousness; his ability to absorb, retain, organize, and use facts; his capacity for effective expression; and his aptitude at making correct decisions on the basis of these facts.

It should be said that Frank avoids any extravagant contention that the legal profession can claim to have created Lincoln. He does note that the lawyer's life at the time and in the place afforded a training ground for those attributes which were to mark Lincoln as a great political President, but he

[4]P. 76.

credits the profession with having done "more to polish than to create his native skills."[5] In this regard, Frank strikes an interesting contradiction. Lincoln was a complicated man personally, but as a lawyer, and as a lawyer who was President, his actions were direct and uncomplicated. Thus, Frank points to Lincoln's ultimate gifts. He could find the heart of the issues and could pursue the heart of the issues with single-mindedness. As President, this meant that he was able to find his own common denominator to the numerous questions which surrounded him. This common denominator was the defeat of the rebellion. And having found the single goal, he pursued it indefatigably, throwing off the distractions which would have pulled him from it. From the beginning, all issues and all men were measured by Lincoln by the single standard: would they help or hurt in the defeat of the Rebellion? This was the cornerstone of Lincoln's conduct of his office and he clung to it as surely no one else could have.

John Frank has accomplished what one might have thought to be impossible. He has provided an original contribution to the study of Abraham Lincoln, well written, scholarly, and in all things exceptional.

The Presidency of Abraham Lincoln

The Presidency of Abraham Lincoln. By Phillip Shaw Paludan. University Press of Kansas, 1994. Pp. xx, 384.

Phillip Shaw Paludan, professor of history at the University of Kansas, has previously written widely and well about the Civil War period. Beginning with an effective chapter describing "The State of the Union: 1860," he now turns his attention to Lincoln's presidency. The facts are not new, but there is a refreshing aura to the book. Perhaps because the book does not purport to cover Lincoln's early life, Lincoln does not appear as the trite, folksy character of popular reputation. Instead, he seems what he surely was: a tough, intense, and skillful politician, successfully leading the nation through an almost impossible challenge.

The author does an unusually good job of setting forth the vast problems of the administration. Almost every decision that had to be made presented a dilemma and the risk of serious harm, even the loss of the war. Unusually intelligent and politically shrewd, Lincoln is seen as the reasonable man, frequently confronting lesser men, including those

[5]P. 172.

who sought to help. The president had a strong and confident sense of himself, the presidency, and power. He was more of a problem solver than a theoretician.

The book succeeds in portraying Lincoln's growth and development on the job. Although all aspects of the administration and Lincoln's performance are described, the war inevitably defined his presidency. Paludan successfully integrates the military history with the social and political history of the period and provides deft, thoughtful portraits of the major civil and military leaders, including Seward, Stanton, Chase, Grant, and McClellan.

The book is marked by appropriate emphasis on the major political issues of the period: Northern dissent, Emancipation, the 1864 election, and Reconstruction. Although recognizing the questionable legality of Lincoln's efforts to cope with dissent—suspension of habeas corpus, press censorship, arbitrary arrest, and trial by military commission—Paludan is generally accepting of Lincoln's theory of necessity in the pursuit of his ultimate obligation of preserving the nation. The complicated evolution of Lincoln's policy regarding slavery is recounted. He began with a willingness to accept a constitutional guarantee of slavery in the states where it existed and proceeded to the Emancipation Proclamation and the Thirteenth Amendment. In regard to the presidential election of 1864, perhaps the Union's major crisis of the war, the author grasps the relationship between Lincoln's chances for reelection and battlefield success or failure of the Federal armies. With respect to Reconstruction, the reader is reminded that the disagreements on this issue arose early in the war and caused sustained conflict between Lincoln and other Northerners, including influential congressional leaders. Lincoln, Paludan believes, was tending just before his death toward a more aggressive policy in behalf of the freedmen: "Lincoln was moving closer to Congress, not away, closer to expanded rights for blacks and to greater protection of those rights" (p. 309). Professor Paludan has given us an important book.

Black Troops, White Commanders, and Freedmen During the Civil War

Black Troops, White Commanders and Freedmen During the Civil War. By
  Howard C. Westwood. Southern Illinois University Press, 1992.
  Pp. xi, 189.

The truth about the role of slavery and the African-Americans in the
Civil War was one of the victims of the Lost Cause, that large coun-
terfactual myth that for 100 years dominated, and still marks, Civil War
history. Designed to decontaminate secession and the Confederacy of
slavery, this myth removed blacks from their true role as the issue, ignored their actual participation in the struggle, and portrayed them as
unconcerned about their own enslavement. Today's generation of historians has sought to exorcise this myth, but American history has not yet
fully recovered from it. Howard C. Westwood's book is another major
step in correcting the record.

The book is a series of topical essays, some of which have been previously published in historical journals. The first four are concerned
with the issue of black enlistment in the Federal army. With fine insight
and thorough familiarity with the facts, the writer details the halting and
sometimes inept Federal course that began in 1861 with a prohibition of
black soldiers but ended with 180,000 of them, largely former slaves, in
the United States armies. Lincoln's role in this politically and socially
complicated story is carefully described, as is the sad tale of discrimina-
tion against these soldiers.

Westwood devotes one chapter to a detailed accounting of the story
of Robert Smalls, the slave wheelman of the Confederate steamer
Planter. In 1862, Smalls and several other slaves captured this vessel in
South Carolina and delivered it to the Federal blockading squadron.
Pronounced by Rear Admiral Samuel F. DuPont as "one of the coolest
and most gallant naval acts of the war," the Smalls incident is well
known, but Westwood tells it in unique and compelling detail.

In other chapters, Westwood goes into the nooks and crannies of the
blacks' role. Here he plows new ground, examining subjects that have previously received little or no attention: the Confederacy's treatment of captured black Federal soldiers, including former slaves; the army's reaction
to black soldiers' mutinies; early and unsuccessful efforts to make land

available for the freedmen; and the only known criminal case enforcing the Emancipation Proclamation. These chapters are fascinating, and they also serve to illuminate the tragic character of race relations at the time that abolition of slavery was finally confronted by the Americans.

Black Troops is a valuable book. Concerned with an important aspect of the Civil War, it is thoroughly researched, finely written, and highly informative. It reminds us that the war cast a long shadow. We stand in that shadow today.

The Confederate Tide Rising

The Confederate Tide Rising: Robert E. Lee and the Making of Southern Strategy, 1861–1862. By Joseph L. Harsh, Kent State University Press, 1998. Pp. xviii, 278.

Joseph Harsh—A Virginian and professor of history at George Mason University—writes in his preface that this book is an introduction to a larger study of General Robert E. Lee's Maryland campaign, published separately at the publisher's suggestion. Consequently, *Confederate Tide Rising* begins with Lee's assignment on June 1, 1862, to command what was to become the Army of Northern Virginia and ends on August 31, 1862, just after the Second Battle of Bull Run, on the eve of the Maryland campaign. Harsh has a strong command of all available historical materials and writes with fine facility.

His book has two essential theses. First, he believes that Lee's strategy was aggressively offensive. Second, he believes that this was undoubtedly the correct strategy. Indeed, he argues the latter point so elaborately that it almost seems too much: Lee advocates typically justify the general's unsuccessful acts on the ground that "he had no alternative." Harsh virtually justifies Lee's penchant for the offensive on this specious ground.

Confederate Tide Rising is essentially a wide-ranging defense of Lee's aggressive and offensive strategy, which some historians have criticized. Harsh writes that "There was a logic in the decisions that Lee made in September of 1862, but it does not emerge until seen in the context of Confederate war aims and grand strategy and until it is viewed as a final step in the arduous journey that carried him to the banks of the Potomac." In short, Lee's Maryland campaign is to be rationalized in the context of the events described in the yet-to-be-published book—then why write this one?

As the foregoing implies, Harsh's tone is defensive, a broad response to the heretics' criticism of the general. Harsh is also a fan of Confederate President Jefferson Davis, whom he finds to be a very effective wartime president. In this connection, he argues that Davis and Lee were agreed on the offensive-defensive Confederate strategy in the Virginia theater. In doing so, Harsh disagrees with the many historians who believe that Davis emphasized defensive operations, whereas Lee concentrated on offensive ones.

Additional arguments supporting Lee appear in Harsh's account. The author contends that prior to the Maryland campaign Lee and his soldiers "shared a trust and confidence"—a common assertion in spite of Lee's constant problem with unusually large-scale straggling and desertion that began during the Peninsula campaign and, Harsh says, that "would hobble his military operations for the remainder of the war." The *Official Records of the War of the Rebellion* abound with Lee's communications concerning this constant problem; he sometimes missed an astonishing one-third to one-half of his men. Lee took unusual methods, such as assigning extra provost marshals and traveling courts-martial tribunals, to try and solve this problem, but none of them succeeded.

Harsh credits Lee with systematically developing his offensive strategy, based on a careful analysis of the logistical factors and his adversaries' circumstances. That strategy, he says, was based on the assumption that the Confederacy, like the Patriots in the Revolution, could only win the war by convincing the enemy that conquering the South would be too painful and costly. According to Harsh, Lee's plan was designed to exact this pain and cost. While Harsh and this reviewer agree that this was the only possible strategy, we disagree as to whether Lee deliberately considered it. In fact, there is persuasive evidence that Lee, in fact, erroneously believed that the South's means of victory was assured in overpowering the North militarily. That belief dictated his self-destructive aggressiveness. His campaigns point to this, and he frequently spoke of "crushing" and "wiping out" Federal armies. In July of 1864, he wrote to Davis: "If we can defeat or drive the armies of the enemy from the field, we shall have peace. All our efforts and energies should be directed to that object." This is unquestionably a statement of belief in the military defeat of the enemy, not of simply wearing that enemy down.

In any event, Lee's aggressiveness, whatever his purpose, was counterproductive because it produced very large, disproportionate, and irreplaceable casualties that ultimately destroyed the viability of his army. Another credible opinion suggests that Lee's aggressiveness was not only mistaken but was also thoughtless; he simply possessed a mindlessly combative personality. Thus, the British military historian, J. F. C. Fuller, states that in 1862 and 1863, "Lee rushed forth to find a battlefield, to challenge a contest between himself and the North." Thomas Buell also writes of Lee's habit of "fighting for the sake of fighting." Harsh's volume plainly rejects any such theory, despite his own admissions that would seem not to vindicate Lee's strategy. For example, Harsh says, contrary to the evidence, that Lee insisted on turning movements as opposed to head-on attacks. "Malvern Hill," writes Harsh, "was the third straight-on attack that should not have been made" on the Peninsula, and that "costly frontal attacks . . . had wasted Confederate resources without commensurate results." Harsh even observes that his Peninsula tactical plans were unworkable and even naive. Further, "Lee contributed to the derangement of his plan" on the Peninsula.

Harsh also addresses another popular criticism of the most famous Confederate general, that he had a Napoleonic notion that he could win the war militarily by crushing the enemy in one great battle or campaign. Given the North's resources and the Federals' commitment to the Union, the idea of such a decisive, war-winning event was totally unrealistic, and Lee's efforts to accomplish it—of which Antietam is an example—was another reason for his desperate and destructive casualties.

Readers may reasonably look forward to Harsh's planned vindication of Lee's Maryland campaign. All but a very few of the most pious of the general's acolytes, such as his biographer Douglas Freeman, acknowledge that campaign as Lee's greatest mistake. If Harsh can convert these heretics, he will have accomplished a great deal.

General Robert F. Hoke: Lee's Modest Warrior

General Robert F. Hoke: Lee's Modest Warrior. By Daniel W. Barefoot. John
    F. Blair Publisher, 1996. Pp. xvii, 452.

As is well known, books about the Civil War crowd the literary market. This is not inappropriate. The sectional discord and the war were surely the defining events in American history. They cast a long shadow over American lives. Indeed, as suggested by today's racial climate, we stand in that shadow still. Surely the historical events are entitled to our attention.

Some of today's scholarship is exceptional. Free of the expressed or implicit racist impulses of a generation ago, some historians are able to avoid the clichéd, romanticized legend of the Margaret Mitchells.

Given the volume of Civil War publishing, it is not surprising that the overall results are mixed. On the one hand, many of the books simply retell a familiar story—Grant and Lee, Gettysburg and Vicksburg are not neglected. On the other hand, occasionally a book appears that imparts relatively new information. Daniel W. Barefoot's biography of Gen. Robert F. Hoke is such a book.

Although a Confederate major general and division commander, Hoke has received little attention in the literature of the war. As the author notes, although Douglas Southall Freeman briefly mentions him, Shelby Foote and Bruce Catton ignore him entirely. A native of Lincolnton, N.C.—also the birthplace of Confederate Gen. Stephen Dodson Ramseur—Hoke was the scion of a wealthy, slaveholding industrial-political family. His formal college education was limited to one year at Kentucky Military Institute.

An unquestioning sectionalist, he enlisted as a second lieutenant and was promoted to a majority in the First North Carolina Volunteers, a six-month organization commanded by D. H. Hill. When that regiment's enlistment expired, he was assigned as a major in the 33rd North Carolina Infantry and was later promoted to colonel of that regiment.

His rise in command was steady. He was commissioned a brigadier general as of January 1863 and assigned to command a brigade in Jubal Early's division of the Army of Northern Virginia. Transferred to A. P. Hill's Light Division in April 1863, he was awarded a major generalship at the age of 26. Hoke was the youngest man ever to hold that rank in the Confederate army.

Although he missed Gettysburg as a result of his wounding at Salem Church during the Chancellorsville campaign, in one or another command capacity Hoke fought at other major battles in the East: on the Virginia Peninsula, Second Bull Run, Antietam, Fredericksburg, and Cold Harbor. He was also on hand during a large part of the Petersburg siege.

Fortunately for the reader, he participated in less well-known battles as well: Big Bethel, New Bern in 1862 and again in 1864, Chantilly, Plymouth, Bermuda Hundred, Drewry's Bluff, the defense of Wilmington, and the last major battle of the war, Bentonville. Further, he was at one time on detached duty in North Carolina responding to Confederate deserter depredations and civilian unrest.

The account of these more obscure activities provides the book with the new information. The book contains no maps, a serious defect highlighted by the fact that the author presents close tactical accounts of all of Hoke's battles. Serious military history readers should read the book with map resources close by.

Mr. Barefoot clearly admires Hoke. He observes that "the Southern people glorified, almost deified, their Confederate heroes," presumably a historian's criticism. But his own characterizations of Hoke on occasion border on this extravagance. However, he acknowledges and describes criticisms of Hoke by other writers such as Richard J. Sommers and Freeman.

Mr. Sommers harshly criticizes Hoke, contending that his promotion to a major-generalship was a mistake. In his "Lee's Lieutenants," Freeman censures Hoke as a major general for failure to cooperate with other divisions at Darbytown Road, Drewry's Bluff, Cold Harbor, Petersburg, and Fort Harrison.

These are highly significant failings, but the author argues that Hoke's conduct on each occasion was defensible. Plainly an admirer of Lee and the Confederate military effort, the author, by his candor, escapes the "Lost Cause" genre of Confederate writers. Thus, he fairly addresses the issue of whether Lee had designated Hoke as his successor as commander of the Army of Northern Virginia in the event of Lee's leaving that role—a still-debated issue.

He further acknowledges Lee's sometimes misplaced aggressiveness, the fact that there was Confederate political discord in North Carolina and, as indicated above, admits that there were Confederate deserters in North Carolina engaged in bushwhacking activities.

The book recounts the story of the deterioration and ultimate downfall of the Confederacy, provoking this reader's sense of the extreme tragedy for both sides arising from the prolonging of the war after it was clearly lost. The casualties at Bentonville, after Lee's surrender and on the eve of Joseph E. Johnston's surrender in North Carolina, are difficult to rationalize.

After Bentonville, anticipating surrender, Hoke's soldiers sometimes engaged in wholesale insubordination or deserted in large numbers. As had been true in Virginia, the surrender in North Carolina was essentially a formality.

Having bid his defeated soldiers farewell on May 1, 1865, Hoke returned to North Carolina. He took the oath of allegiance in 1866, married successfully and was an effective parent.

Starting as a manual-laboring farmer, he proceeded to prosperous mining, railroad and mineral-springs enterprises, dividing his time between Raleigh and Lincolnton. He did not participate in politics. Although not intensely involved in postwar Confederate memorial activities, he did serve on the committees established in the 1890s to erect monuments to Lee and Jefferson Davis, and to establish the Confederate memorial in Washington. He died in 1912. The extent of his own reconstruction is suggested by the fact that he was offered a brigadier generalship in the United States Army during the Spanish-American War.

Mr. Barefoot's protagonist was indeed a modest man. He left no wartime letters or memoirs and was not prone to publishing his wartime activities. Despite these handicaps, Barefoot's scope of research is impressive and his use of sources is excellent. He also writes gracefully. He has made a fine contribution to the literature of the war.

Battle Cry of Freedom

Battle Cry of Freedom: The Civil War Era. By James M. McPherson. Oxford University Press, 1988. Pp. xix, 904.

The Civil War is at last remote in time. Thoughtful people, North and South, have forgiven each other and themselves. The explosion in communications and transportation has contributed to the growth of a national culture. Finally, racial attitudes have changed markedly. Although race relations are far from ideal, reasonable people acknowledge the equality of blacks and whites as the appropriate ideal. These rather recent changes have permitted a new view of the Civil War and its preliminaries and aftermath. Much of the best scholarship on the period is taking place now.

James M. McPherson's *Battle Cry of Freedom* is a symbol, perhaps the apogee, of this advance in historiography. The book therefore reflects two premises: that the war was about black slavery and that it was in no sense a romantic event.

As his title suggests, McPherson understands that in terms of cause and effect the central issue of the war was the status of black people. However flawed and inept the trial, freedom was at stake. McPherson therefore rejects the implicitly racist rationales that have trivialized that issue in favor of once-fashionable cultural and economic explanations of the war. He has put black people back on the center of the stage, paying needed attention to their military contribution and to abolition and the survival of the Union.

As regards the romance of the war, by discarding the clichés of "the Blue and the Gray" McPherson makes it plain that the war was nothing less than a tragedy. It was an abject failure of American politics and the source of untrammeled harm in human terms. Thus, unlike much previous writing, the book does not glorify the events of the war.

The book is remarkable in another respect. Pervasive events like the Civil War tend to receive specific treatments. One book is a military history. Another is a political history. Still others present social or economic histories. In addition to offering significant insights into the ordeal, McPherson skillfully synthesizes its many aspects. In this reviewer's experience only one prior historian has had this faculty for dealing with the Civil War as a whole. This was Allan Nevins in his multivolumed works of a generation ago, *The Ordeal of the Union* and *The War for the Union*.

McPherson's analysis is questionable with respect to a special interest of Hoosiers. This concerns his treatment of dissent in the North, especially among the Democrats in the Middle West, including Indiana. Although he devotes needed attention to the complicated economic and political sources of the Copperheads' attitudes, his choice of sources leads McPherson to overstate both the extent and the nature of dissent. Depending on which data one consults, Indiana ranked either first or second among the Northern states in the percentage of its military population that enrolled in the Northern armies, and these soldiers were overwhelmingly volunteers. Gilbert R. Tredway's *Democratic Opposition to the Lincoln Administration in Indiana* establishes that the Democratic Congressional Districts consistently furnished more volunteers in proportion to their population than the Republican districts. In short, the evidence contradicts the once-prevailing view that the Indiana Democratic party was rife with pro-Confederate feeling. There were surely some disloyal party spokesmen and a disloyal fringe group, but the mainstream, although racist and politically irresponsible, supported the Union. There is a difference between being wrong and being disloyal.

Despite this exception, McPherson's book is superb. Beautifully written, it is a book for scholars and those of the general public who would understand this watershed event of American history.

Acknowledgments

AMERICAN BLUE & GRAY ASSOCIATIONS. "General Lee–A Different View" from *The Color Bearers*, 1995.

AMERICAN HISTORICAL REVIEW. "Generals Lee and Jackson" from review in Vol. 98, No. 2, April 1993.

BUTTERNUT PRESS. "The Twenty-Fourth Michigan of the Iron Brigade" from the introduction to the 1984 reprint of O. B. Curtis, *History of the Twenty-Fourth Michigan of the Iron Brigade* (Detroit, 1891).

CIVIL WAR TIMES. "Giants in Tall Black Hats" from Vol. 3, No. 8, 1961.

COLUMBIAD. "The Confederate Tide Rising" from review in Vol. 2, No. 2, 1998. "Historians' Perspectives on Lee" from Vol. 2, No. 4, 1999.

FARNSWORTH HOUSE. "Reynolds of Gettysburg" from Michael A. Riley, *'For God's Sake, Forward!,'* 1995.

GETTYSBURG MAGAZINE. "Three Flags at Gettysburg" from Issue No. 1, July 1989.

GREENWOOD PUBLISHING GROUP, INC., Westport, CT. Copyright © 1993 by Dennis S. Lavery and Mark. H. Jordan. "Iron Brigade General: John Gibbon" from Dennis S. Lavery and Mark. H. Jordan, *Iron Brigade General: John Gibbon, A Rebel in Blue*, 1993.

HARVARD LAW SCHOOL BULLETIN. "Lawyer Lincoln–Myth and Fact" from November 1964 issue.

INDIANA HISTORICAL SOCIETY. "Ex Parte Milligan: A Curb of Executive and Military Power" from *We The People: Indiana and the United States Constitution*, 1987.

INDIANA LAW JOURNAL. "Lincoln as a Lawyer" from review in Vol. 38, No. 4, 1962–63

INDIANA MAGAZINE OF HISTORY. "Atlanta, Pea Ridge, and Chickamauga" from review in Vol. 89, No. 4, 1993. "Battle Cry of Freedom" from review in Vol. 85, No. 4, 1989. "Black Troops, White Commanders, and Freedmen During the Civil War" from review in Vol. 88, No. 4, 1992. "Commanders of the Army of the Potomac" from review in Vol. 59, No. 2, 1963. "Indiana in the War of the Rebellion" from review in Vol. 57, No. 4, 1961. "Lee and Grant: A Dual Biography" from review in Vol. 86, No. 2, 1985. "The North Fights the Civil War" from review in Vol. 90, No. 4, 1994. "Old Abe the War Eagle" from review in Vol. 83, No. 1, 1987. "Tennessee's War" from review in Vol. 62, No. 3, 1966. "War in Kentucky" from review in Vol. 91, No. 4, 1995.

INDIANA UNIVERSITY PRESS, Bloomington and Indianapolis. "John Brawner's Damage Claim" from Alan T. Nolan and Sharon Eggleston Vipond, eds., *Giants in Their Tall Black Hats*, 1998.

KENT STATE UNIVERSITY PRESS. "R. E. Lee and July 1 at Gettysburg" from Gary W. Gallagher, ed., *First Day at Gettysburg: Essays on Confederate and Union Leadership*, 1992.

MADISON HOUSE PUBLISHERS, INC. "Considering *Lee Considered:* Robert E. Lee and the Lost Cause" from John Y. Simon and Michael E. Stevens, eds., *New Perspectives on the Civil War*, 1998.

MORNINGSIDE HOUSE. "Brave Men's Tears: The Iron Brigade at Brawner Farm" from Alan D. Gaff, *Brave Men's Tears: The Iron Brigade at Brawner Farm*, 1988. "In the Bloody Railroad Cut at Gettysburg" from Lance J. Herdegen and William J. K. Beaudot. *In the Bloody Railroad Cut at Gettysburg*, 1990.

PENNSYLVANIA HISTORY. "Generals McClellan and Hancock" from review in Vol. 57, No. 2, 1990.

REGISTER OF THE KENTUCKY HISTORICAL SOCIETY. "The Presidency of Abraham Lincoln" from review in Vol. 93, No. 2, 1995.

STANFORD LAW REVIEW. "A. Lincoln, Prairie Lawyer" from review in Vol. 13, 1961.

STATE HISTORICAL SOCIETY OF WISCONSIN. "History of the Sauk County Riflemen" from the introduction to the 1984 reprint of Philip Cheek and Mair Pointon, *History of the Sauk County Riflemen* (State Historical Society of Wisconsin, 1909). "Rufus Dawes' Service with the Sixth Wisconsin Volunteers" from the foreword to the 1962 reprint of Rufus Dawes, *Service with the Sixth Wisconsin Volunteers* (Alderman and Sonsi, 1890).

UNIVERSITY OF NORTH CAROLINA PRESS. Copyright © by the University of North Carolina Press: 1995, 1996, 1991. "Confederate Leadership at Fredericksburg" from Gary W. Gallagher, ed., *The Fredericksburg Campaign: Decision on the Rappahannock*, 1995. "Joshua Lawrence Chamberlain" from Alice Rains Trulock, ed., *In the Hands of Providence: Joshua L. Chamberlain and the American Civil War*, 1996. "The Price of Honor: R. E. Lee and the Question of Confederate Surrender" from Alan T. Nolan, *Lee Considered: General Robert E. Lee and Civil War History*, 1991.

VIRGINIA COUNTRY MAGAZINE. "Virginia's Unwelcome Visitors" from Vol. 4, 1967.

VIRGINIA MAGAZINE OF HISTORY AND BIOGRAPHY. "Why the Confederacy Lost" from review in Vol. 101, No. 4, 1993.

THE WASHINGTON TIMES. New World Communications, Inc. "General Robert F. Hoke: Lee's Modest Warrior" from review in issue of August 24, 1996. "Stonewall Jackson: The Man, the Soldier, the Legend" from review in issue of March 8, 1997.

Index

LaVergne, TN USA
23 February 2010
174008LV00002B/42/P